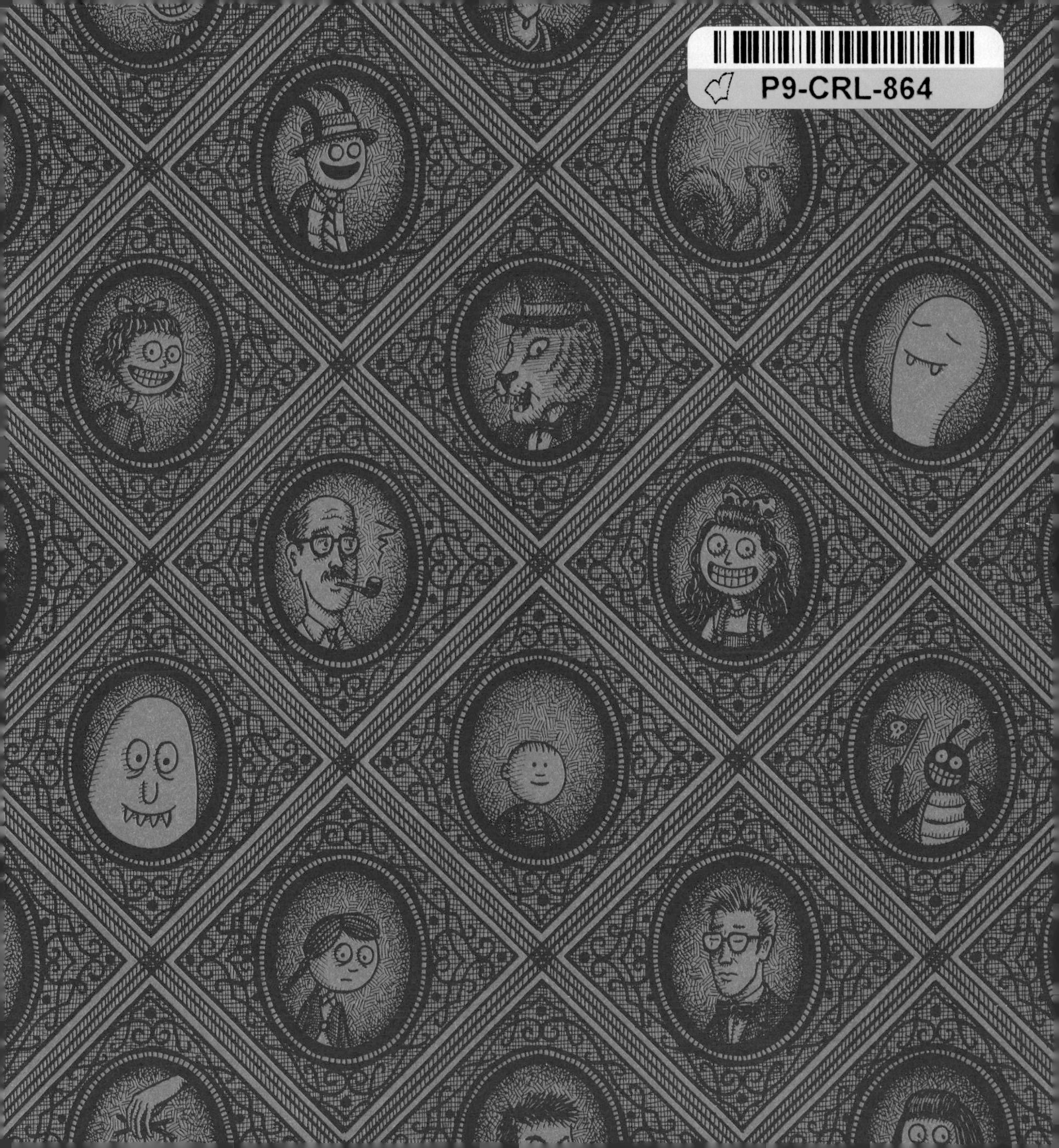

THE ENVIOUS SIBLINGS

THE ENVIOUS SIBLINGS

AND OTHER MORBID NURSERY RHYMES

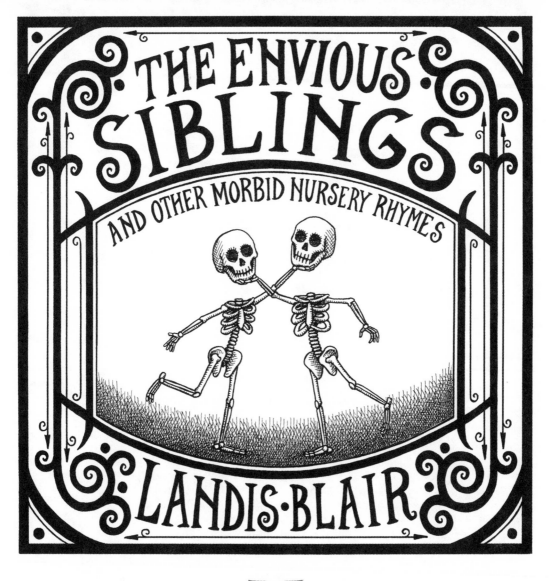

LANDIS·BLAIR

W. W. NORTON & COMPANY

Independent Publishers Since 1923

For information about permission to reproduce selections from this book,
write to Permissions, W. W. Norton & Company, Inc.,
500 Fifth Avenue, New York, NY 10110

For information about special discounts for bulk purchases, please contact
W. W. Norton Special Sales at specialsales@wwnorton.com or 800-233-4830

Manufacturing by Versa Press
Production manager: Lauren Abbate

Library of Congress Cataloging-in-Publication Data

Names: Blair, Landis, author, artist.
Title: The envious siblings : and other morbid nursery rhymes / Landis Blair.
Description: First edition. | New York : W. W. Norton & Company, [2019]
Identifiers: LCCN 2019020039 | ISBN 9780393651621 (hardcover)
Subjects: LCSH: Nursery rhymes, American. | American wit and humor, Pictorial. | Black humor.
Classification: LCC PS3602.L3364 E58 2019 | DDC 811/.6—dc23
LC record available at https://lccn.loc.gov/2019020039

W. W. Norton & Company, Inc., 500 Fifth Avenue, New York, N.Y. 10110
www.wwnorton.com

W. W. Norton & Company Ltd., 15 Carlisle Street, London W1D 3BS

1 2 3 4 5 6 7 8 9 0

For David Koss, who couldn't care less about this book despite being culpable for its existence.

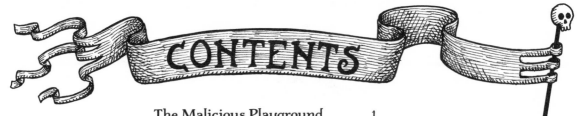

CONTENTS

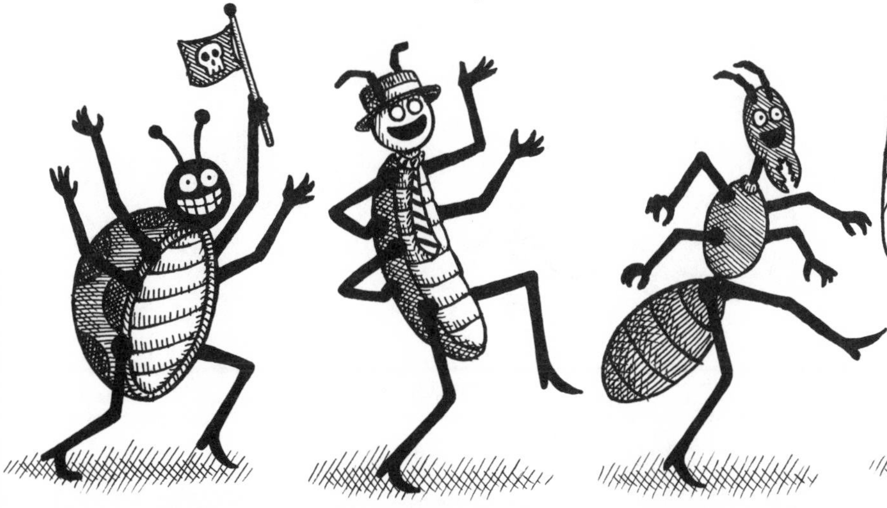

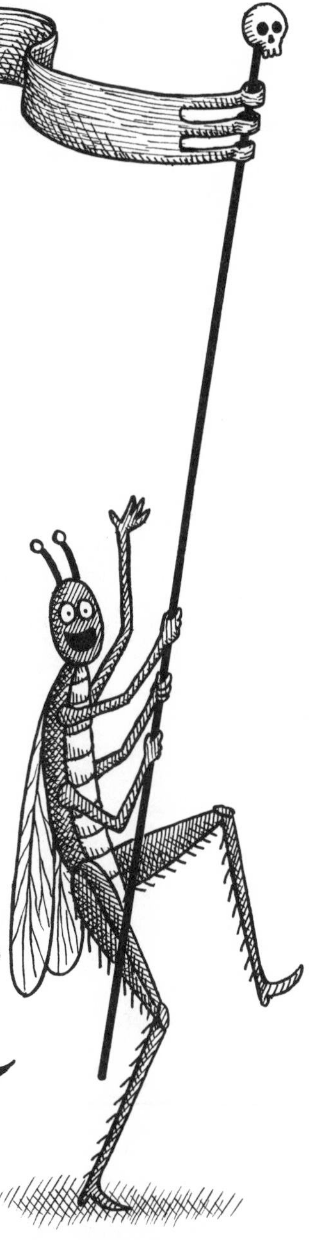

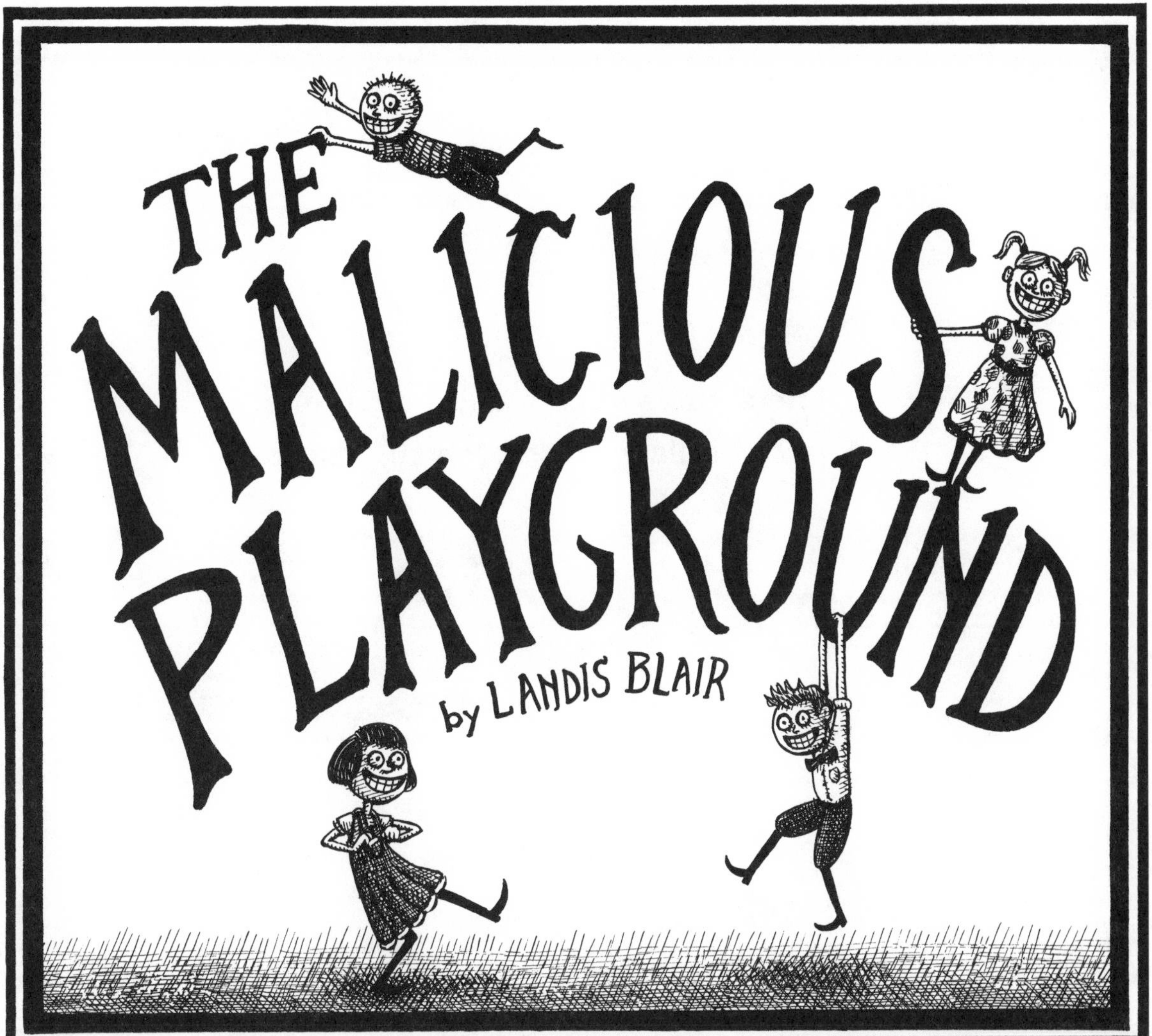
THE
MALICIOUS
PLAYGROUND
by LANDIS BLAIR

The slide is such a good design,
A perfect place to stretch the spine.

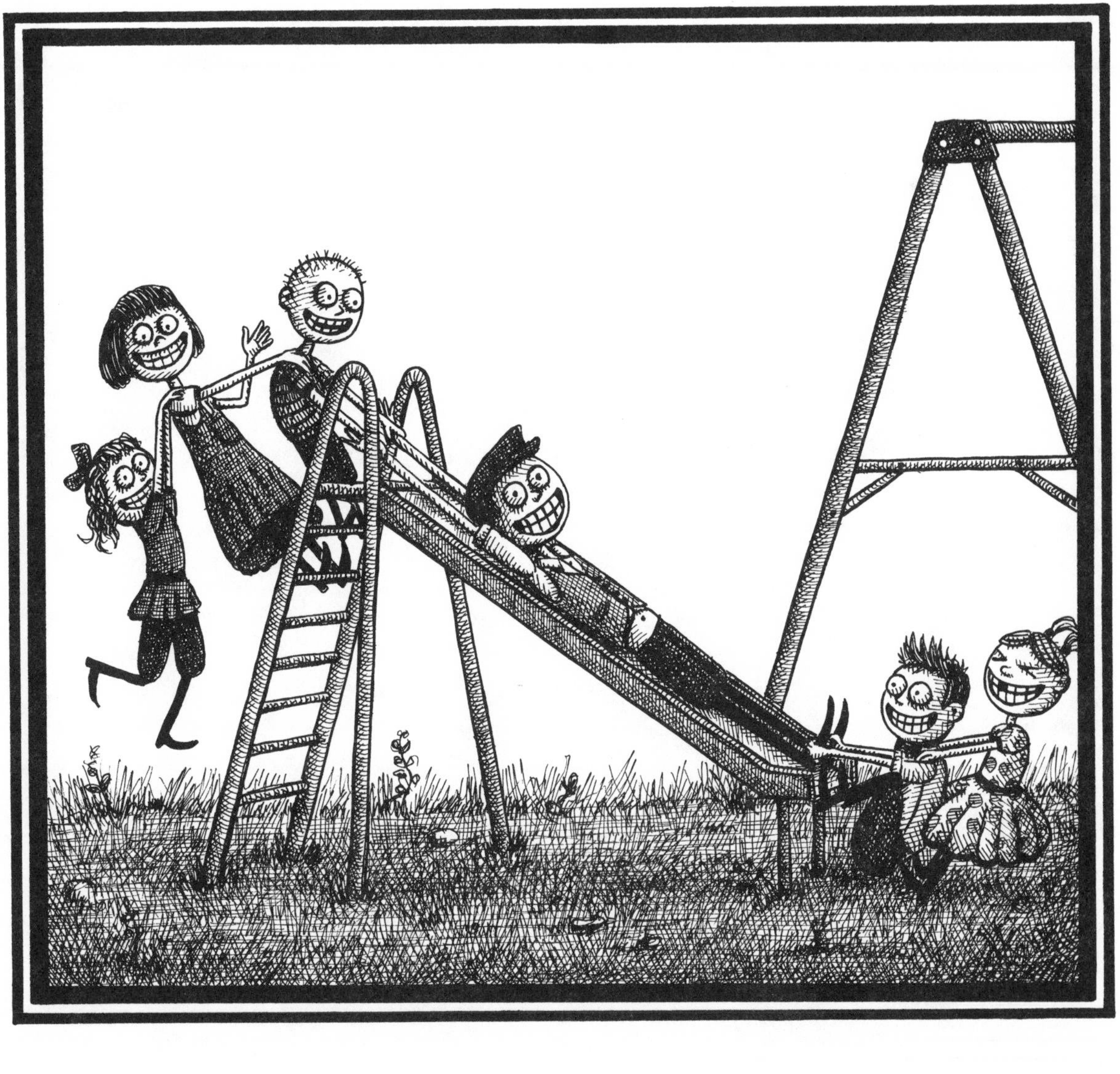

The sandbox sure can satisfy
The urge for sand kicked in the eye.

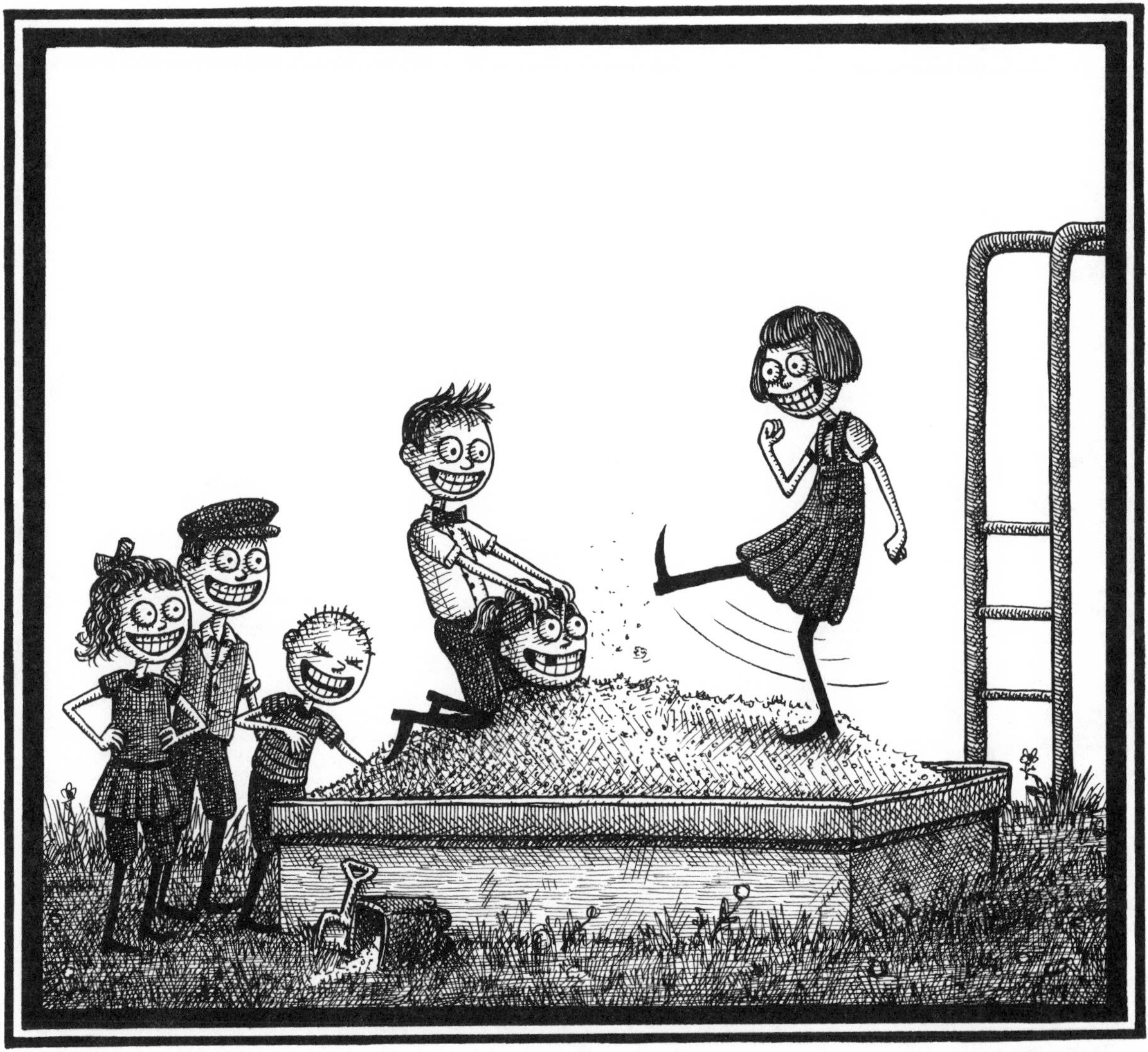

A teeter-totter has some use,
In making jaws go extra loose.

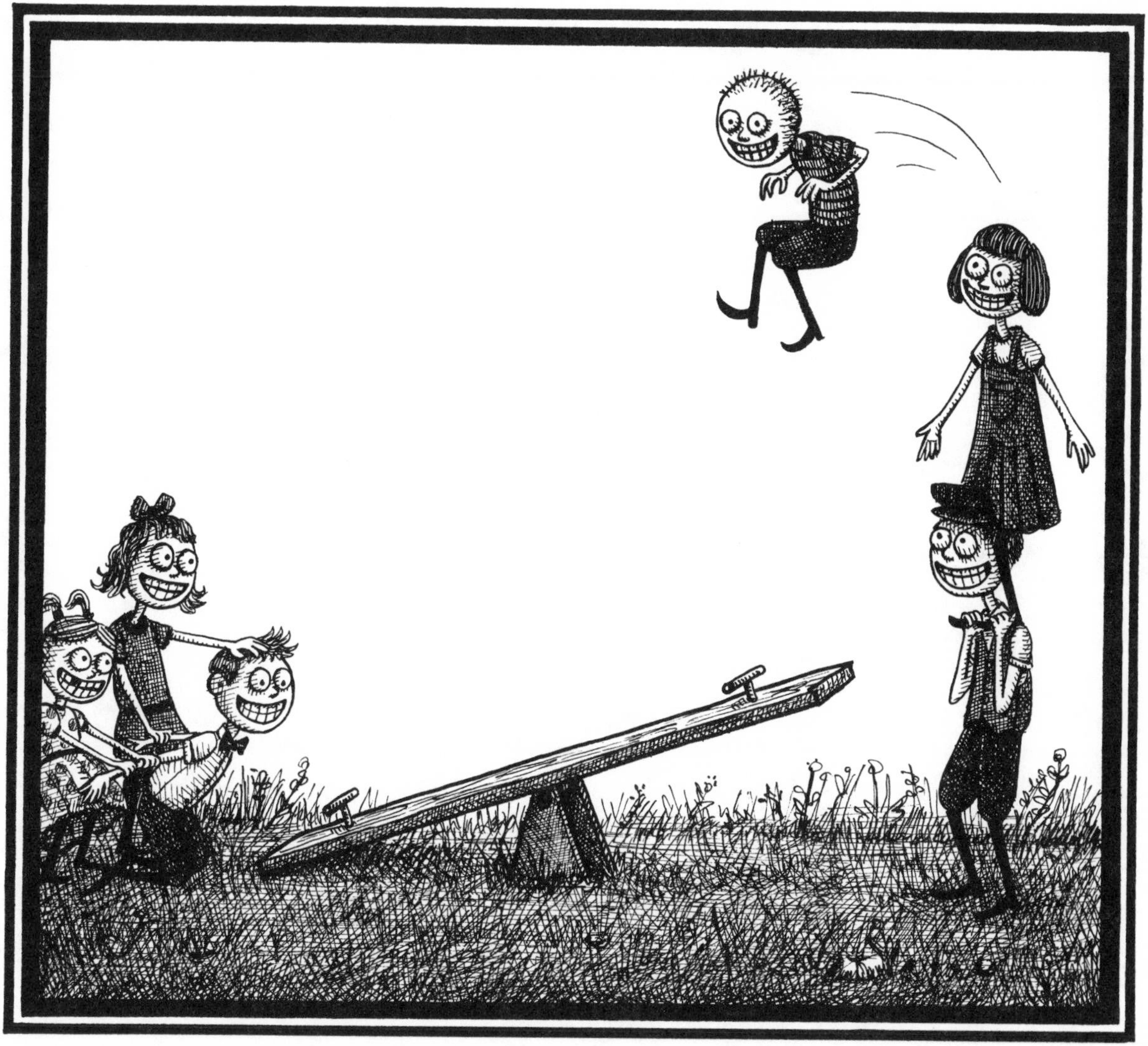

A swing set is a giddy place
To find a good kick in the face.

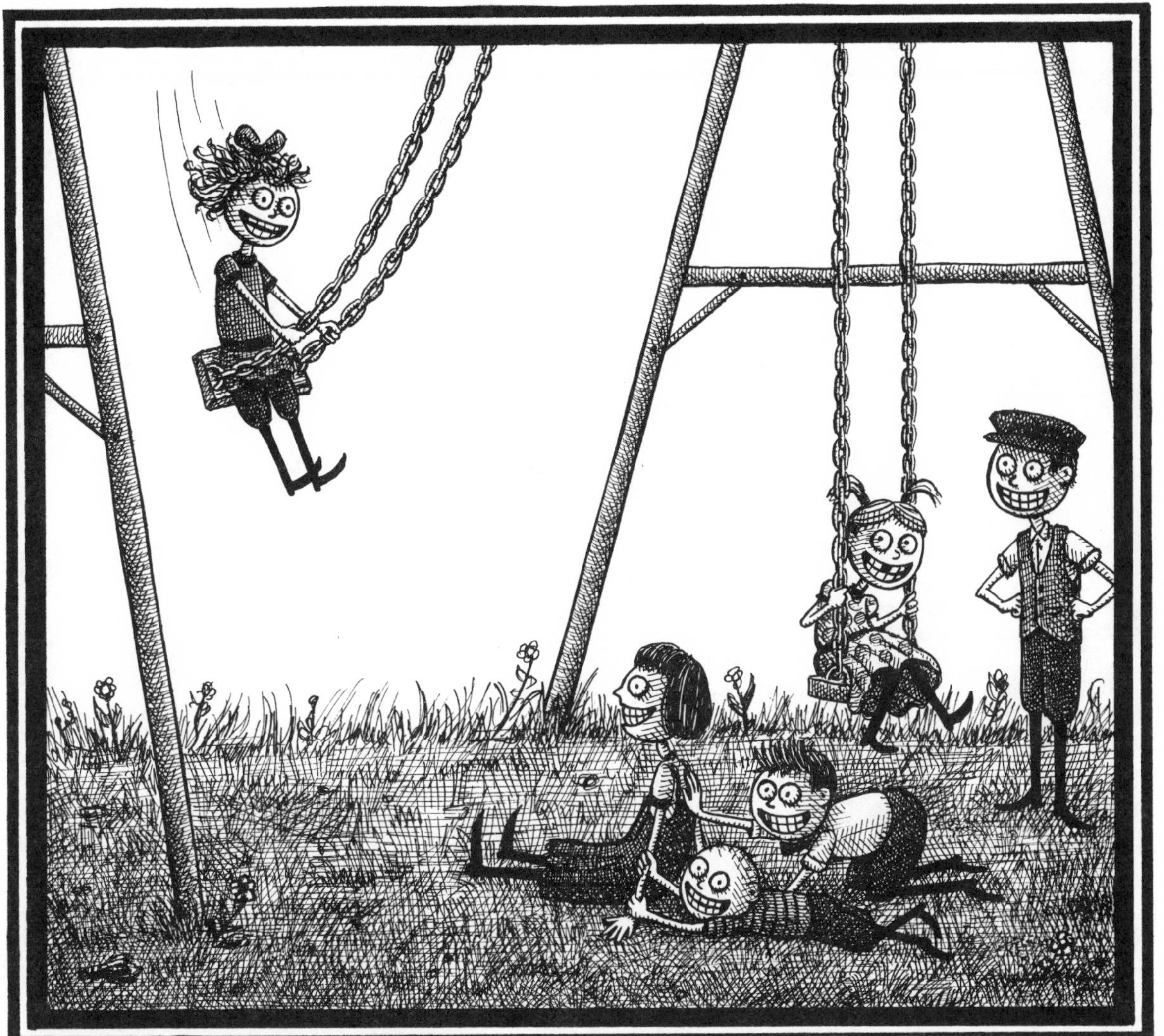

Monkey bars become efficient,
Making shoulder blades deficient.

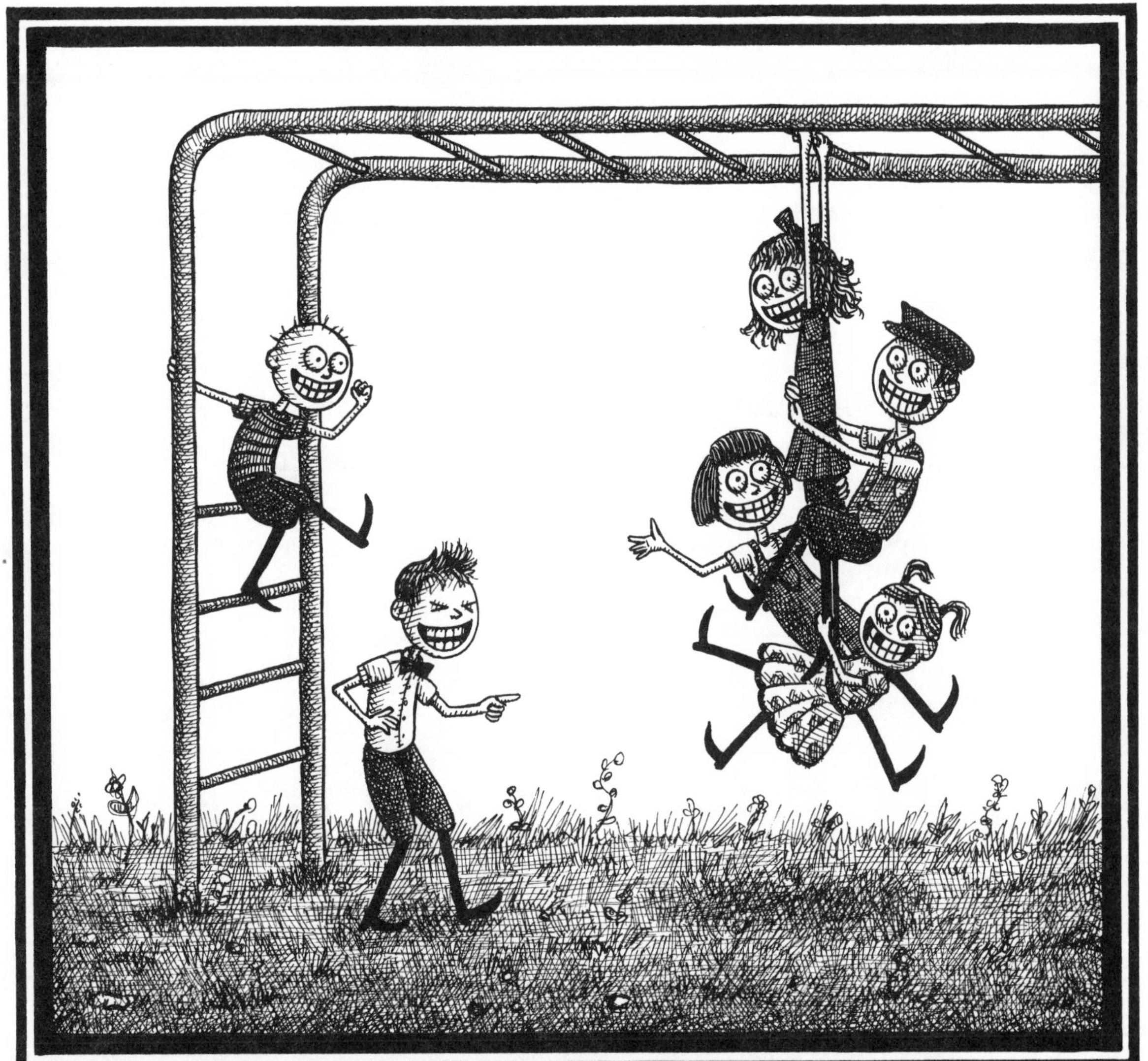

Some think spring riders kind of dull,
But with such ease they crack a skull.

With rope bridges no time lingers,
Snapping off all tiny fingers.

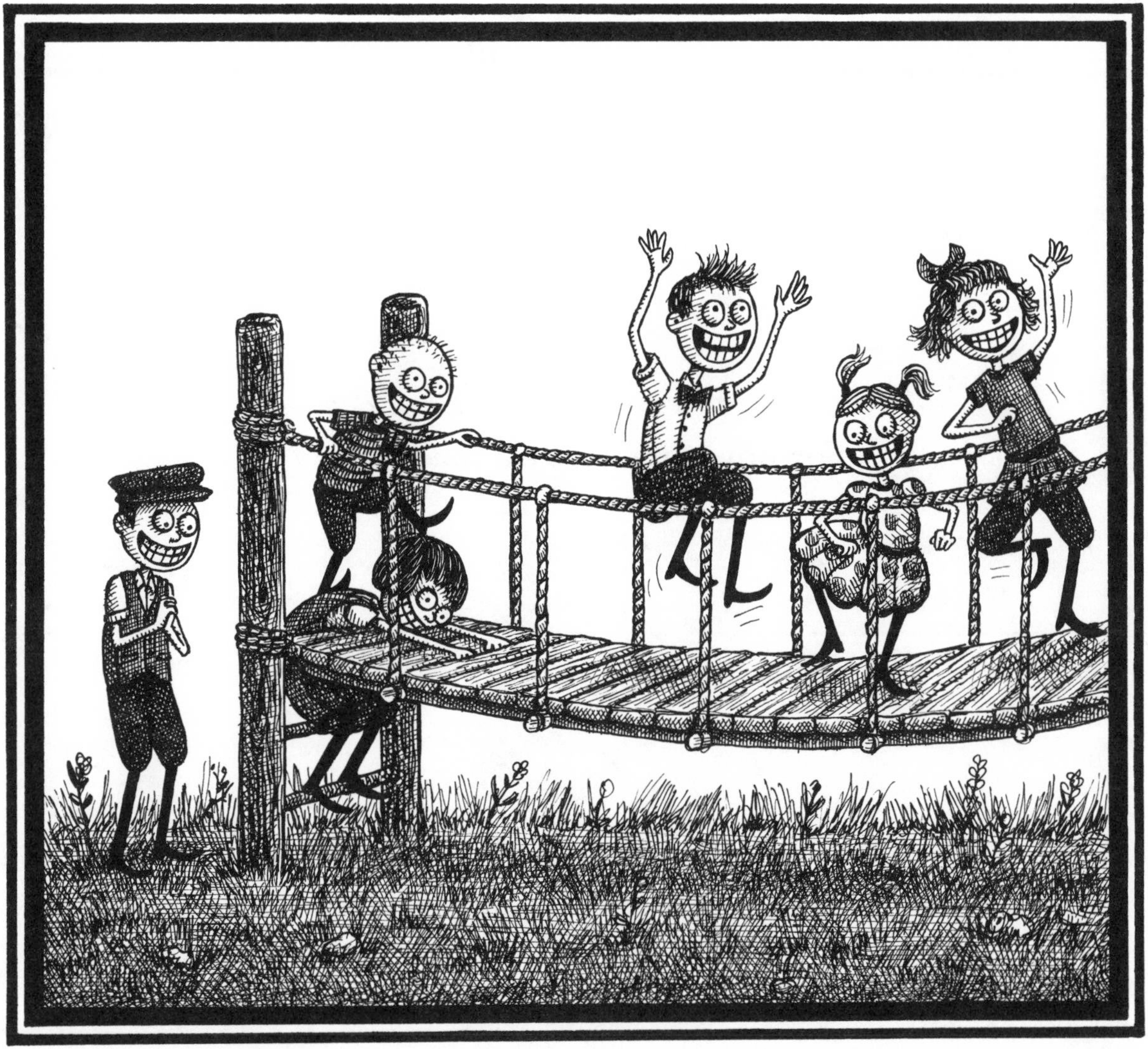

Merry-go-rounds create such awe,
For how they leave a face so raw.

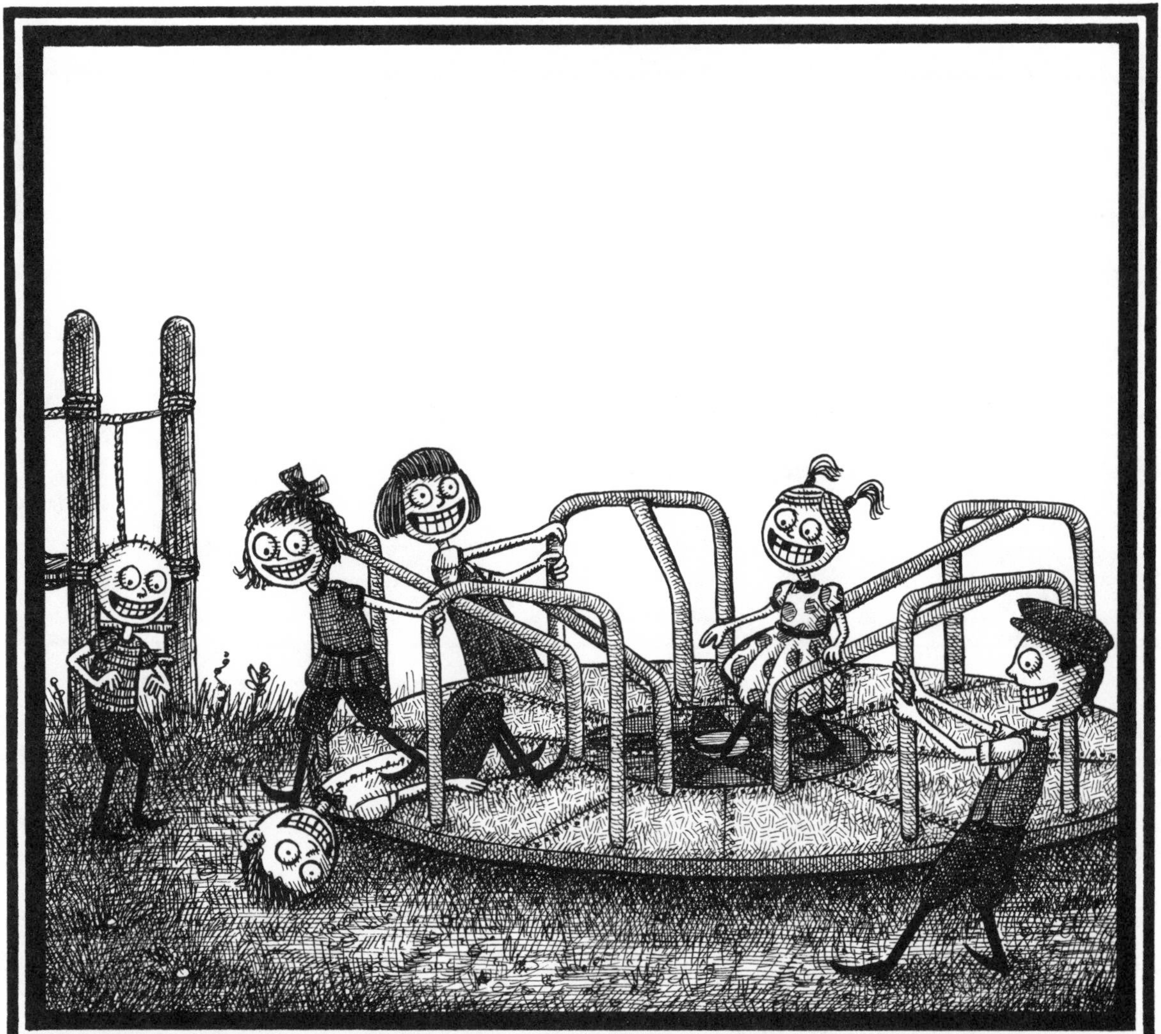

Diggers are such useful givers,
In extracting your friends' livers.

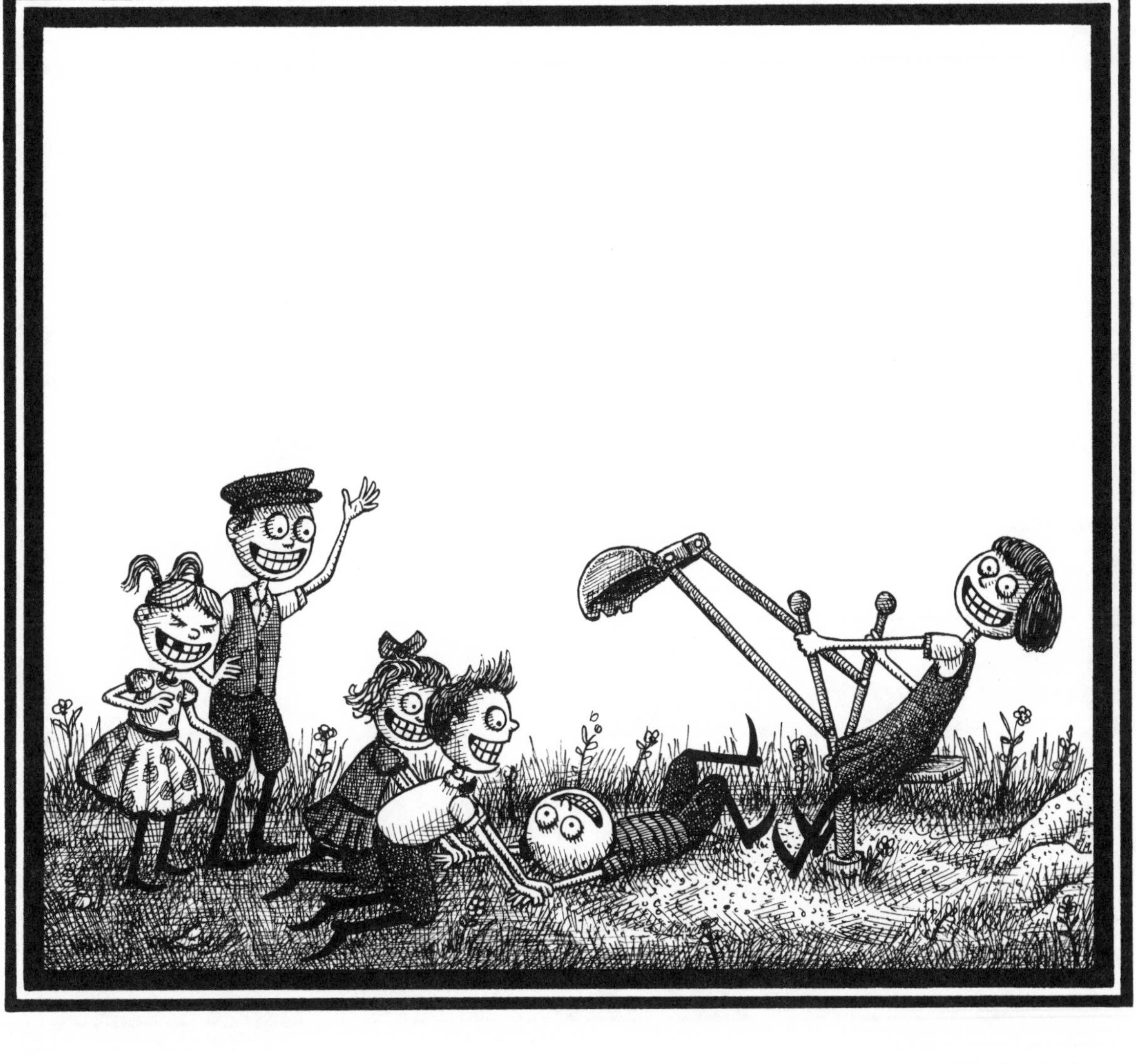

The jungle gym at best condones
The shattering of all your bones.

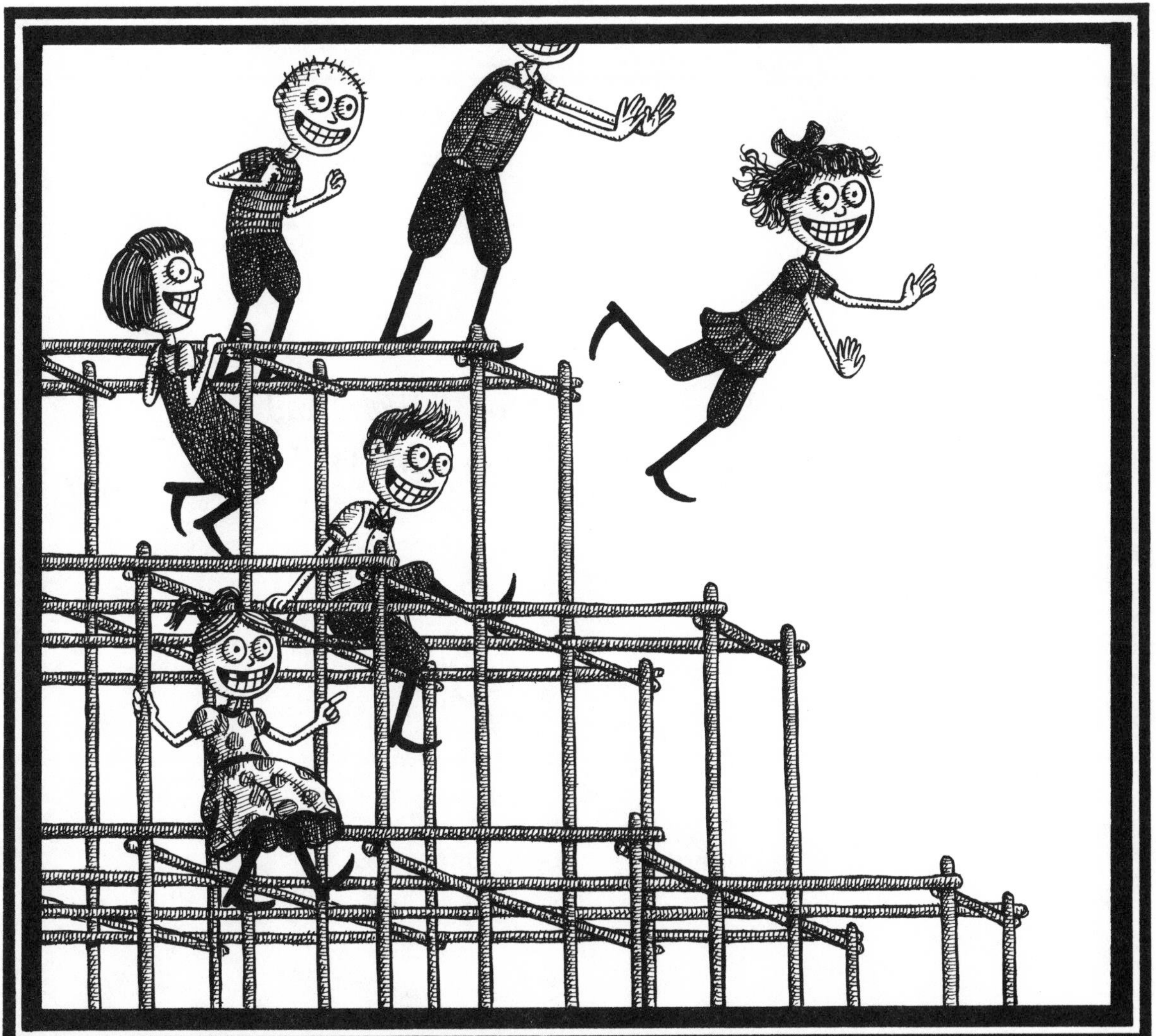

And when the fun has all been had,
It's time to go and play with Dad.

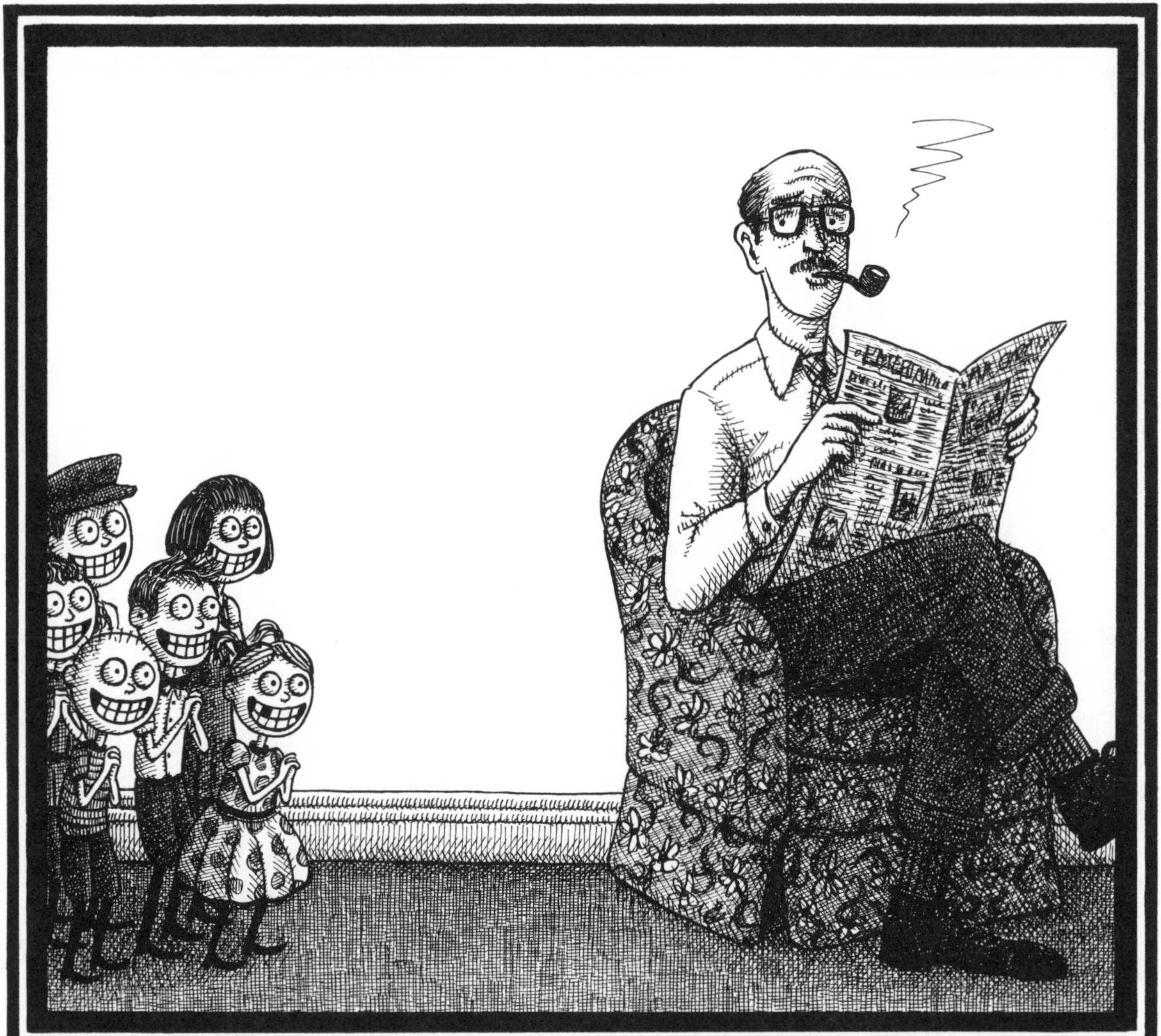

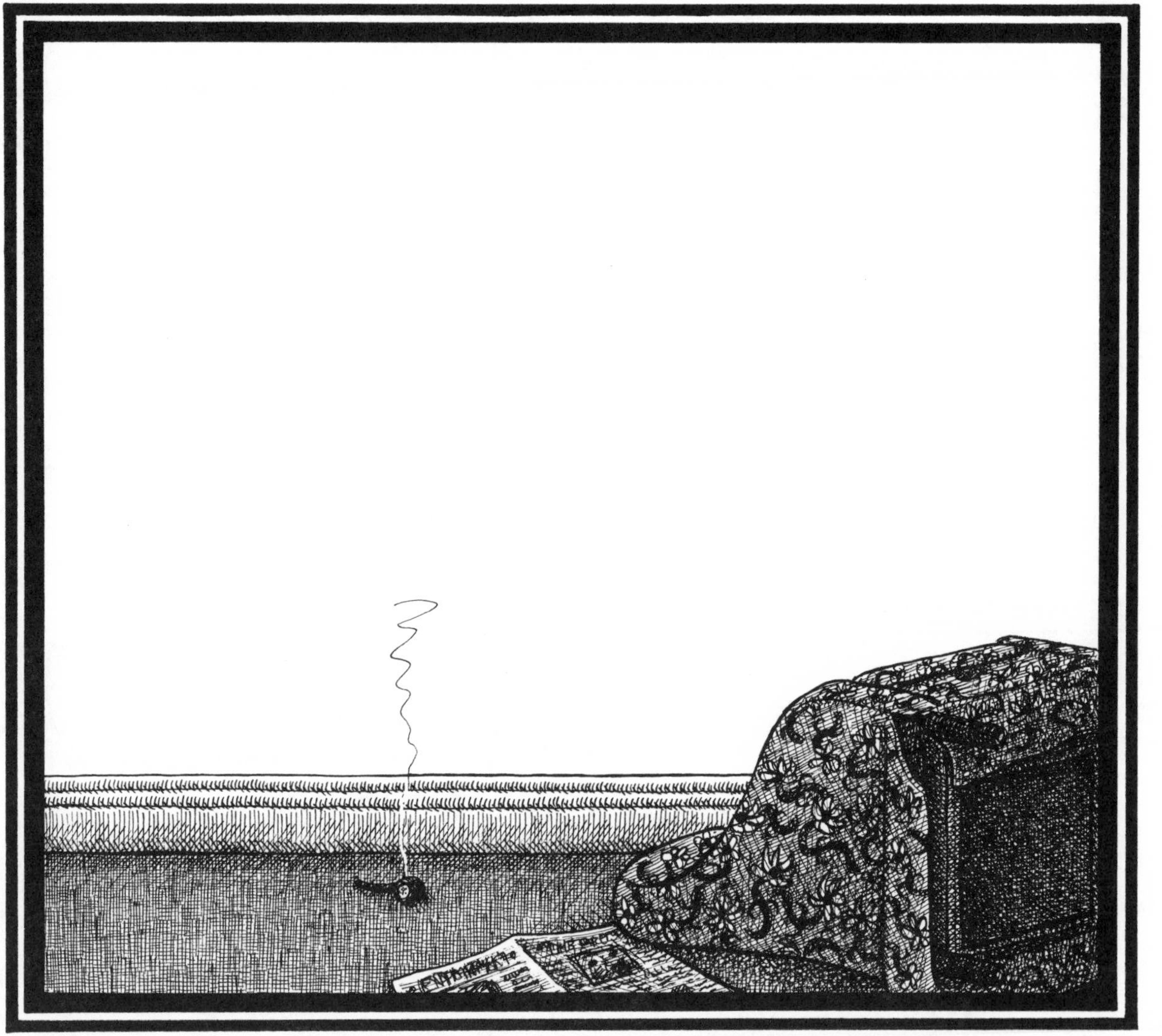

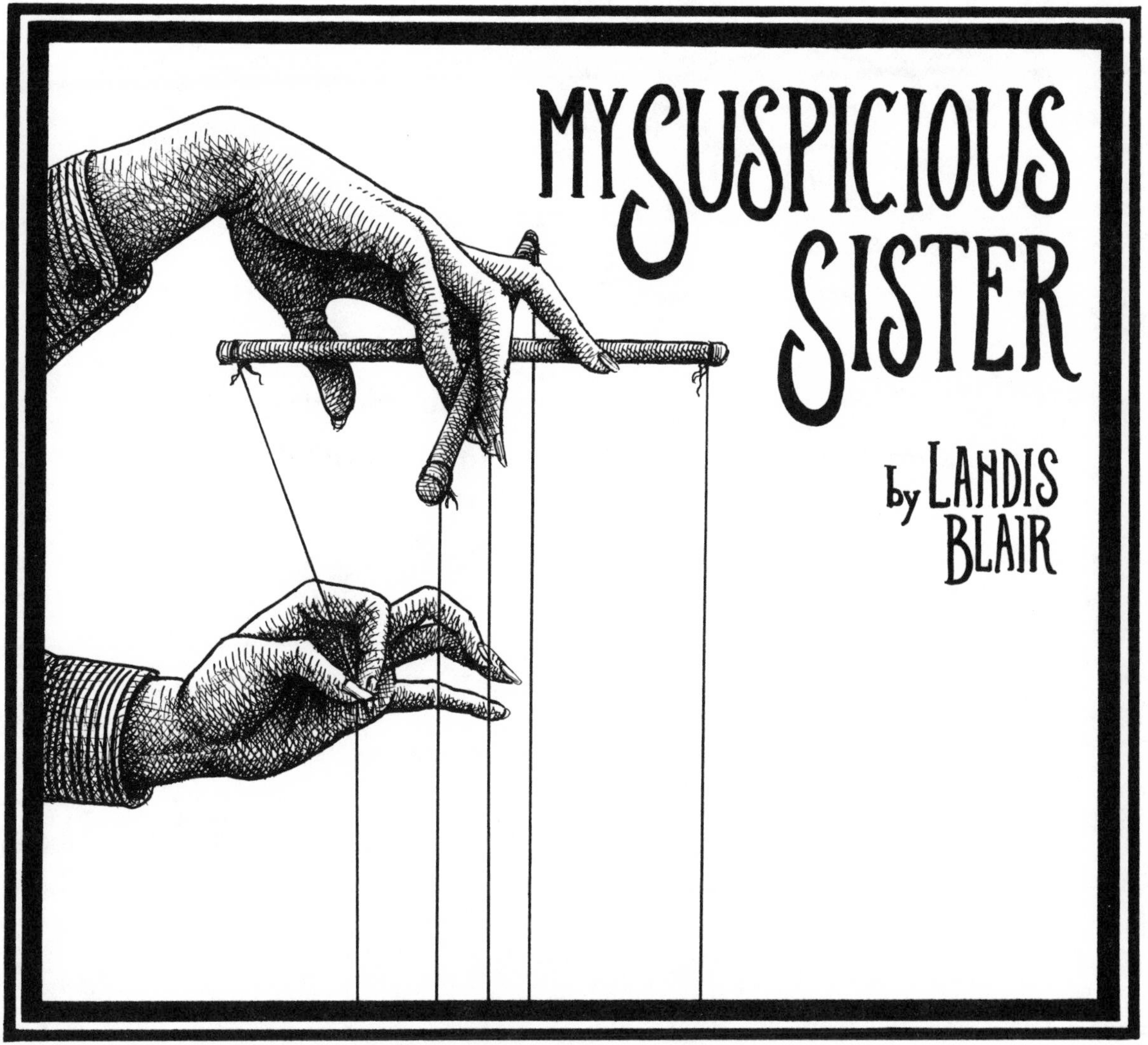
MY SUSPICIOUS SISTER
by LANDIS BLAIR

I have an older sister, or so my parents say,
But I sometimes wonder if there may have been foul play.

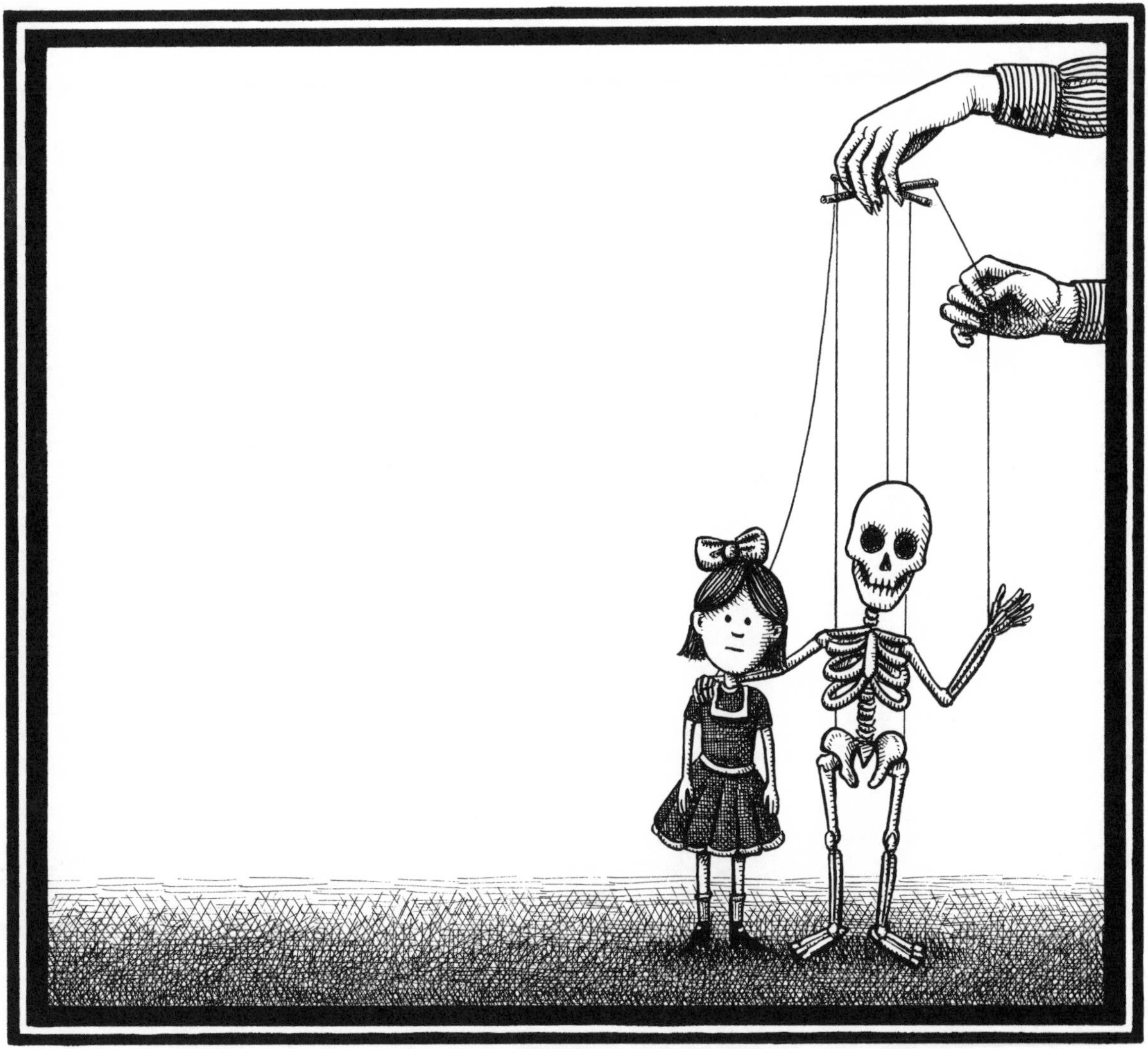

I have an older sister with whom I walk each day,
But every time she sees the dog she has to run away.

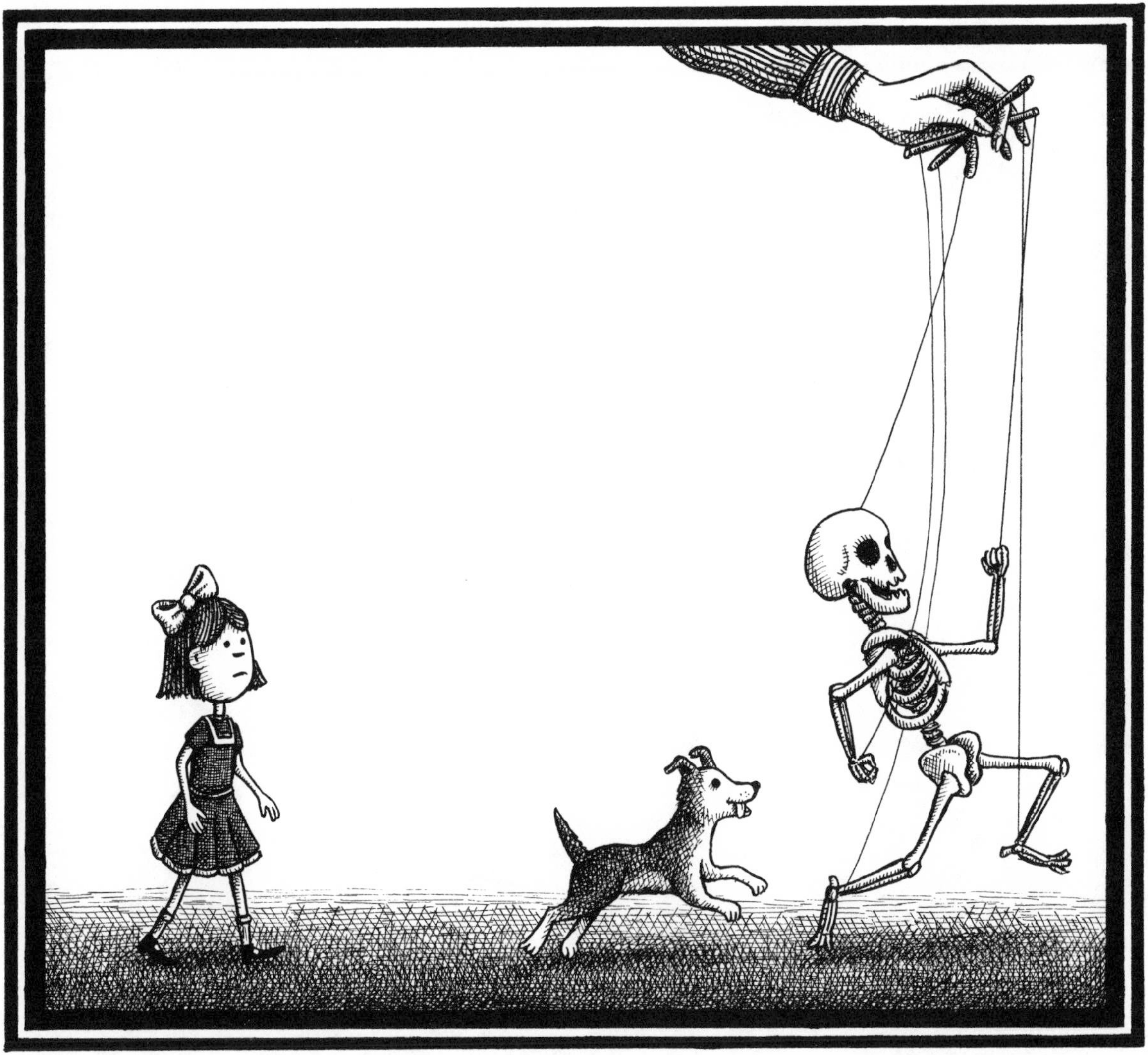

I have an older sister who doesn't mind rough play,
But then I have to help her find the parts that she mislays.

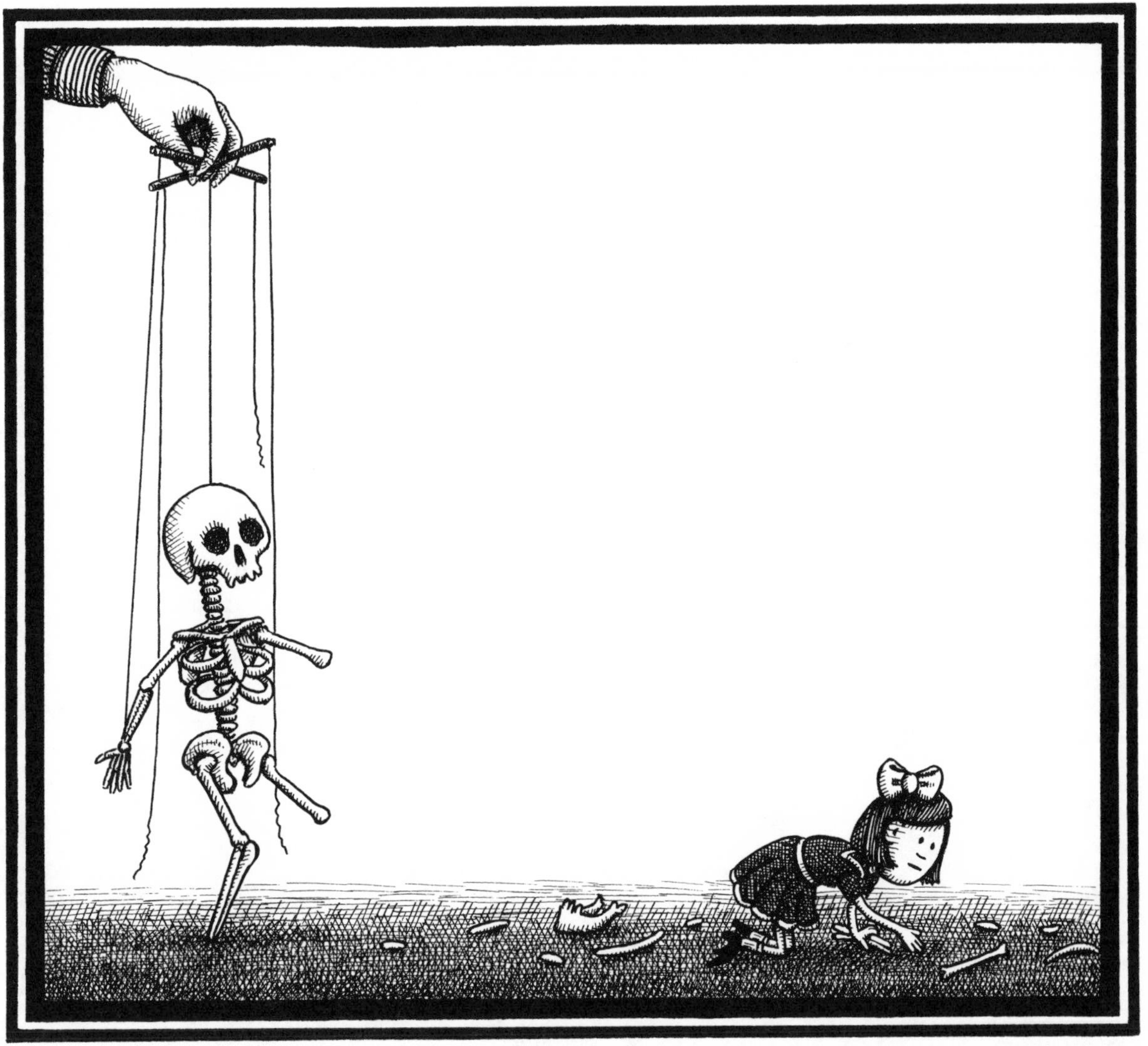

I have an older sister, we meet in the cafe,
But she eats so little that it's her whom I outweigh.

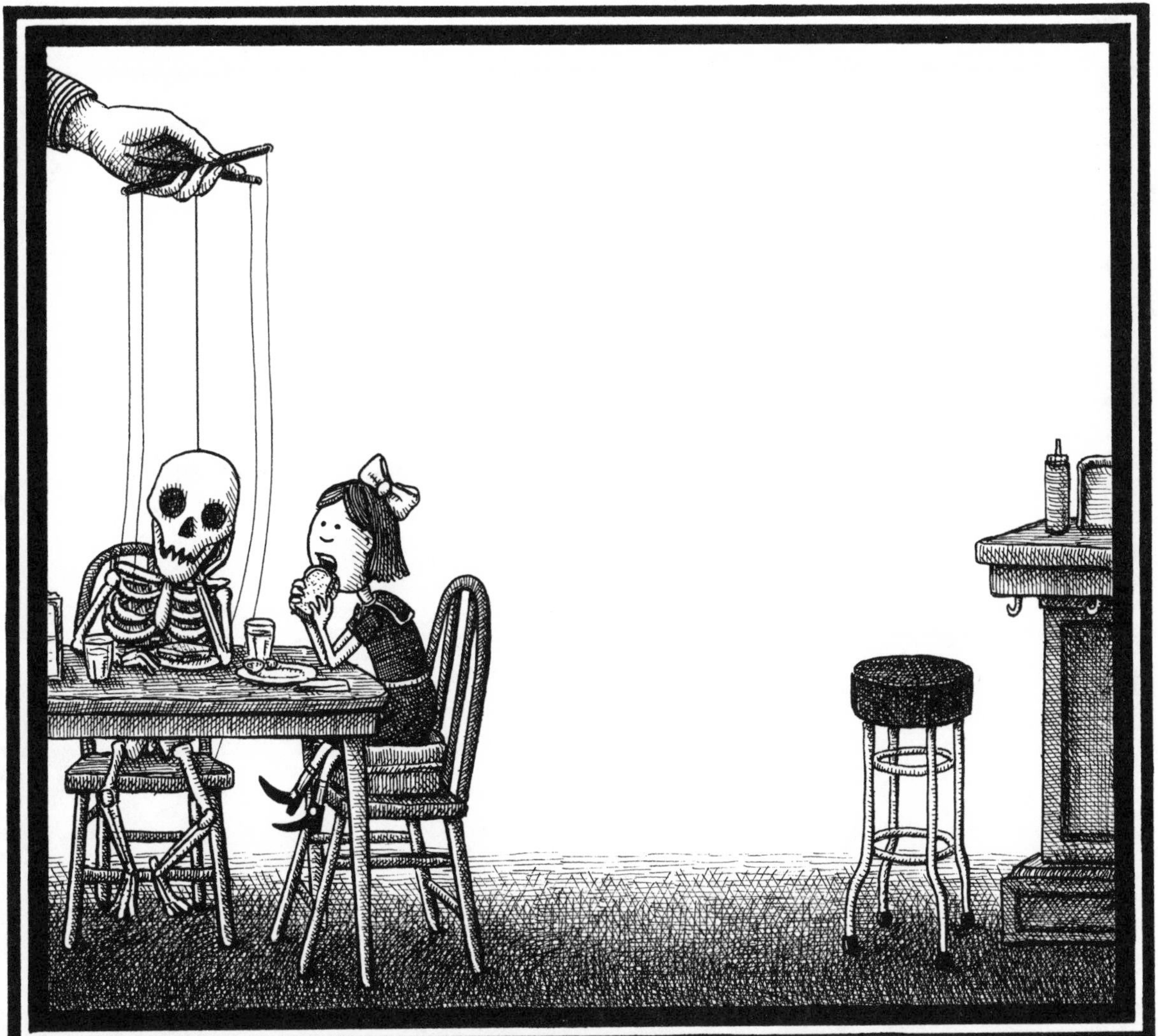

I have an older sister, we rode the train one day,
But she didn't like it 'cause it made her joints all splay.

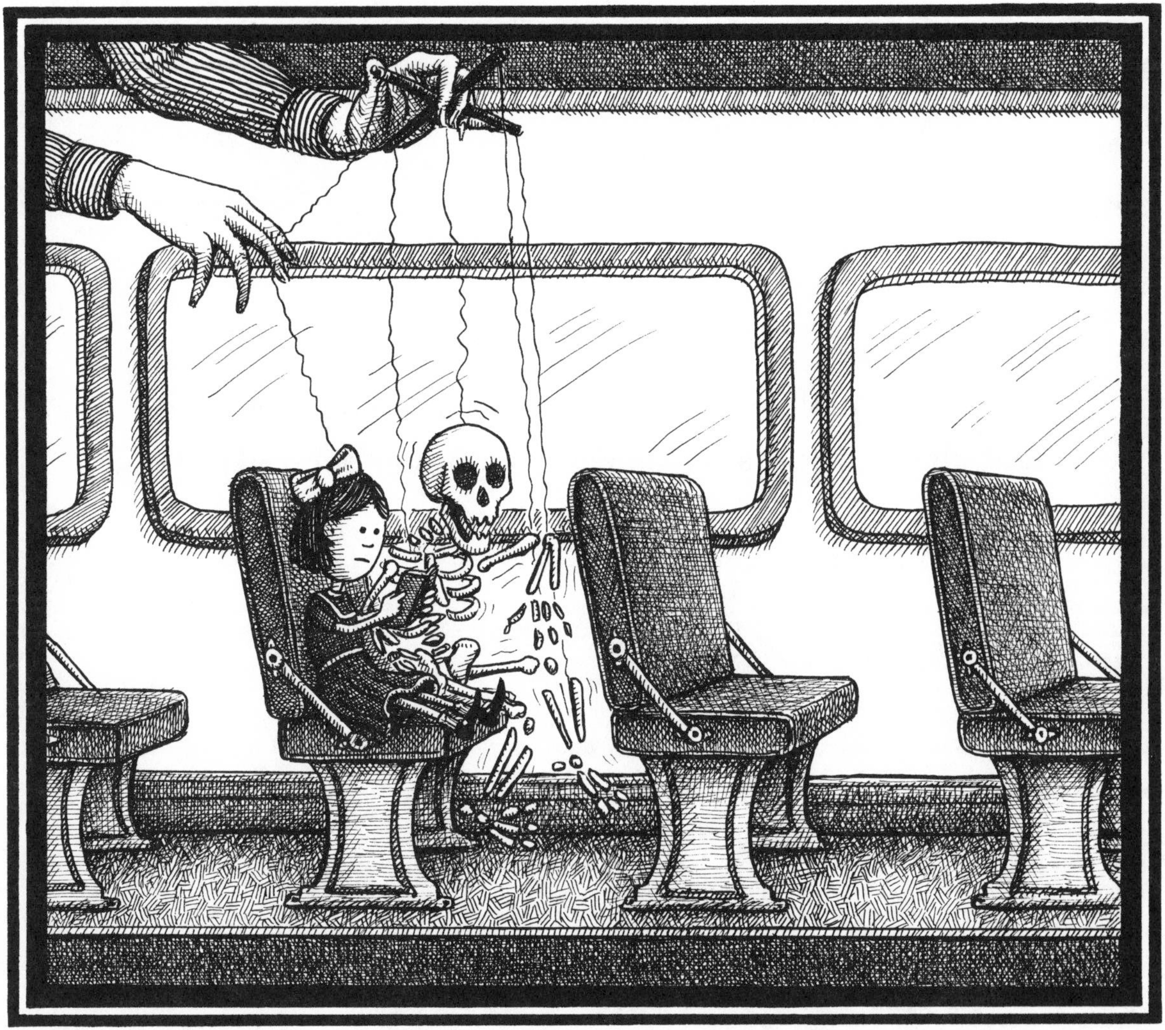

I have an older sister, she likes to kneel and pray,
But she might just be asleep; I've never seen her stray.

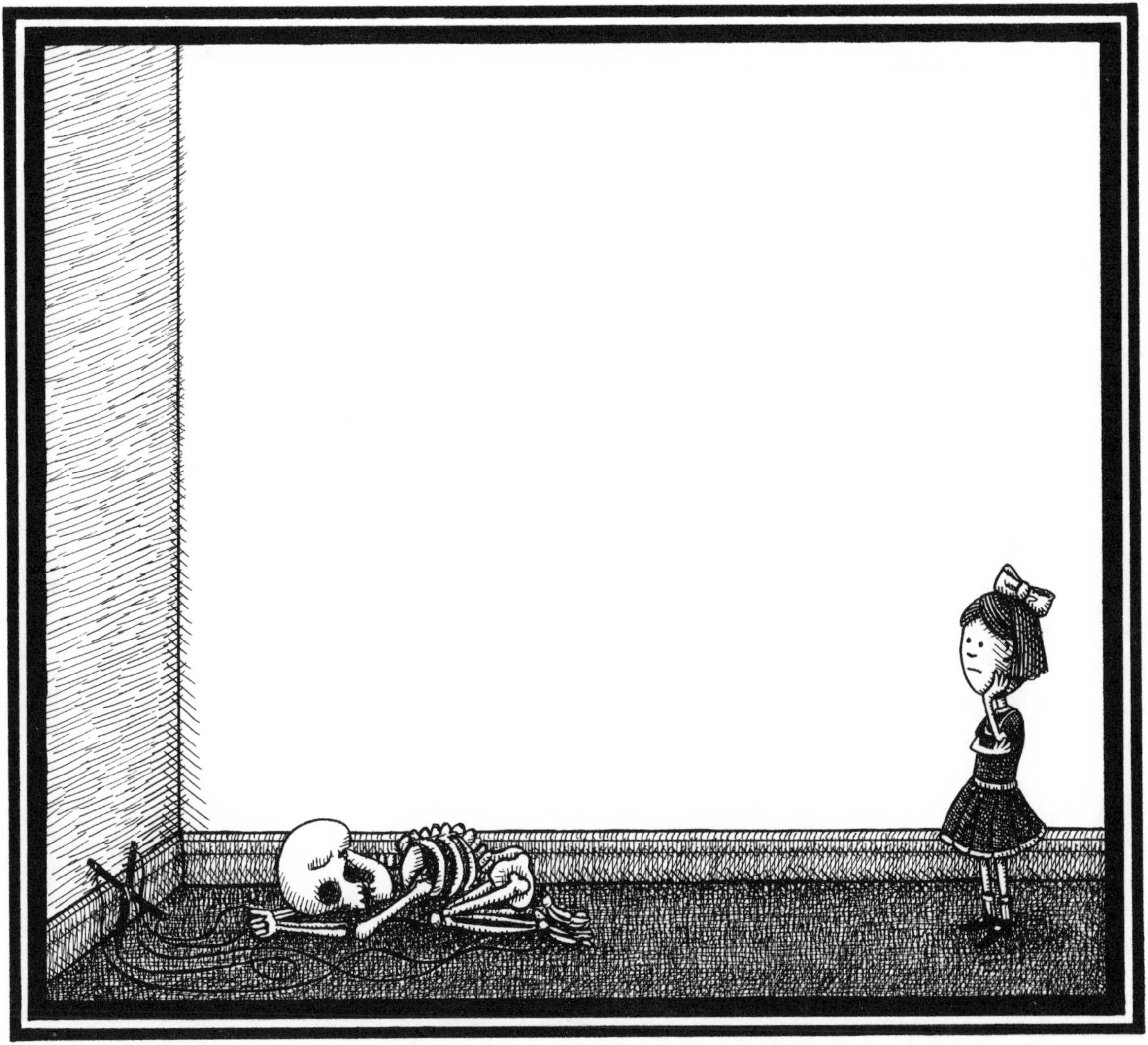

I have an older sister, who has some pet blue jays,
But she doesn't feed them, so I think they're stowaways.

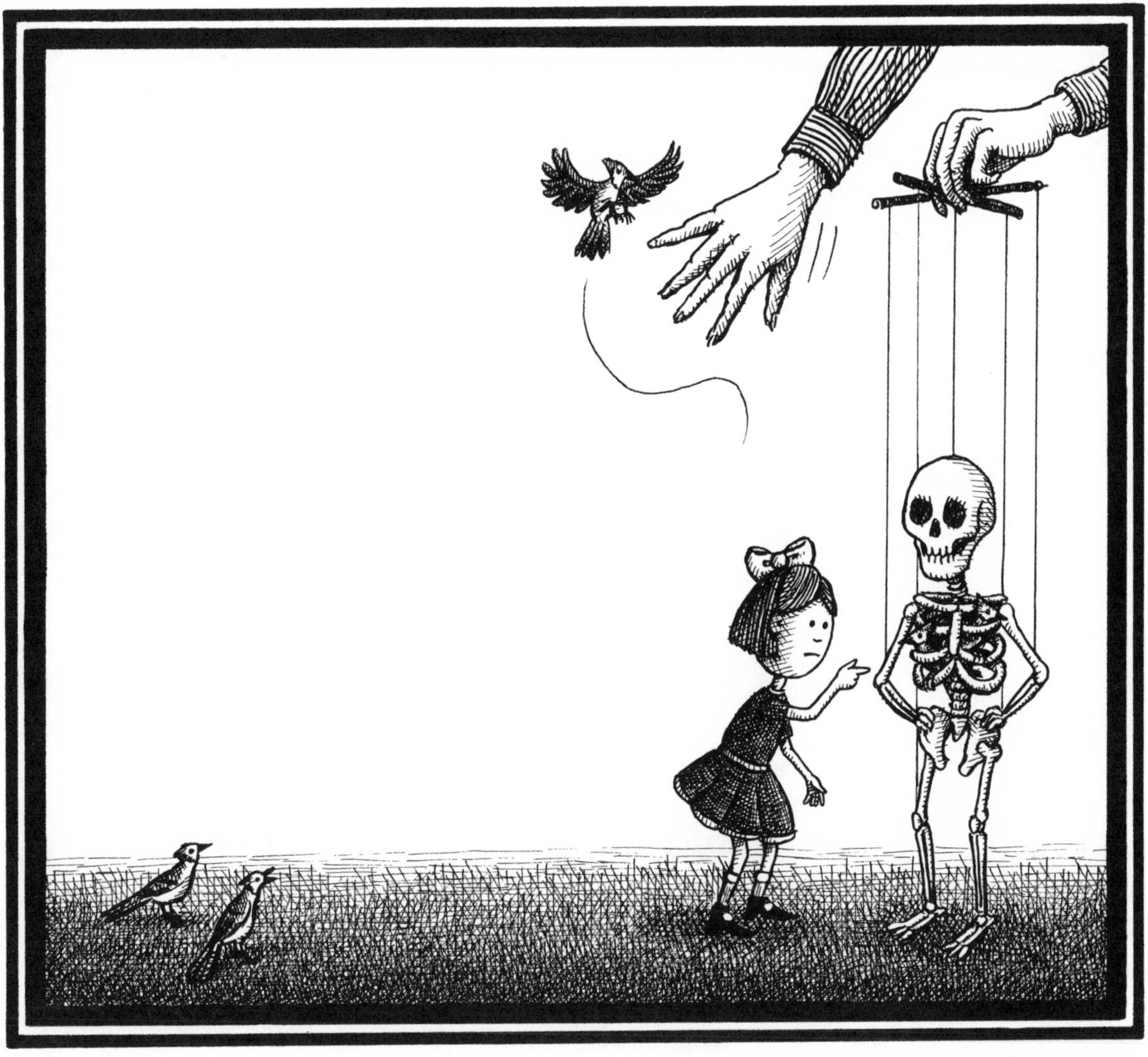

I have an older sister, who powders every day,
But I doubt it helps, since her complexion is so gray.

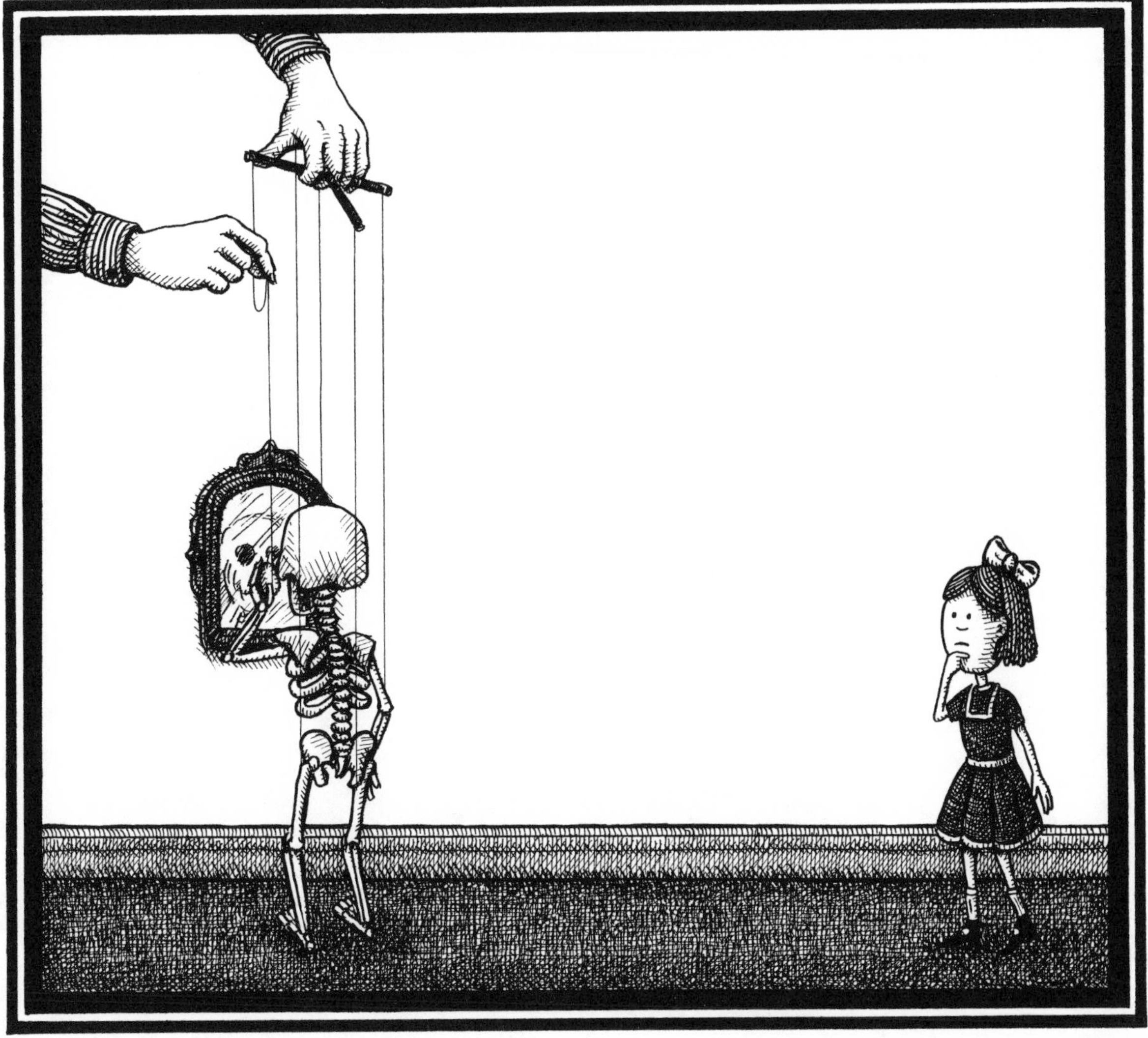

I have an older sister, and I'm her protégé,
But of late I wonder if she's leading me astray.

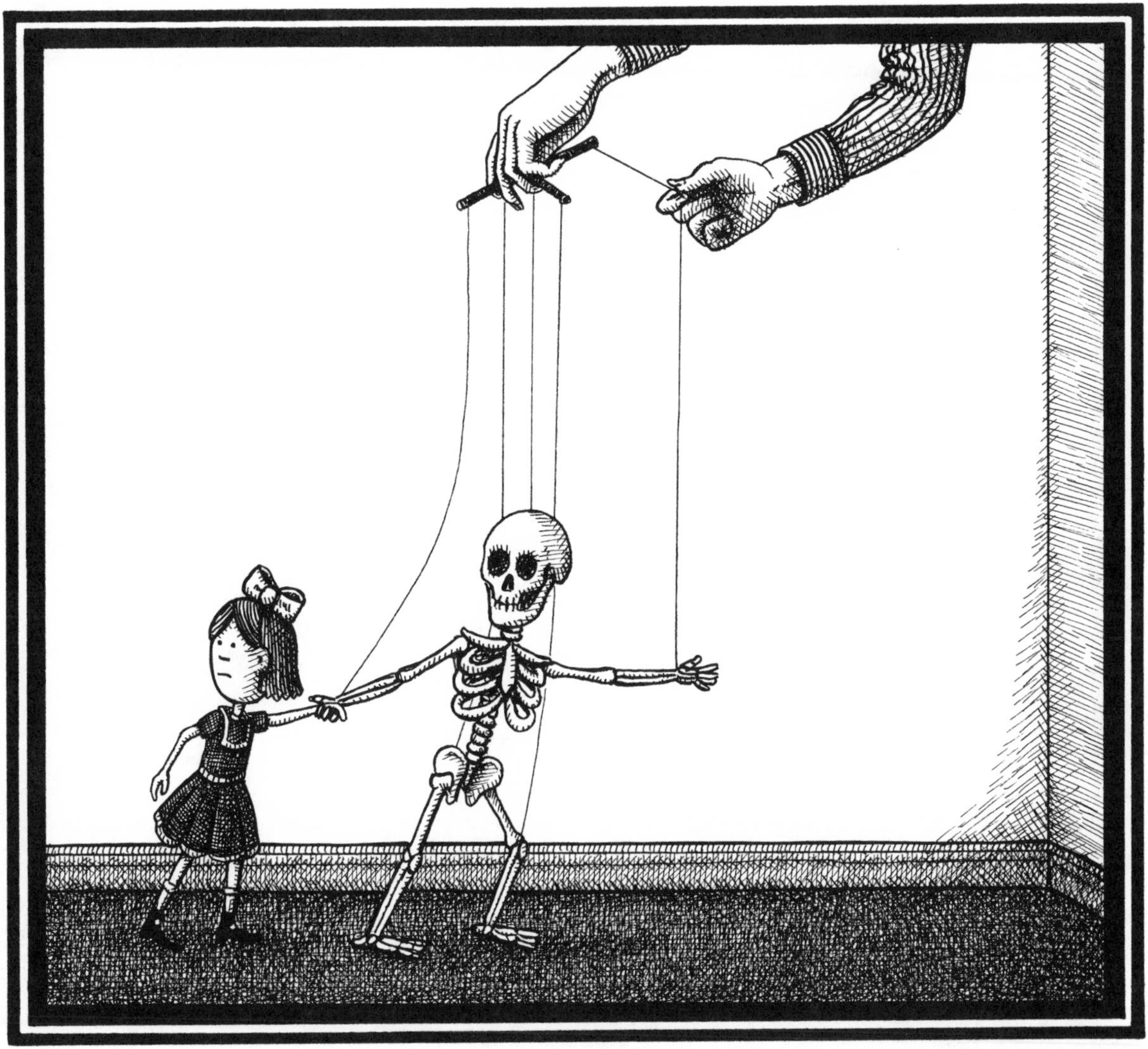

I have an older sister, whom I cannot disobey,
She wants me now to follow her, I hope I'll be okay.

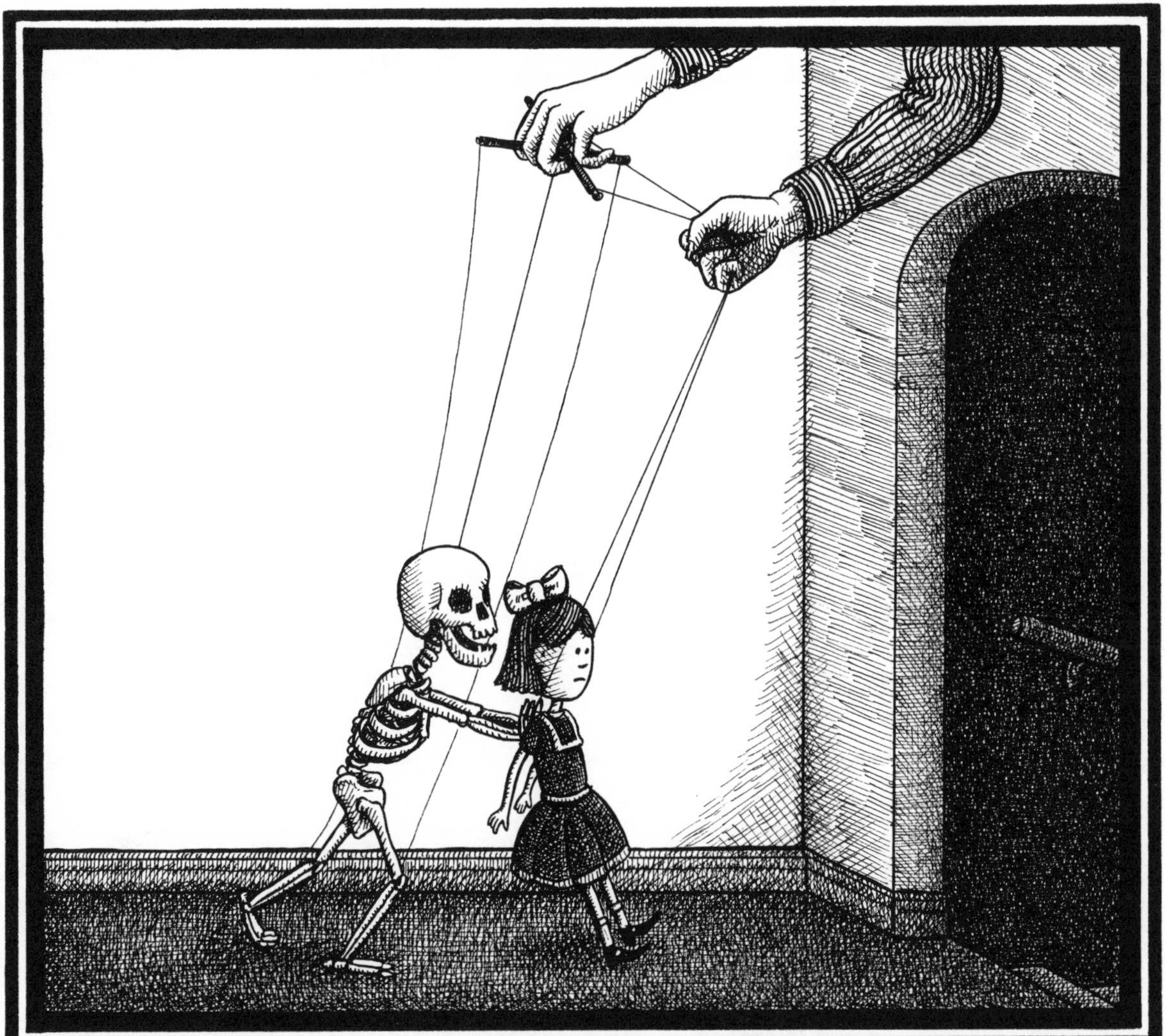

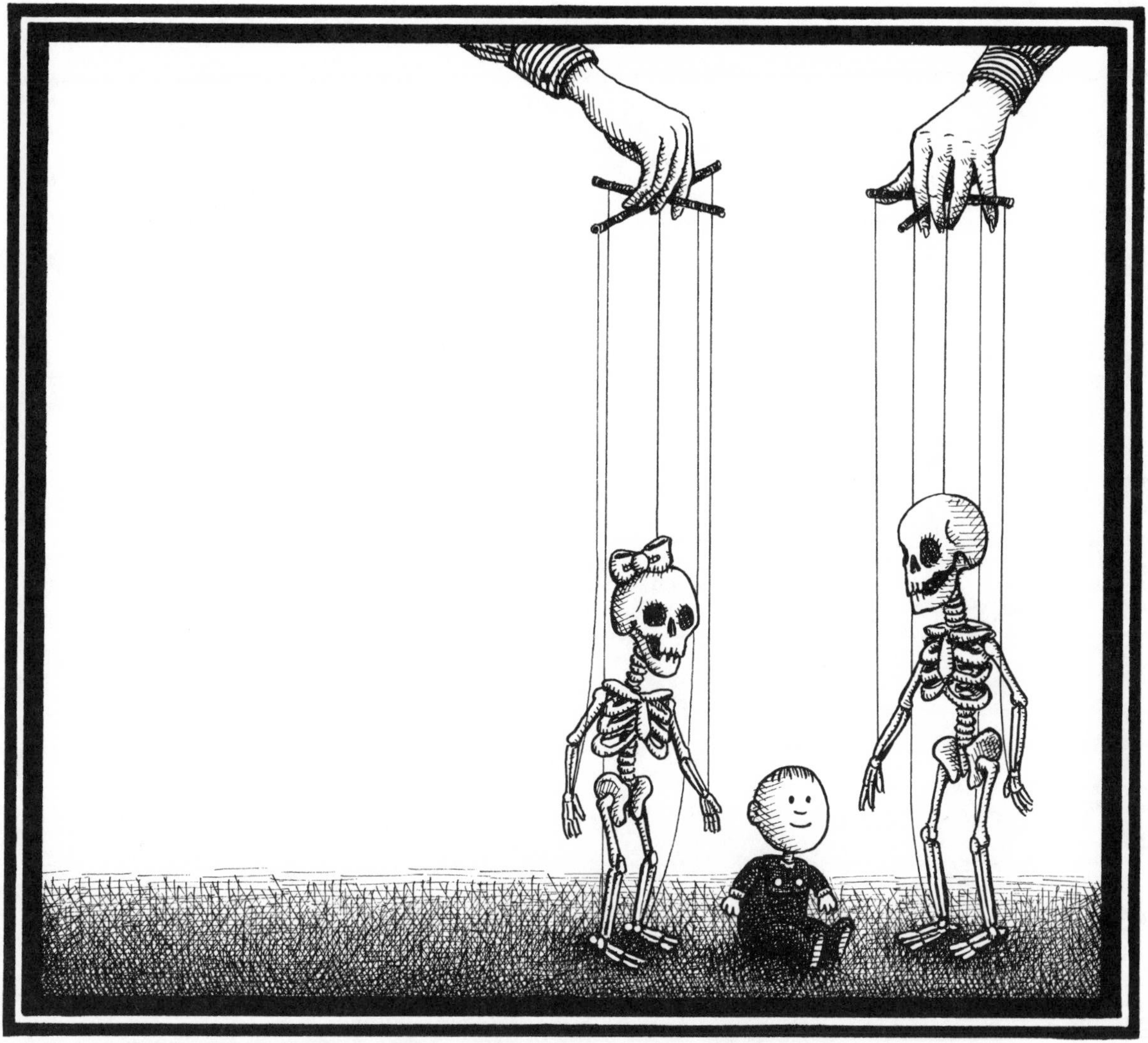

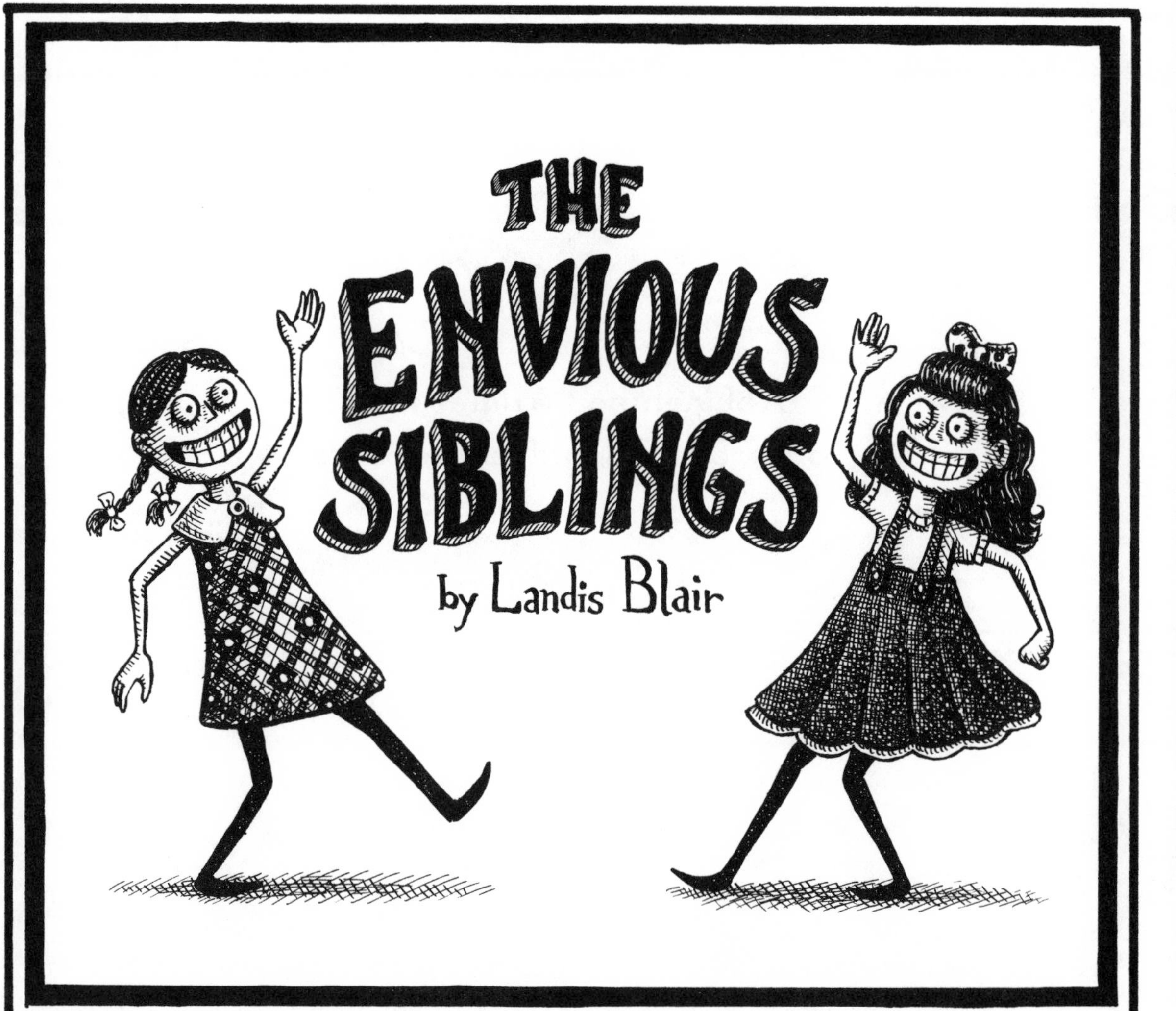
THE
ENVIOUS
SIBLINGS
by Landis Blair

Abby envied Angie's hair,
Sheared it all and left her bare.

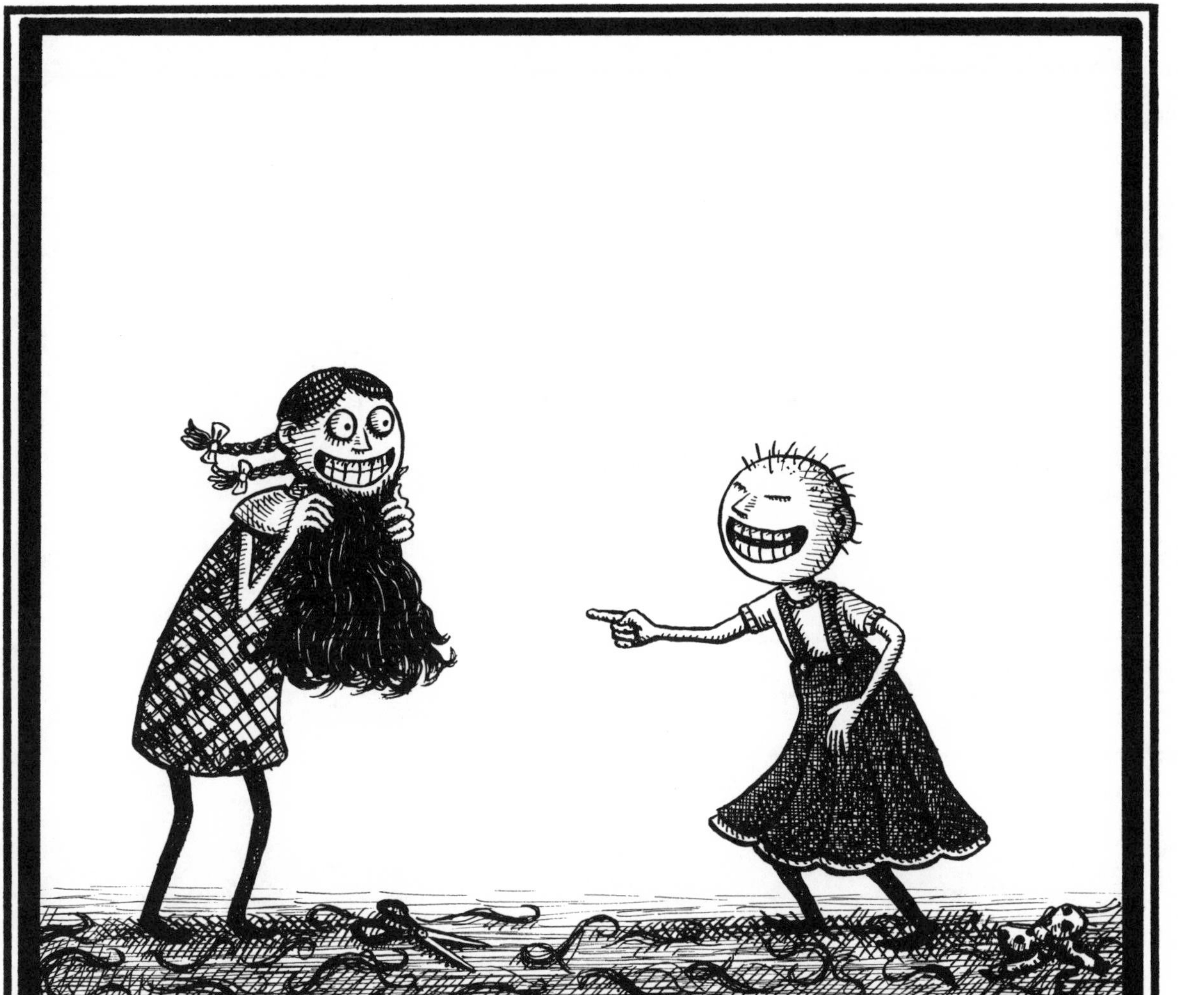

Angie envied Abby's teeth,
Pried them forth and made a wreath.

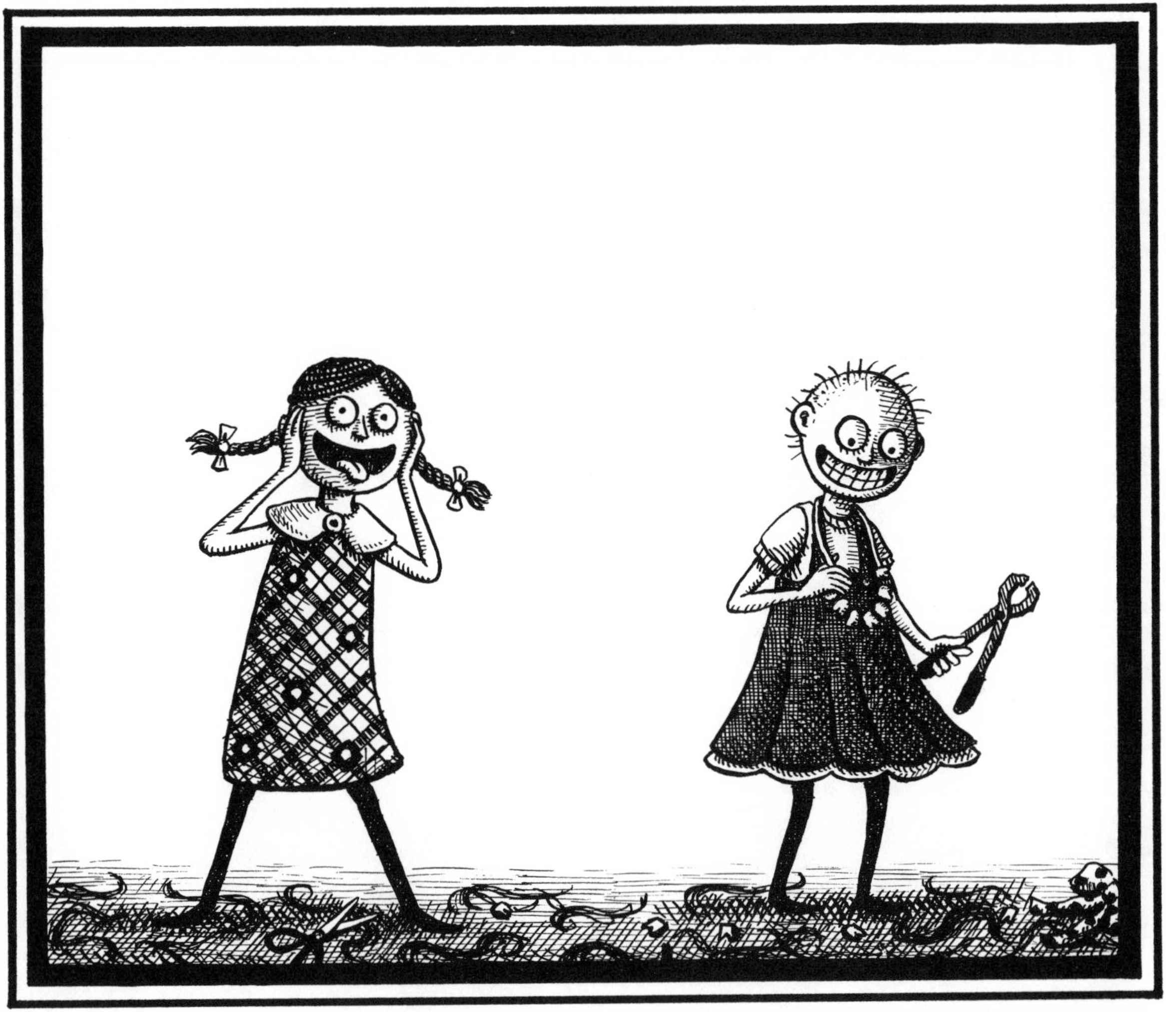

Abby envied Angie's hand,
Lopped it off and formed a band.

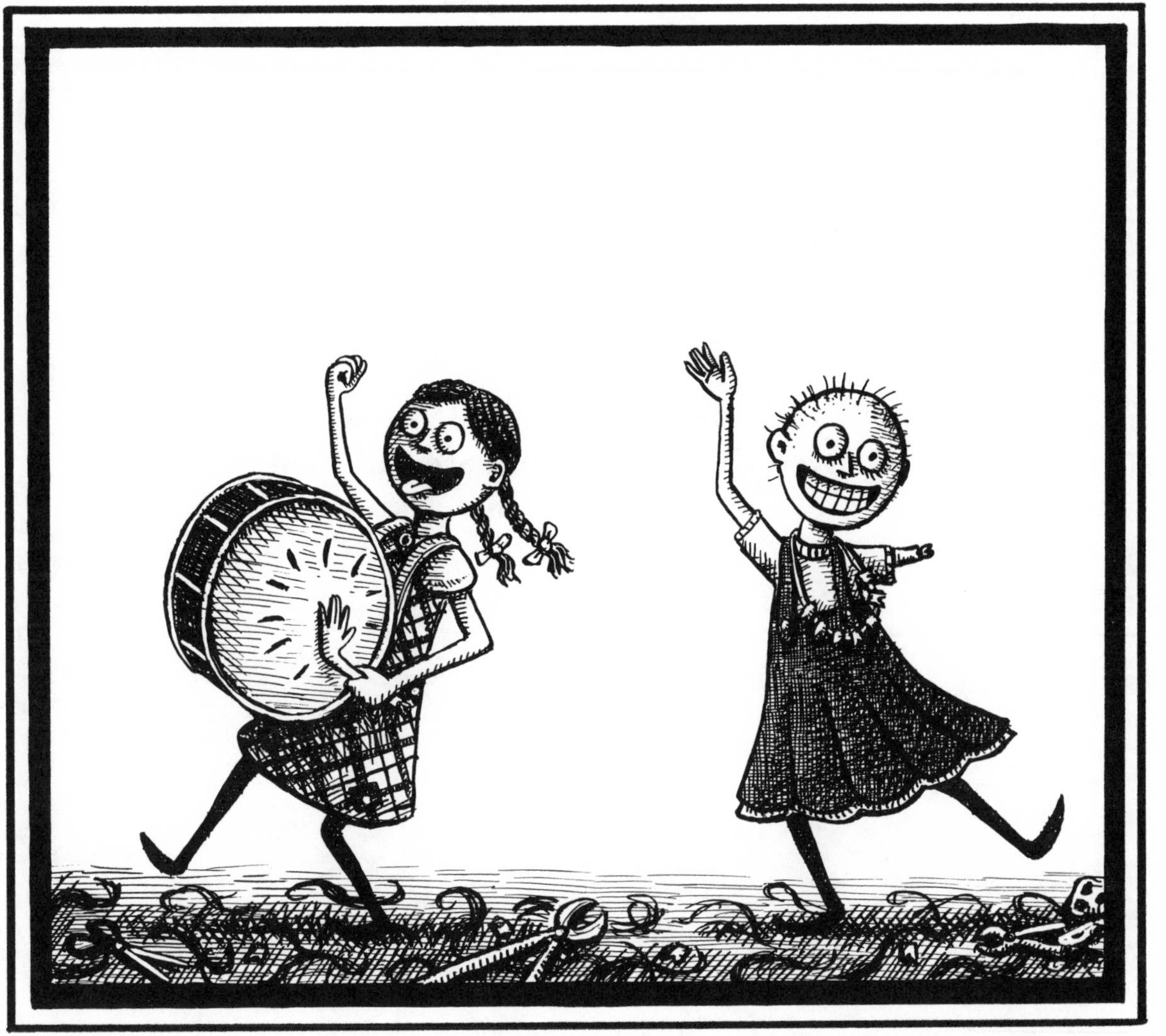

Angie envied Abby's feet,
Sawed them down and ate the meat.

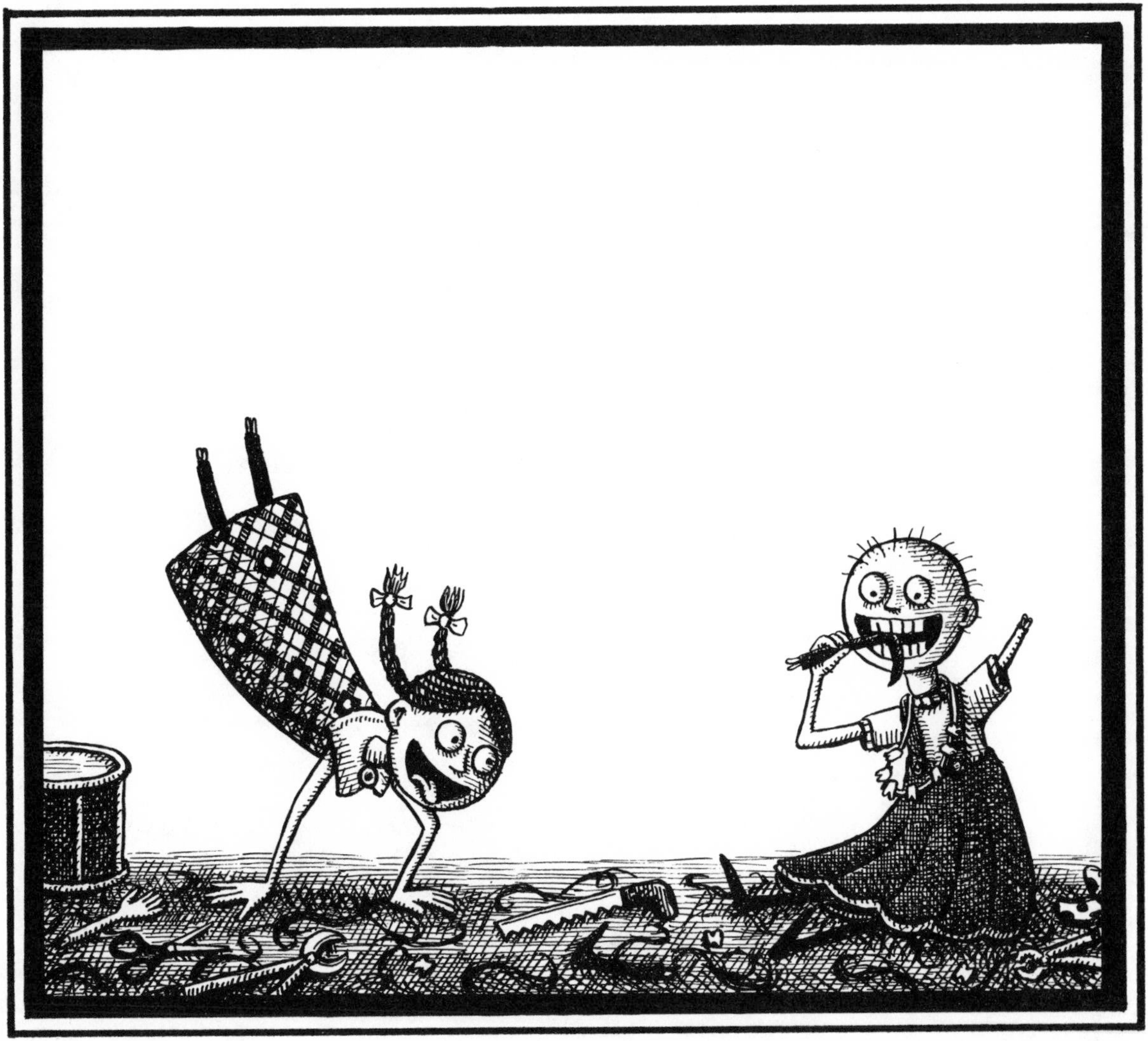

Abby envied Angie's lips,
Sliced them thin and made some whips.

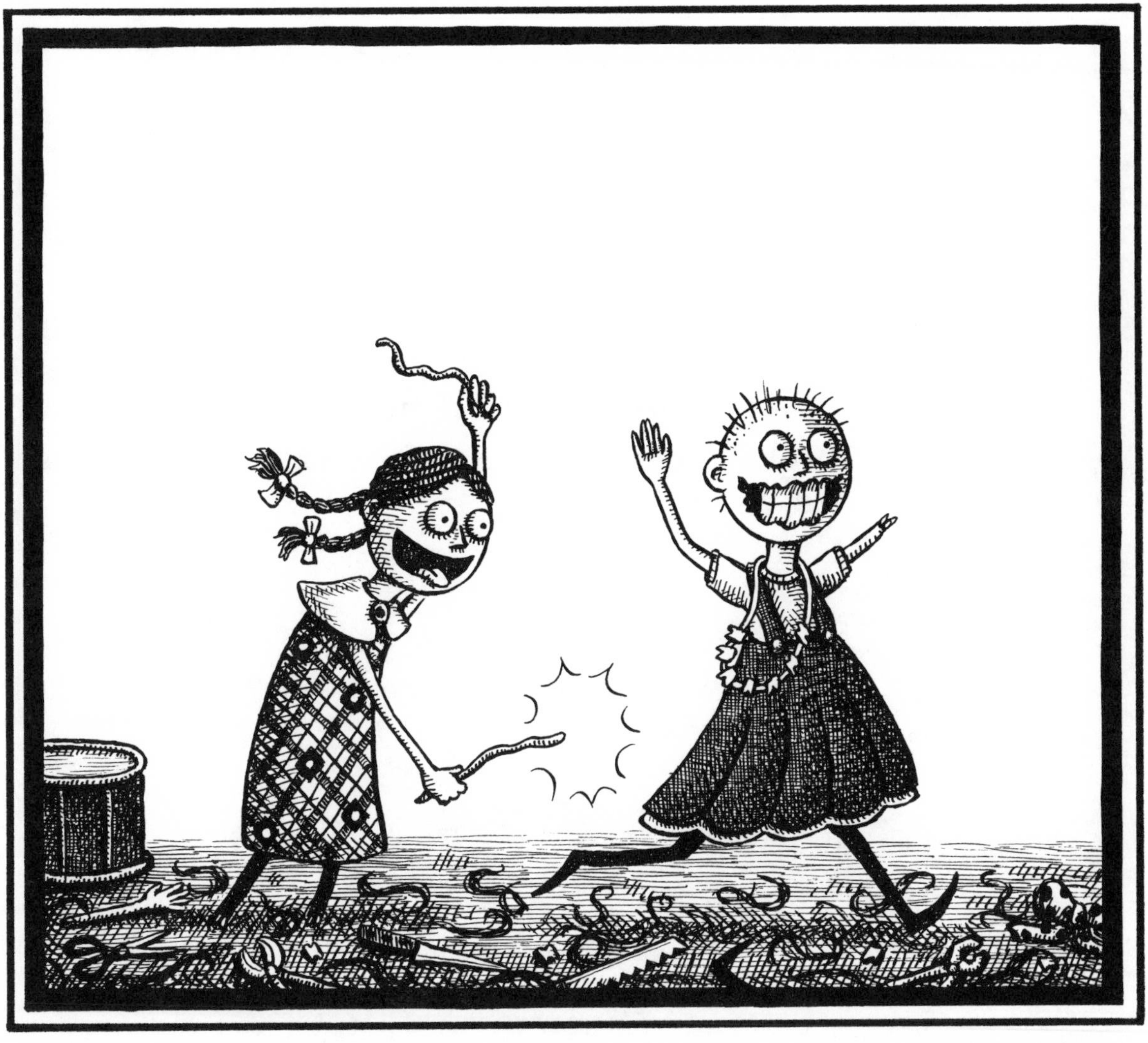

Angie envied Abby's nose,
Broke it loose and fed the crows.

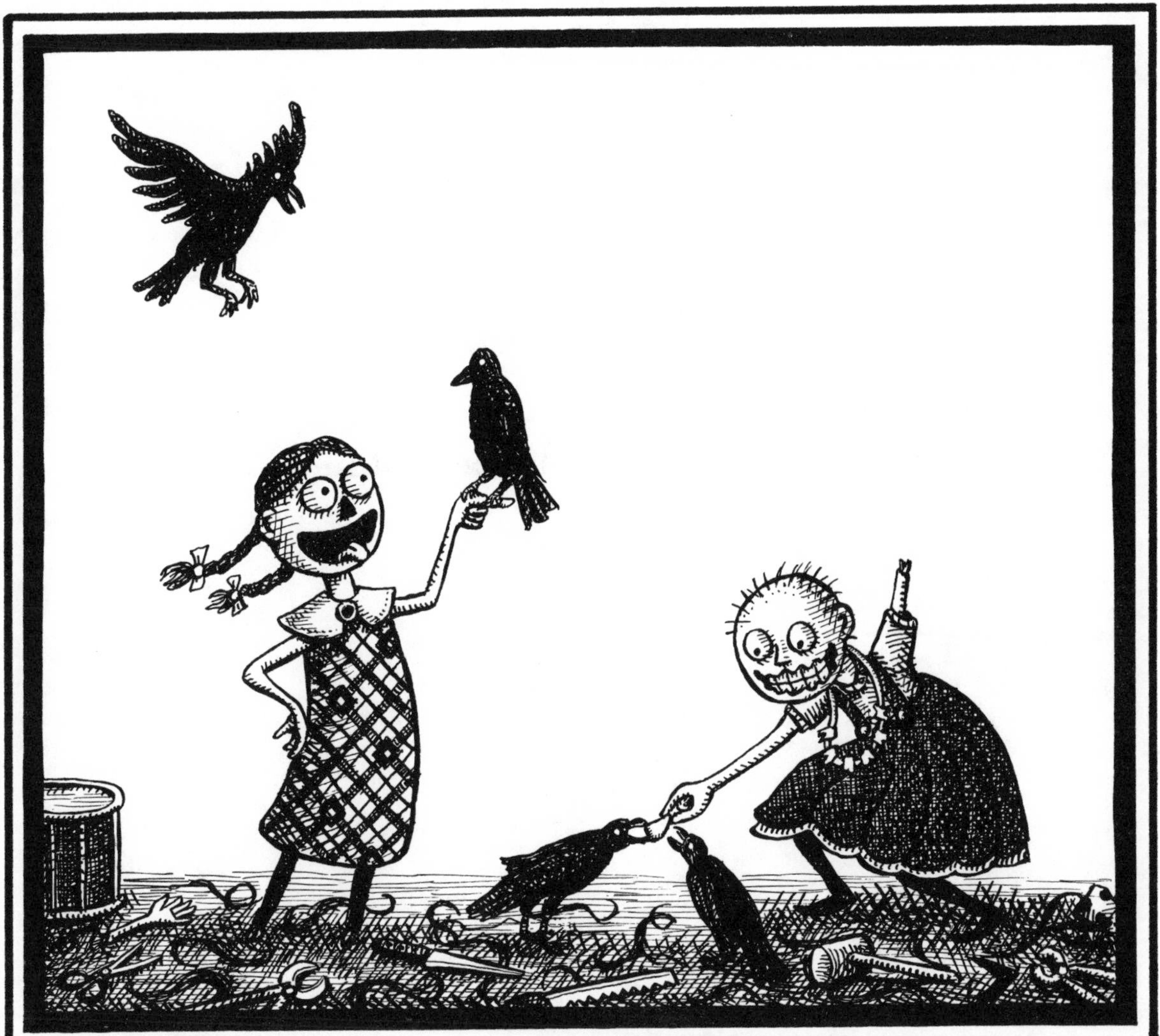

Abby envied Angie's eye,
Plucked it out and bounced it high.

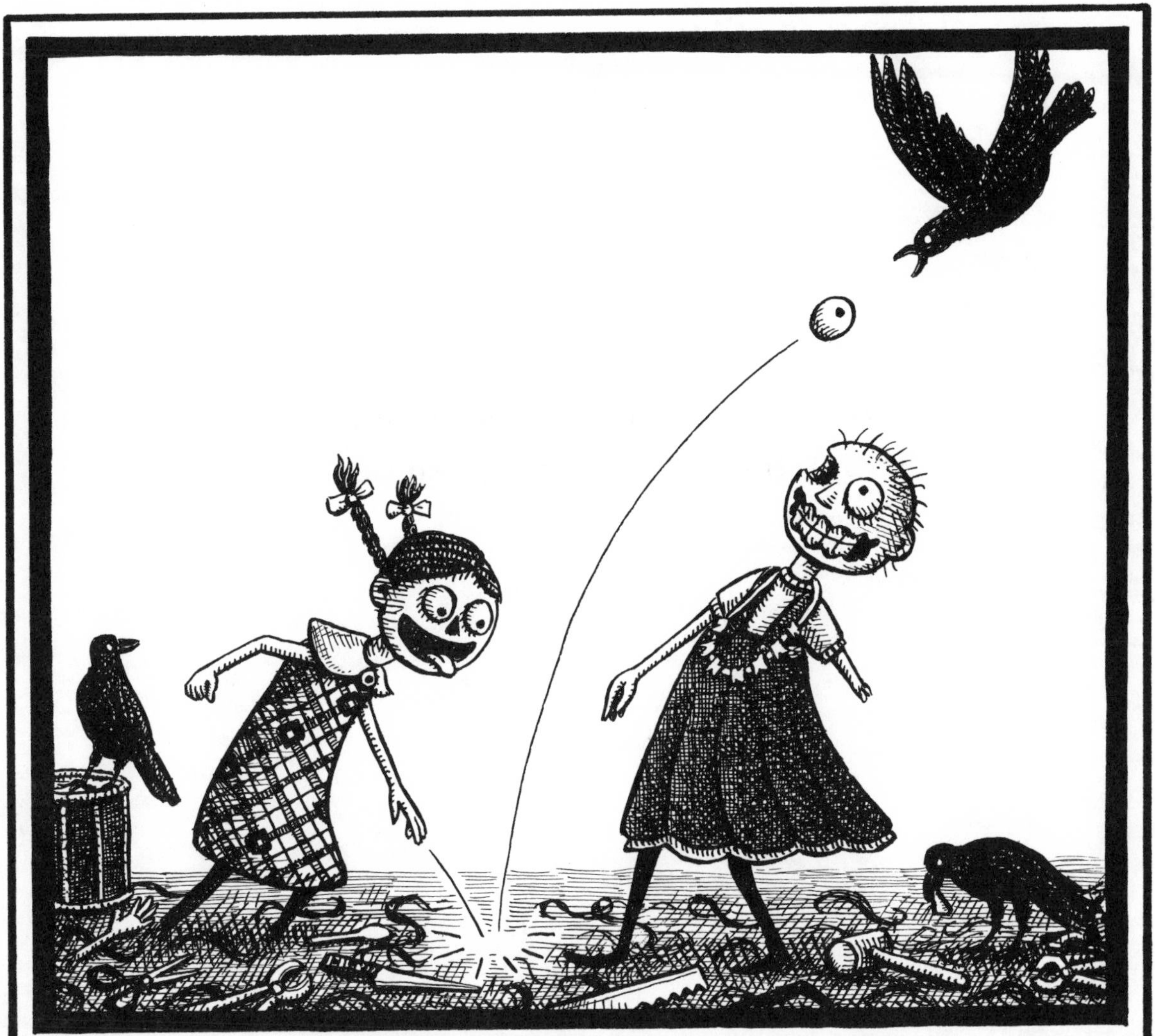

Angie envied Abby's ear,
Stretched it free and topped her rear.

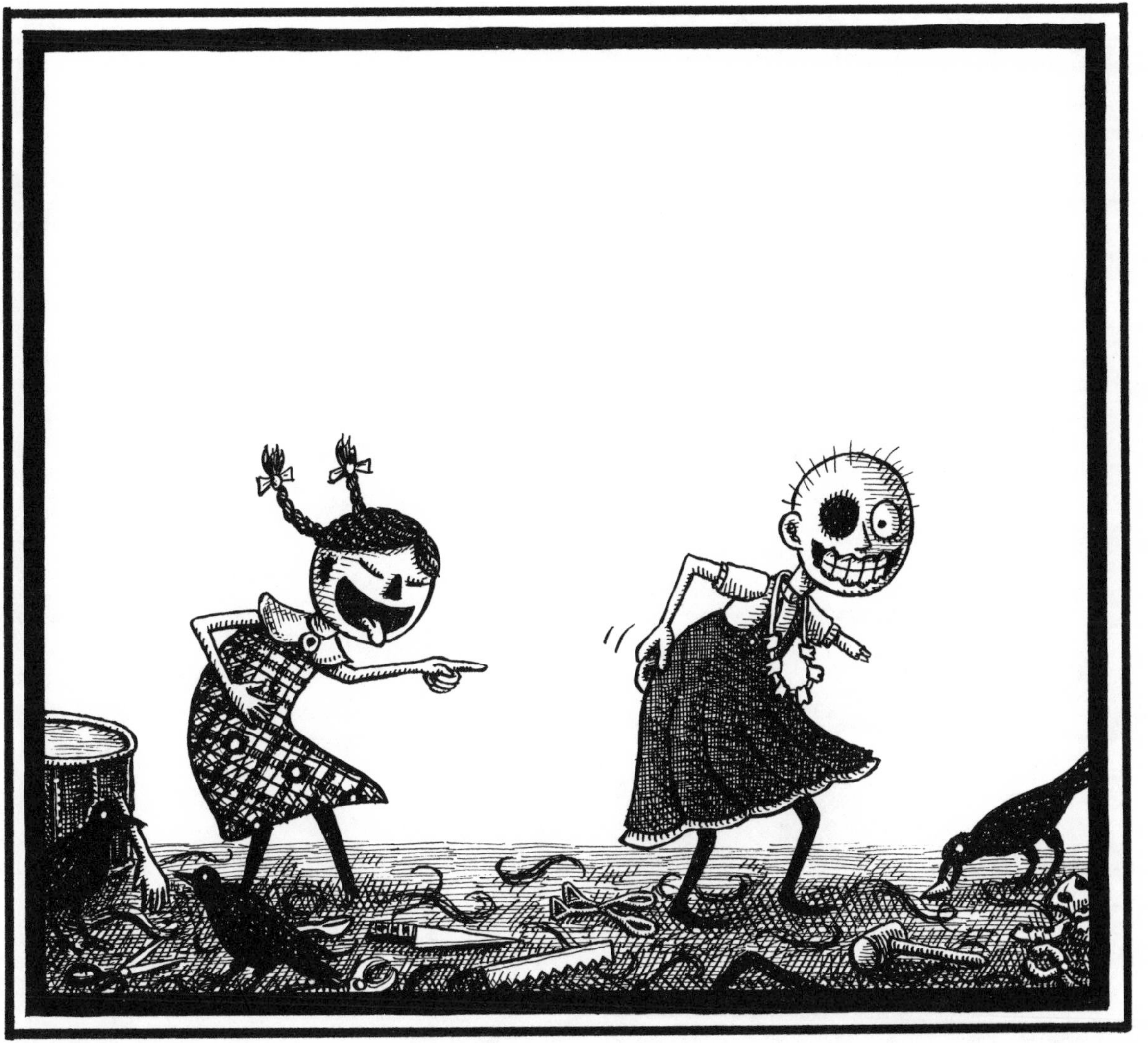

Abby envied Angie's skin,
Peeled it raw and lined a bin.

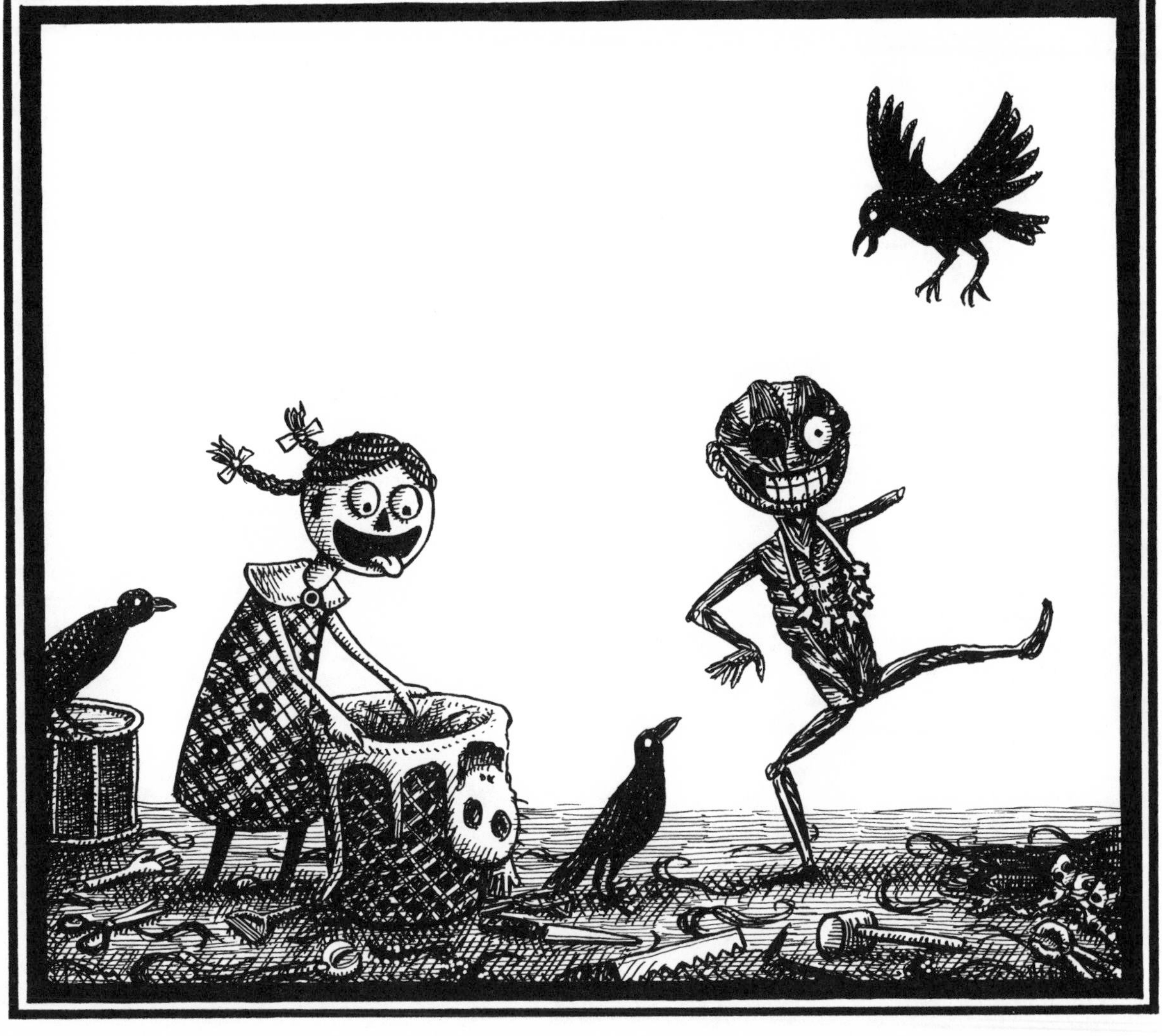

Angie envied Abby's tonque,
Yanked it clean and had some fun.

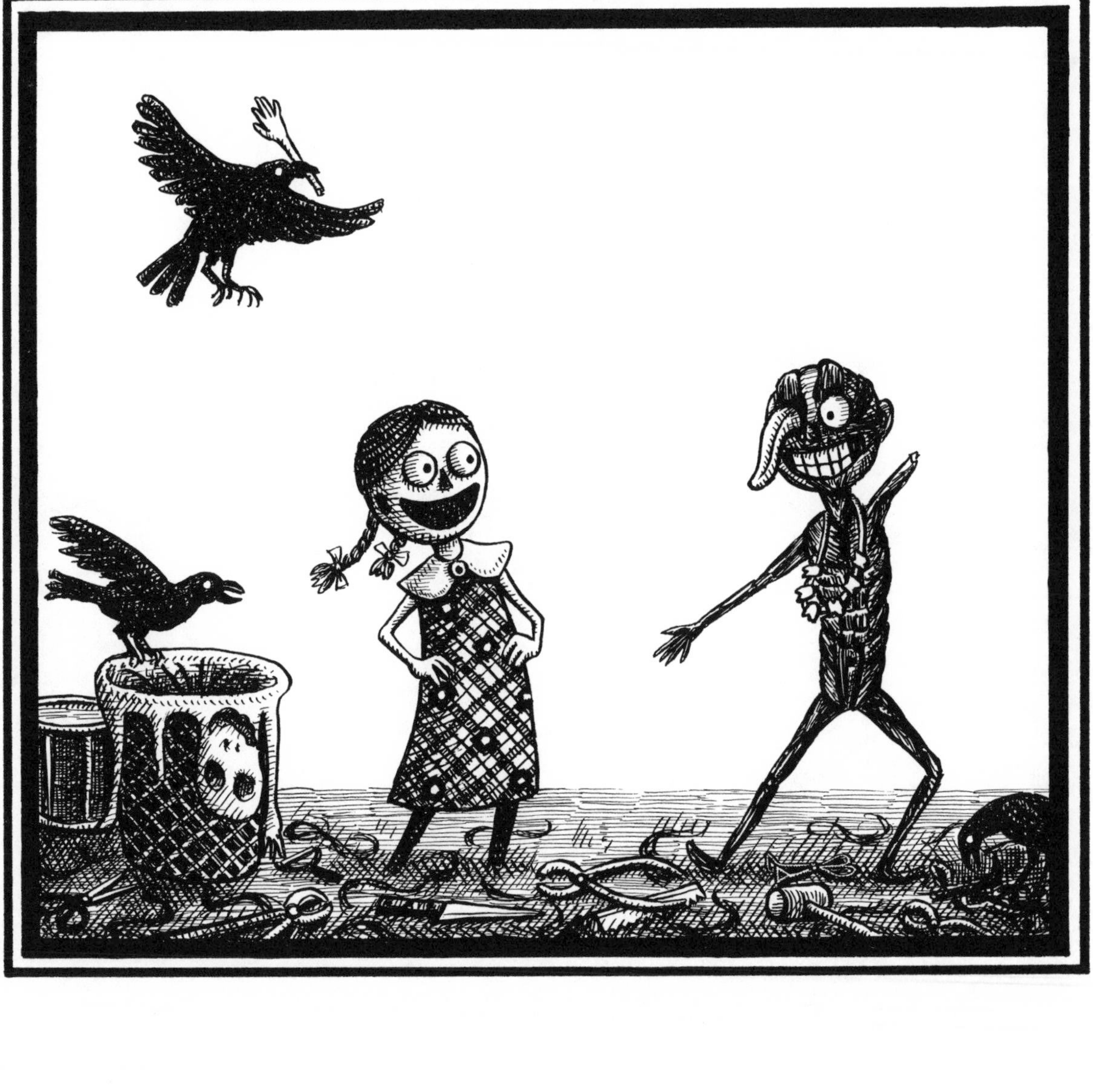

Mother, tiring of the fuss,
Murdered both and envy thus.

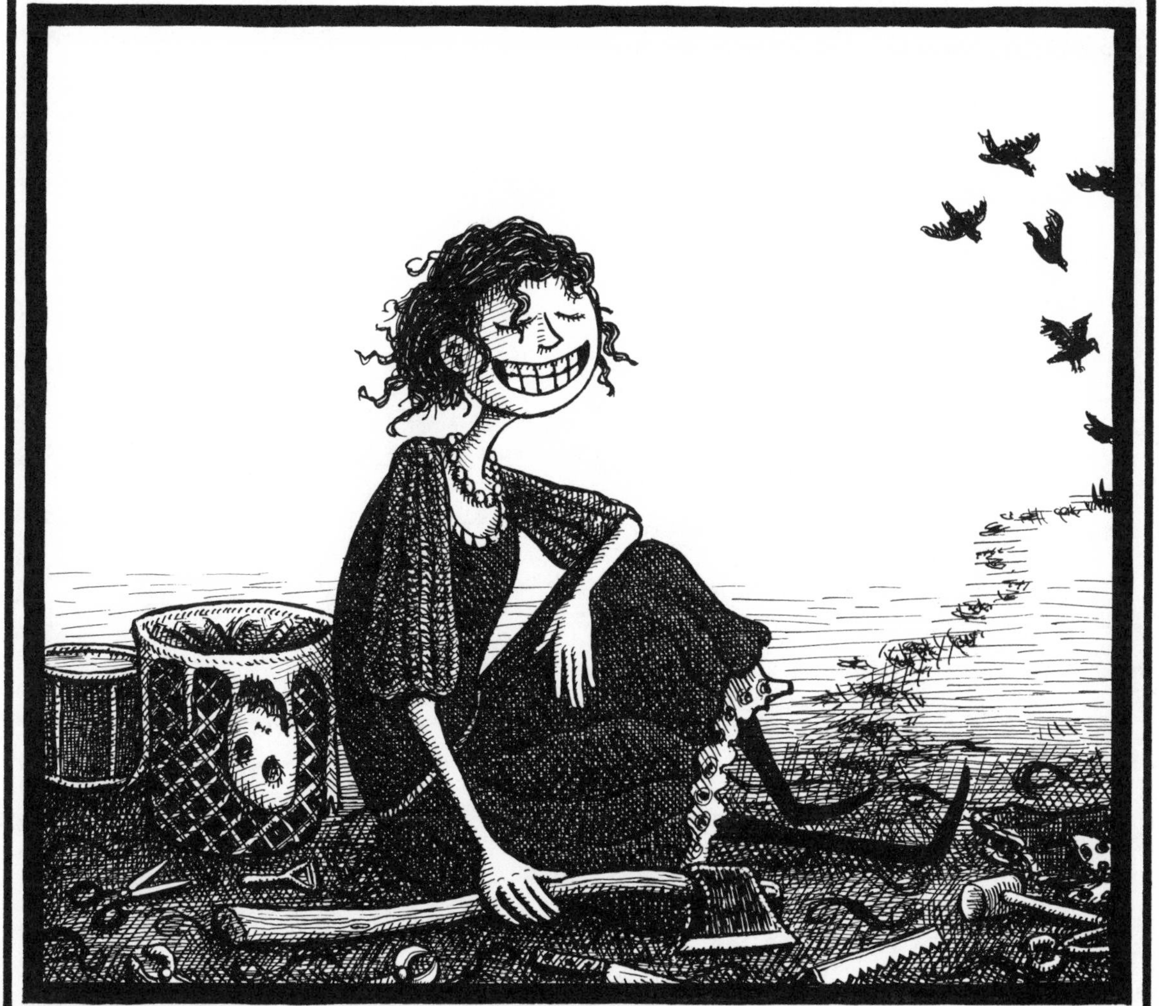

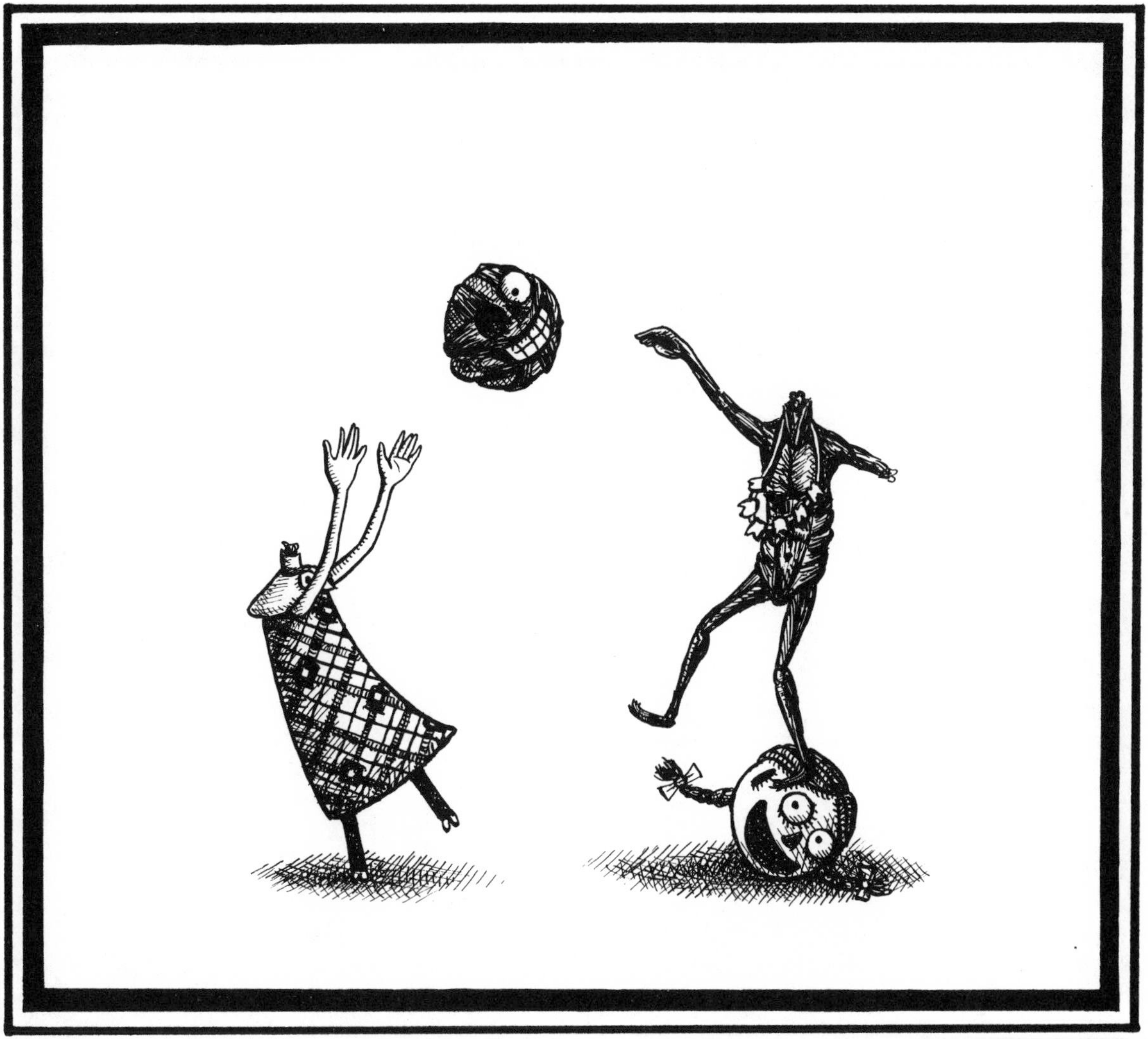

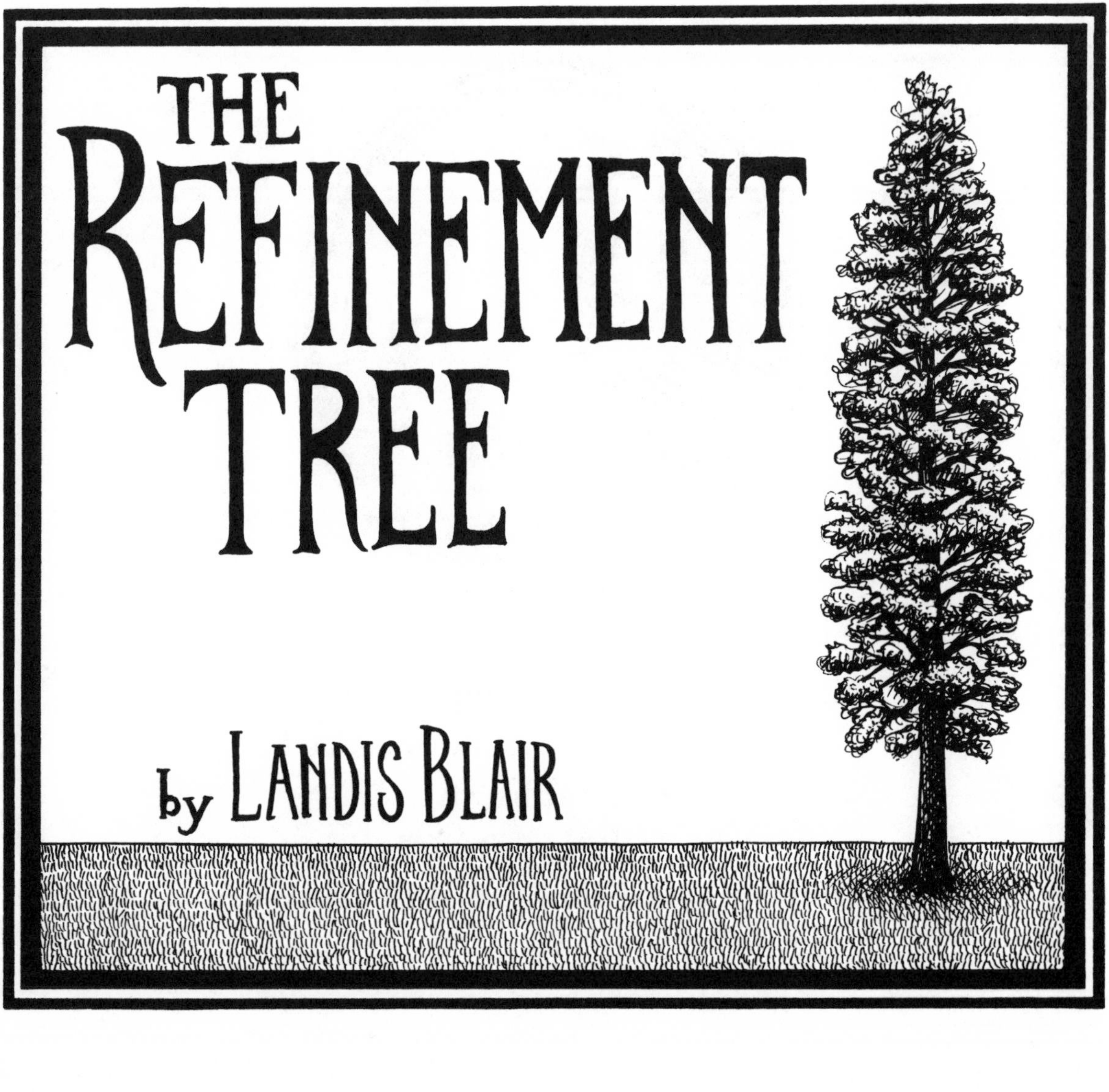
THE REFINEMENT TREE
by LANDIS BLAIR

Young Simon was drawn to the trees,
Of this he could not be appeased.
Defiant he ran
And felt a grown man,
Declaring he'd climb what he pleased.

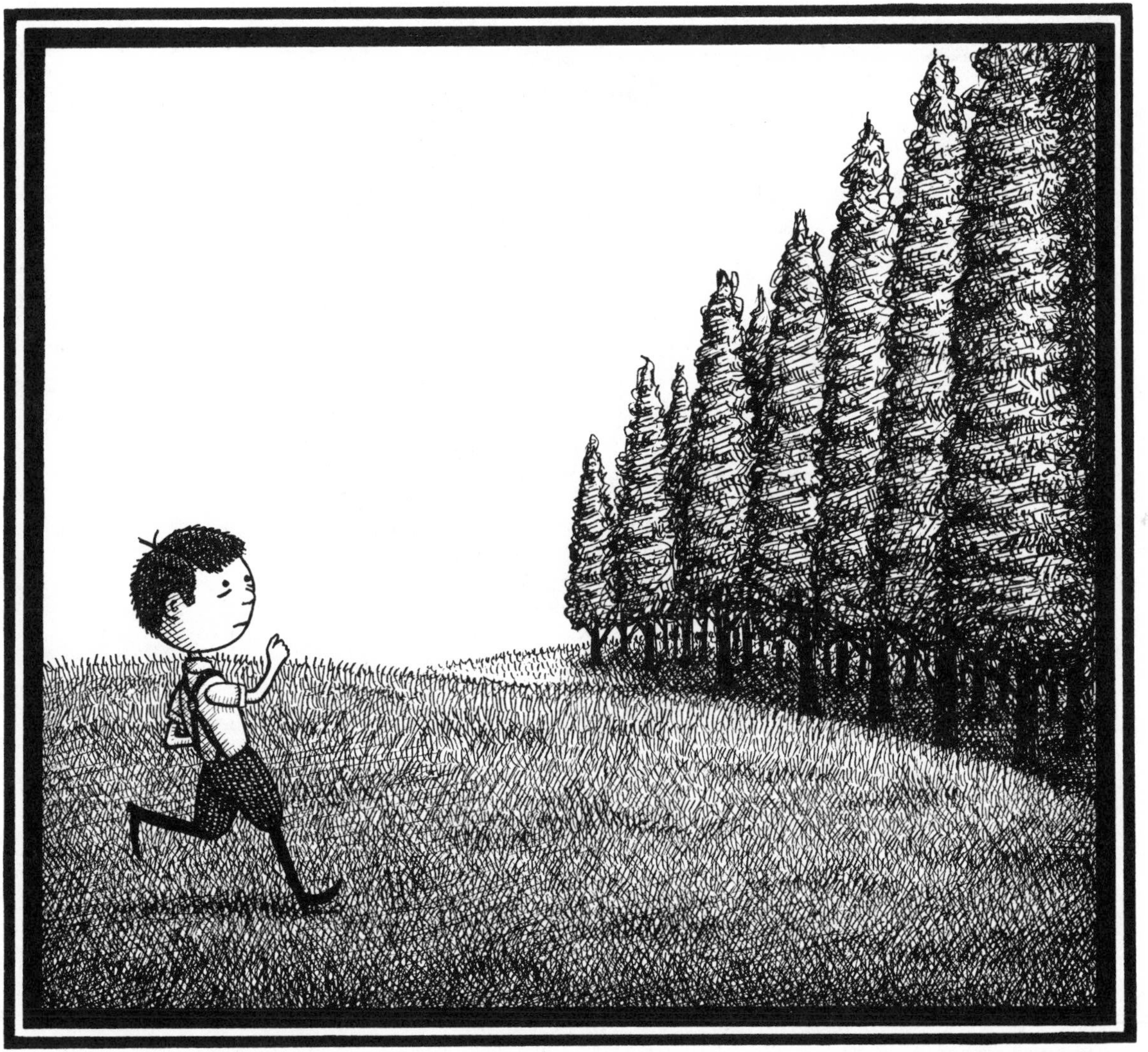

Surrounded by trunks everywhere,
Young Simon selected with care
A giant in girth
With roots through the earth,
And promptly ascended with flare.

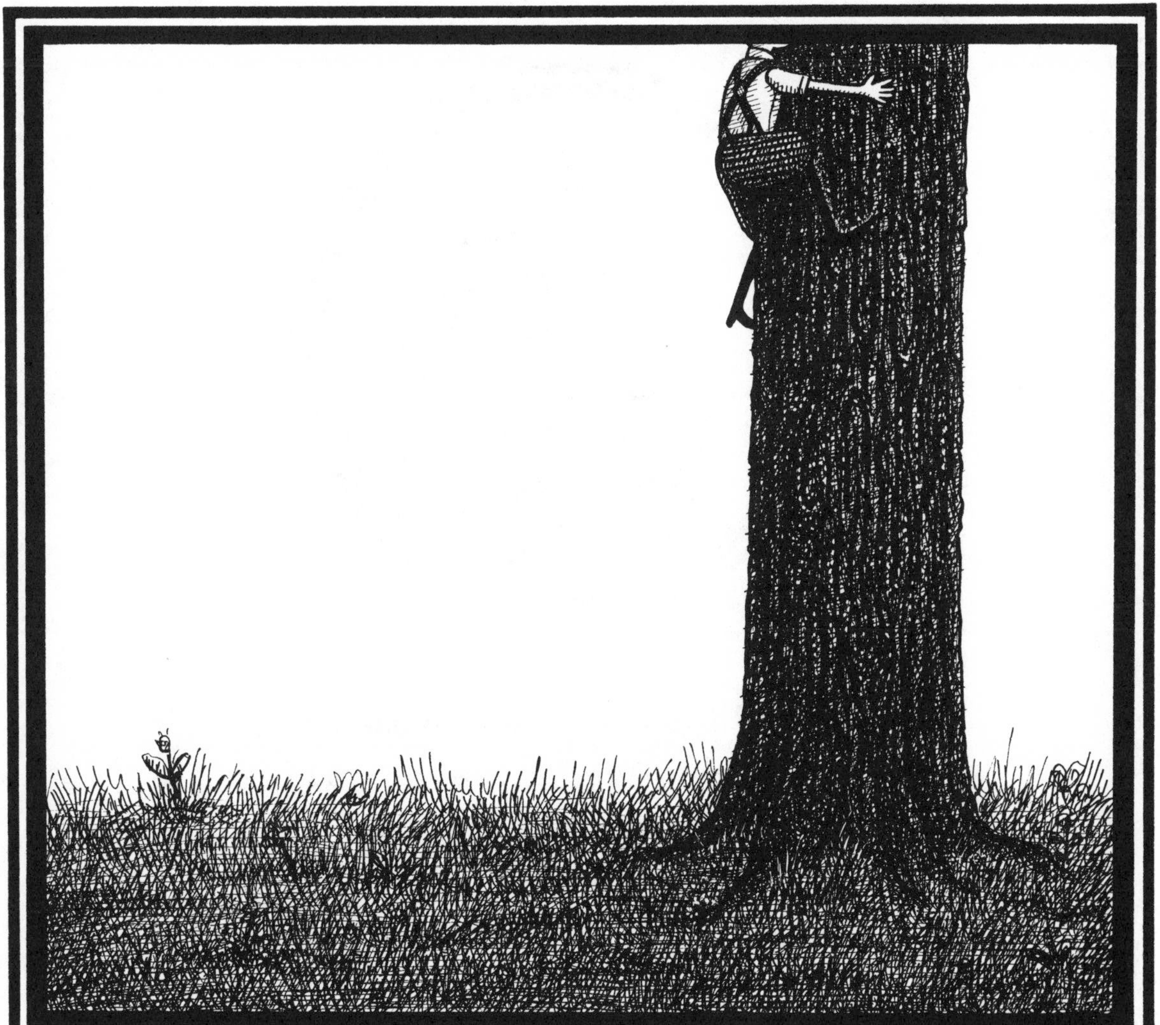

Approaching the summit with pride,
He was king over all that he spied.
But the tree was quite old,
Releasing its hold—
Young Simon's throne was denied.

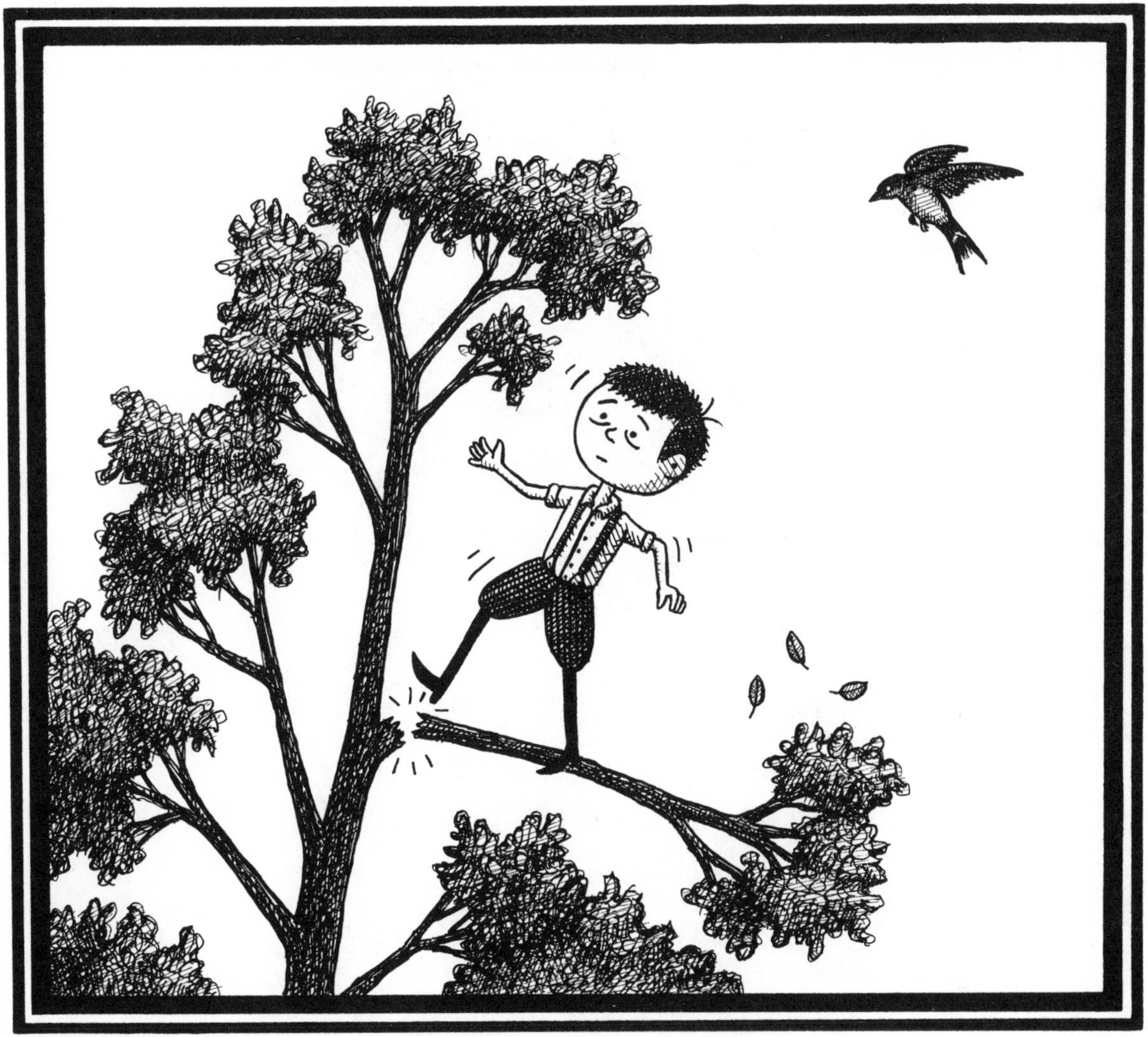

Then crashing his nose on the tree,
He was robbed of an old memory,
His late grandma's smell
And the stories she'd tell
Young Simon before he was three.

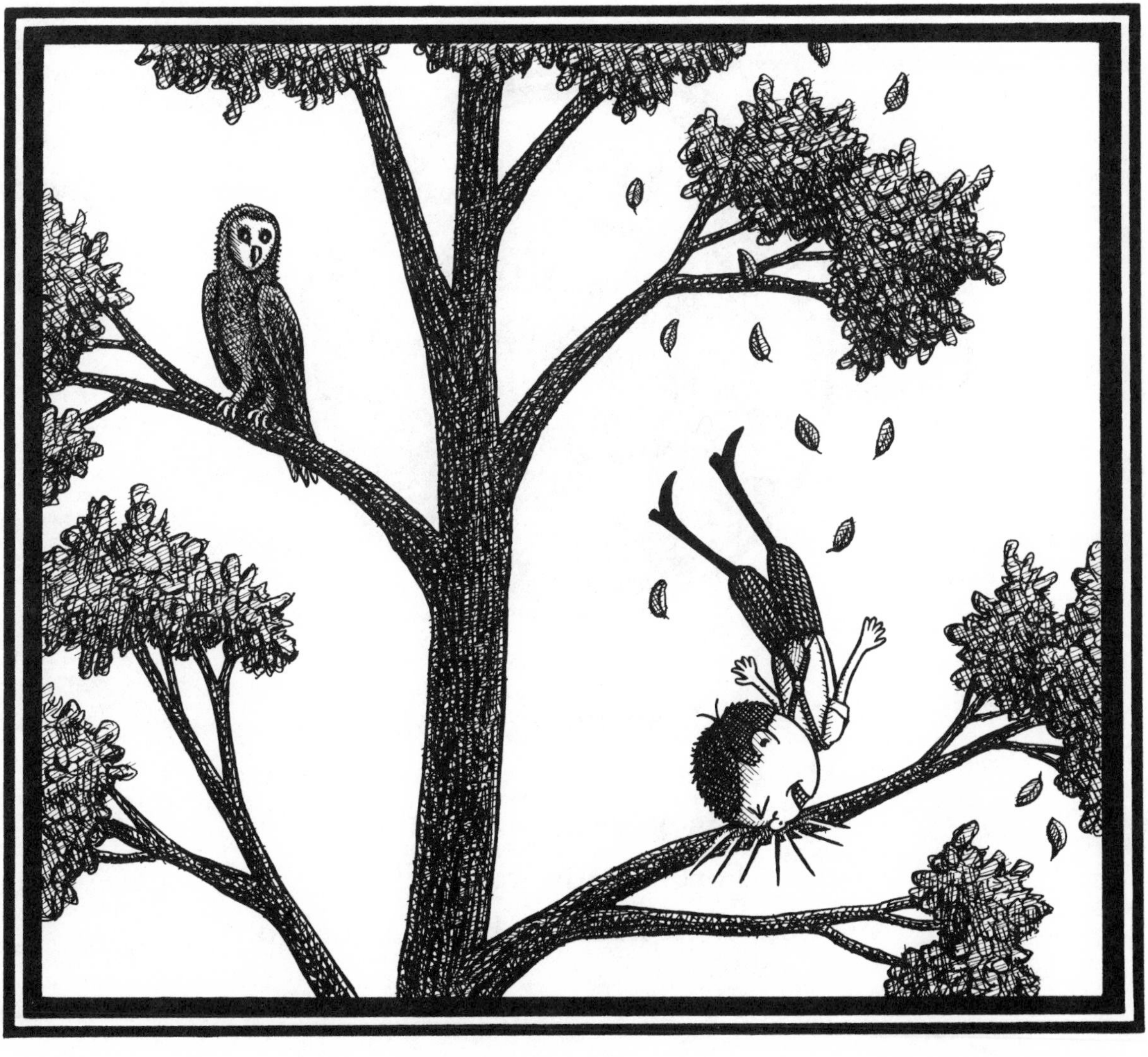

Feeling his right foot displaced,
More thoughts from his mind were erased.
His parents with gall
Forbade him football,
While Simon in church was encased.

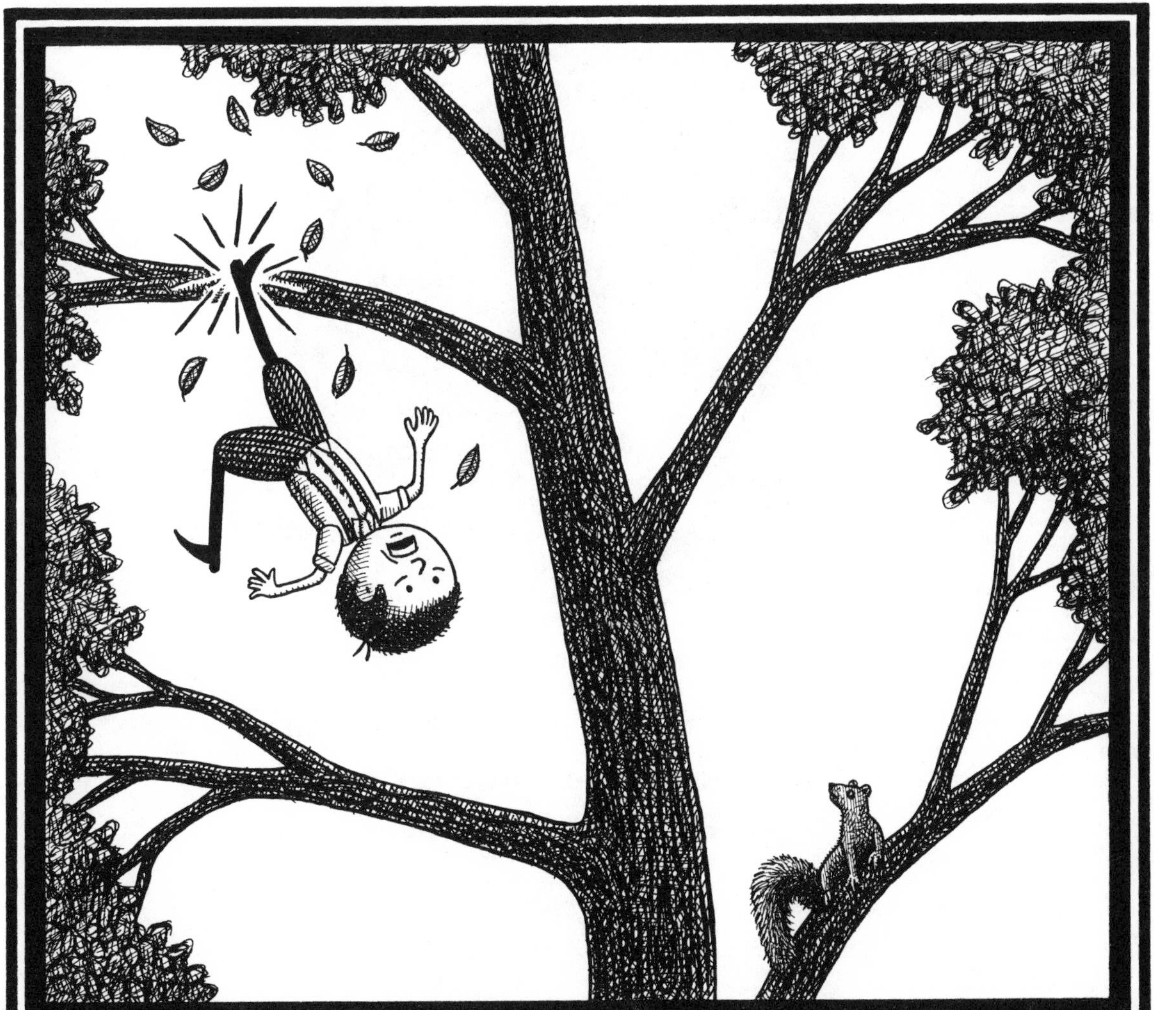

Young Simon then hovered some time,
Before he plunged onto his spine,
The stars he had spied
While lying outside
Entirely fell from his mind.

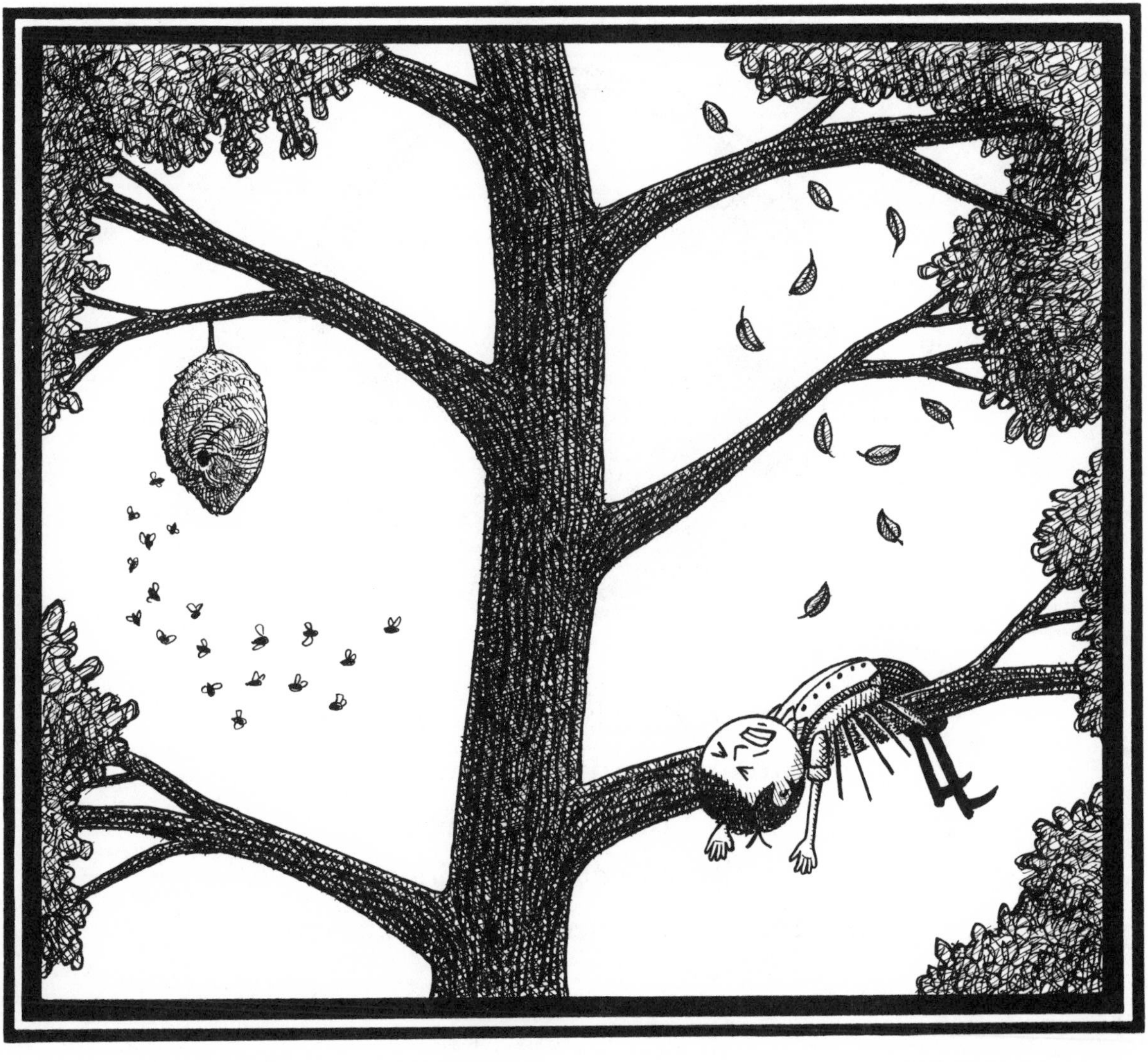

A shattering blow met his arm,
Causing young Simon alarm.
Fur, drool, and sticks
With affectionate licks—
He forgot his loyal friend's charm.

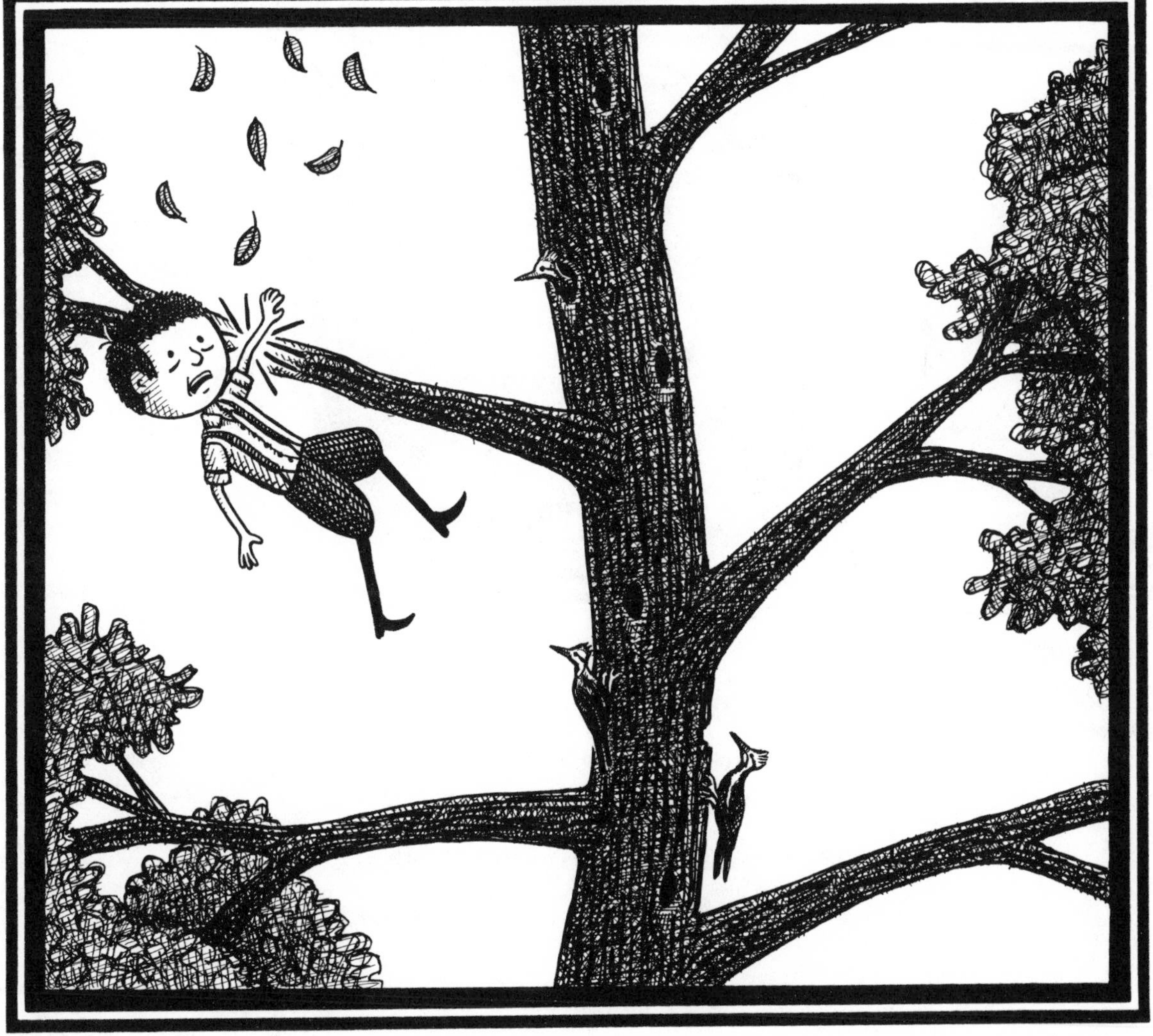

Then pointed twigs ripped at his hide,
Causing more thoughts to subside,
The shame he had felt
And the horrible belt,
From Simon were forcibly pried.

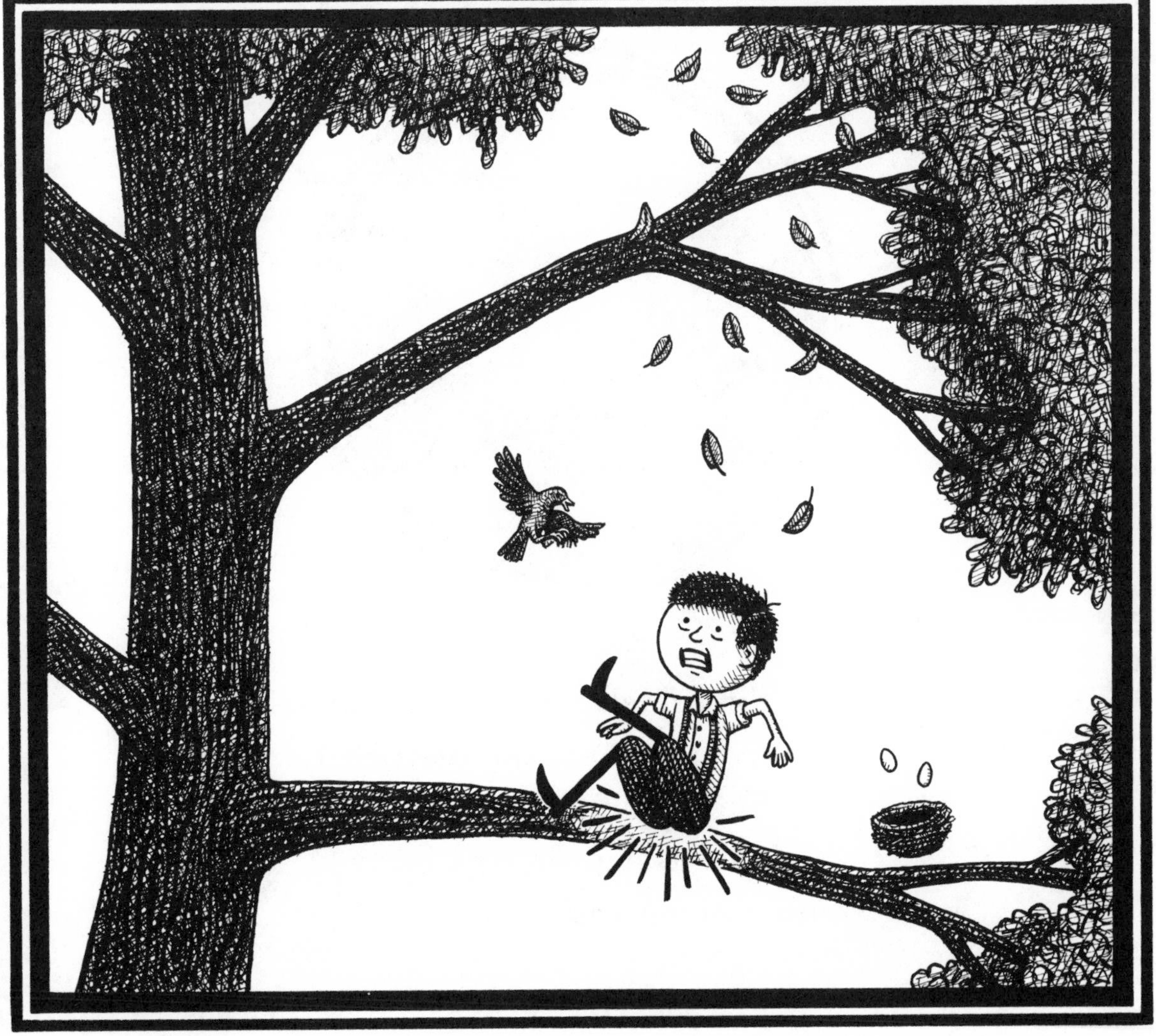

Young Simon felt lips smacked apart,
Removing his passionate heart,
The kiss he had shared
With the girl at the fair,
Budding love and emotion depart.

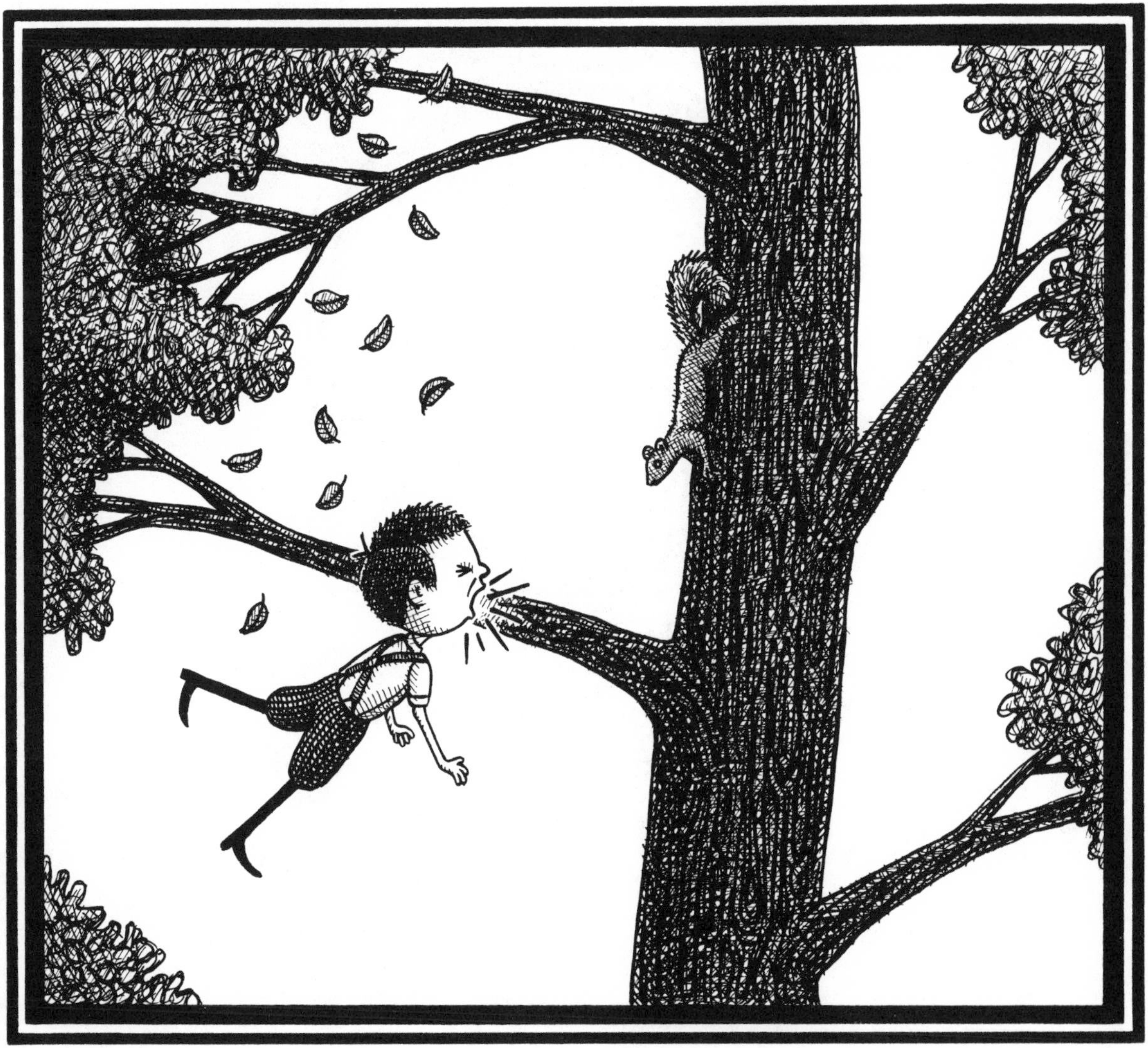

With his head now a growing expanse,
His shins became known to a branch,
The flourish of feet
Along with a beat,
Young Simon forgot how to dance.

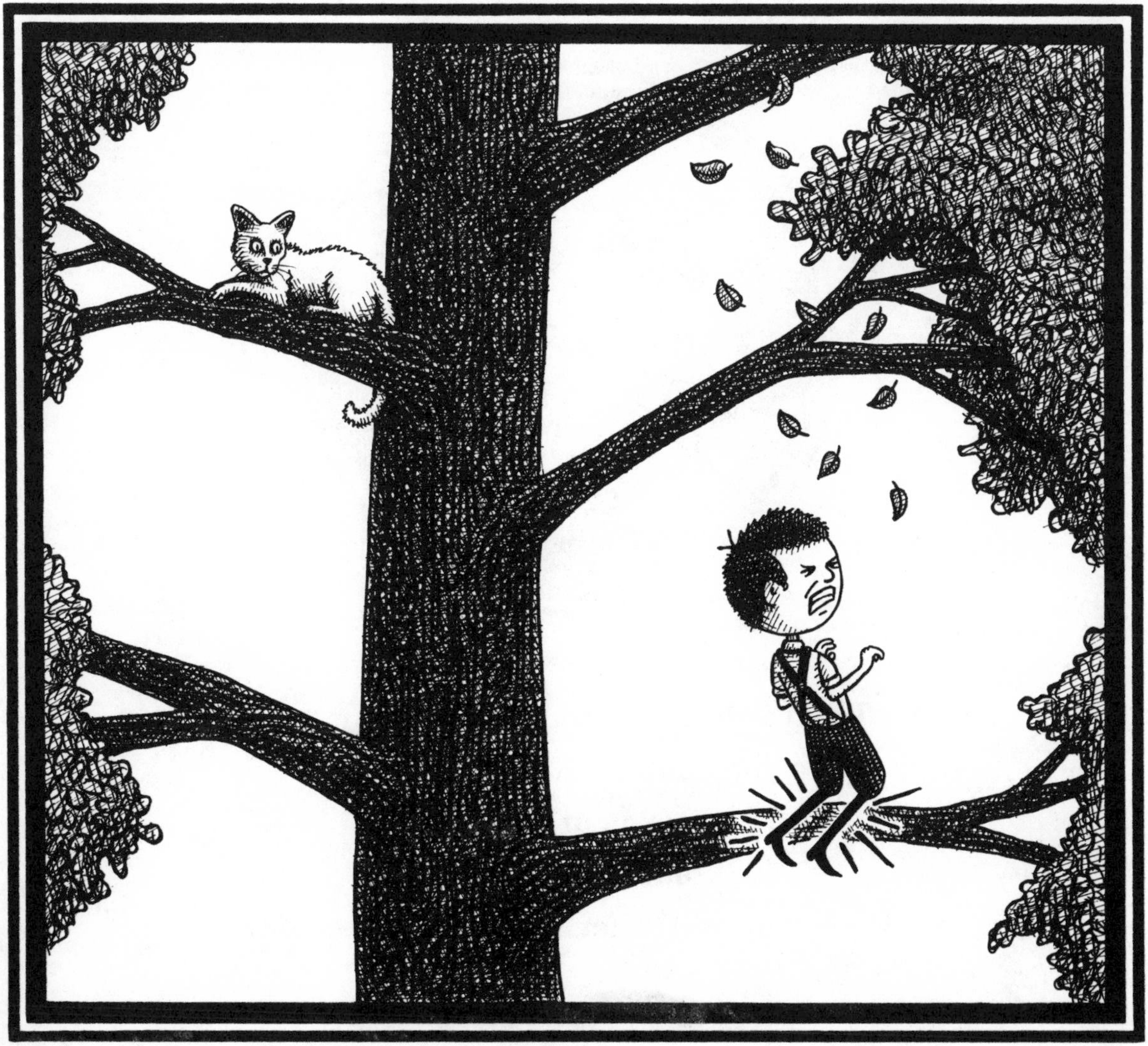

Then into the tree his hand thrust,
Young Simon let go of disgust.
The words of his mother
To clean up his brother
Were lost with her love and her trust.

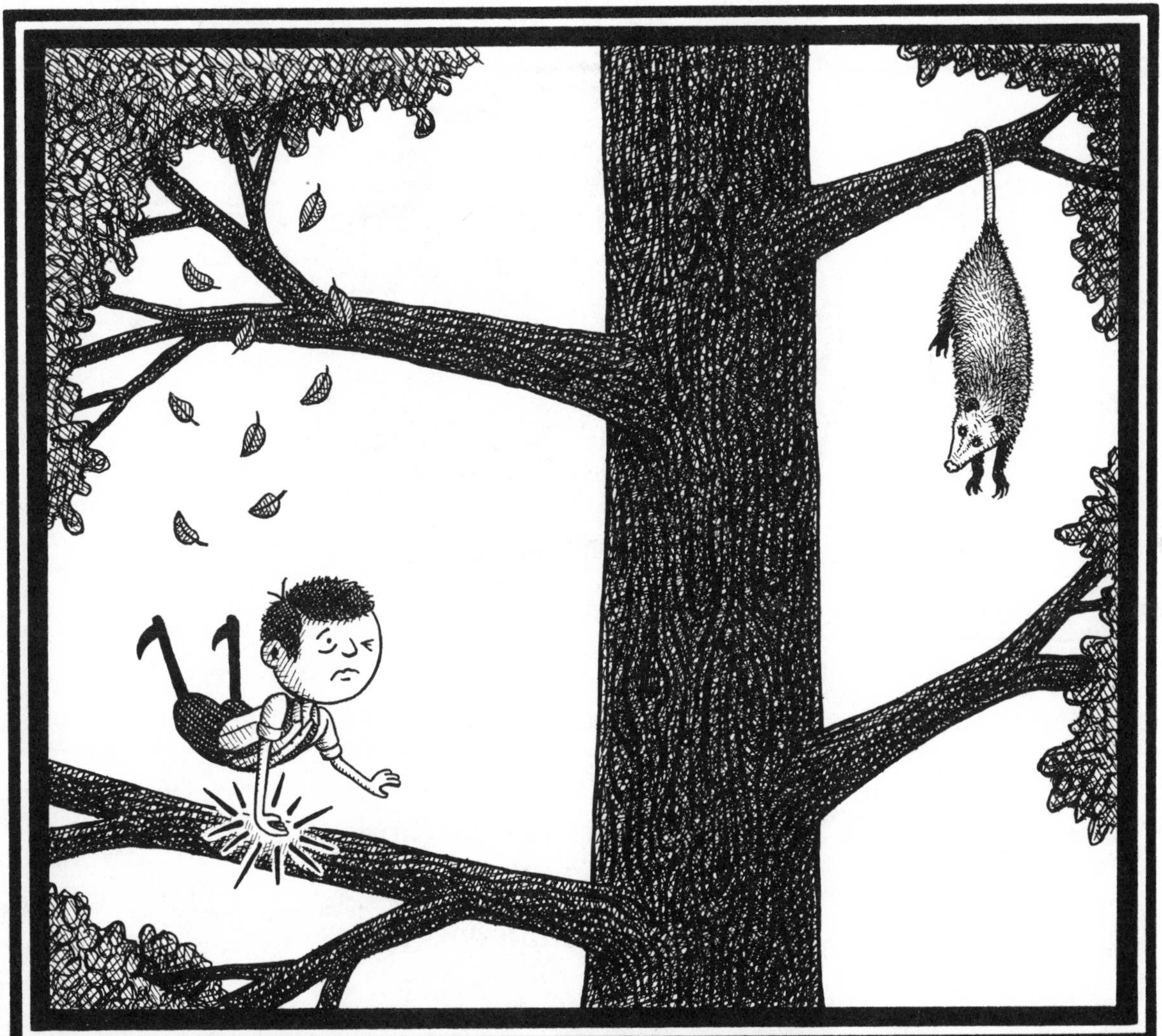

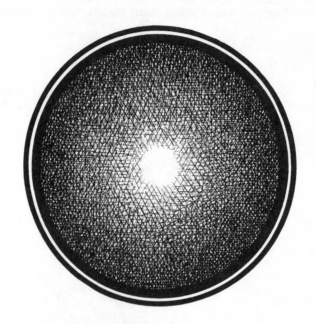

And downward and downward he fell,
Young Simon now empty, a shell.
He crashed to the ground
And grinned all around,
Content but unable to tell.

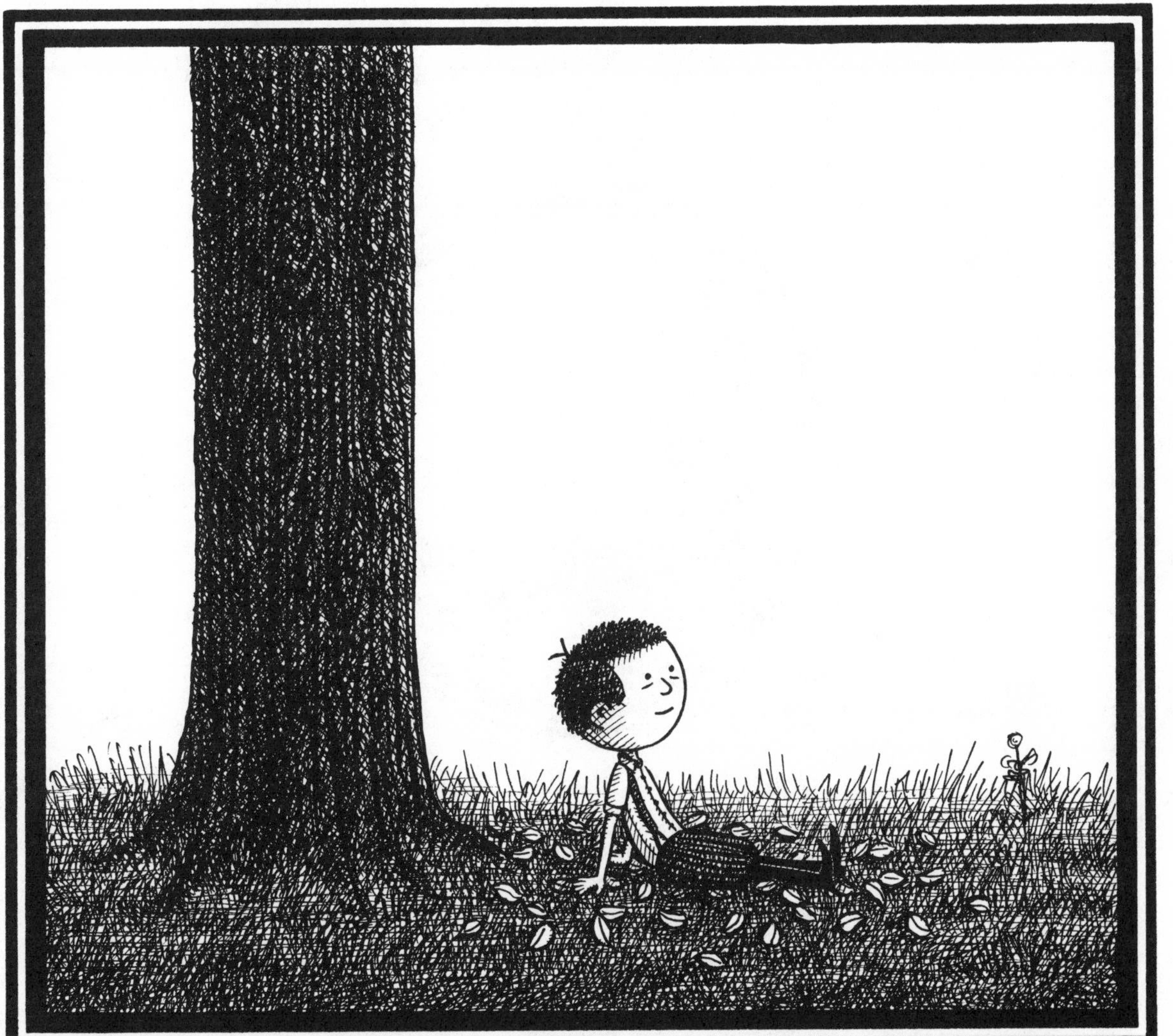

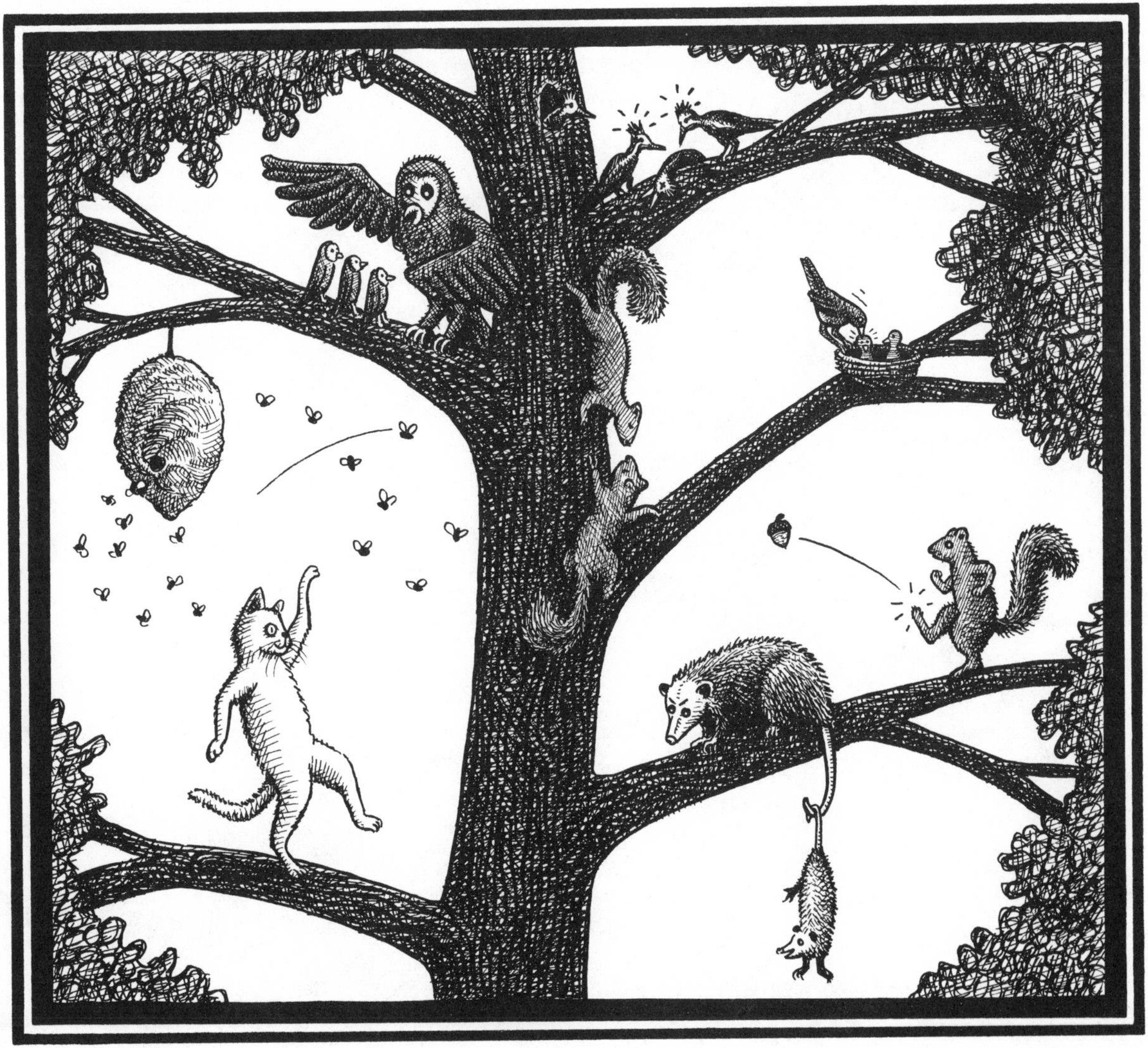

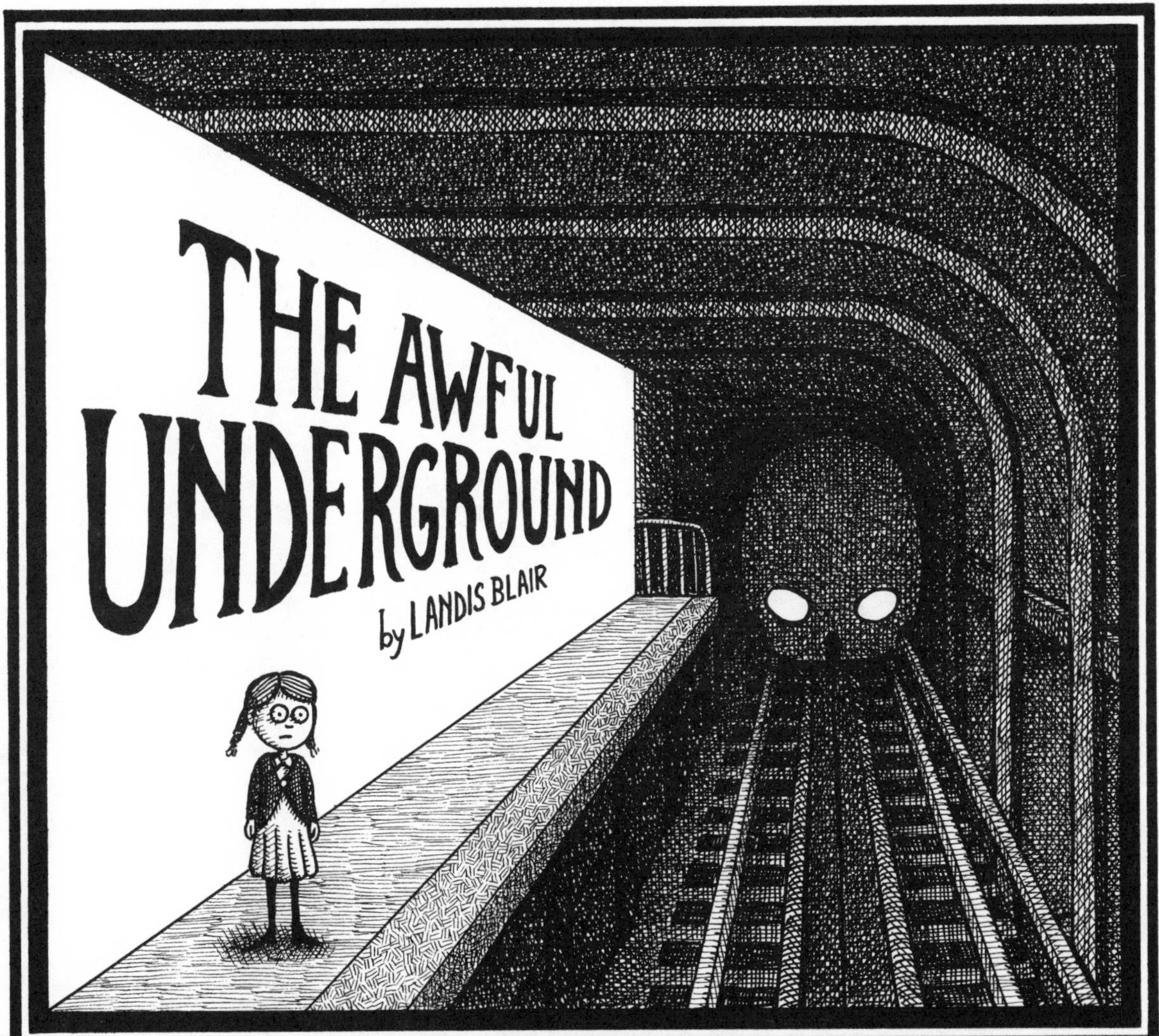
THE AWFUL
UNDERGROUND
by LANDIS BLAIR

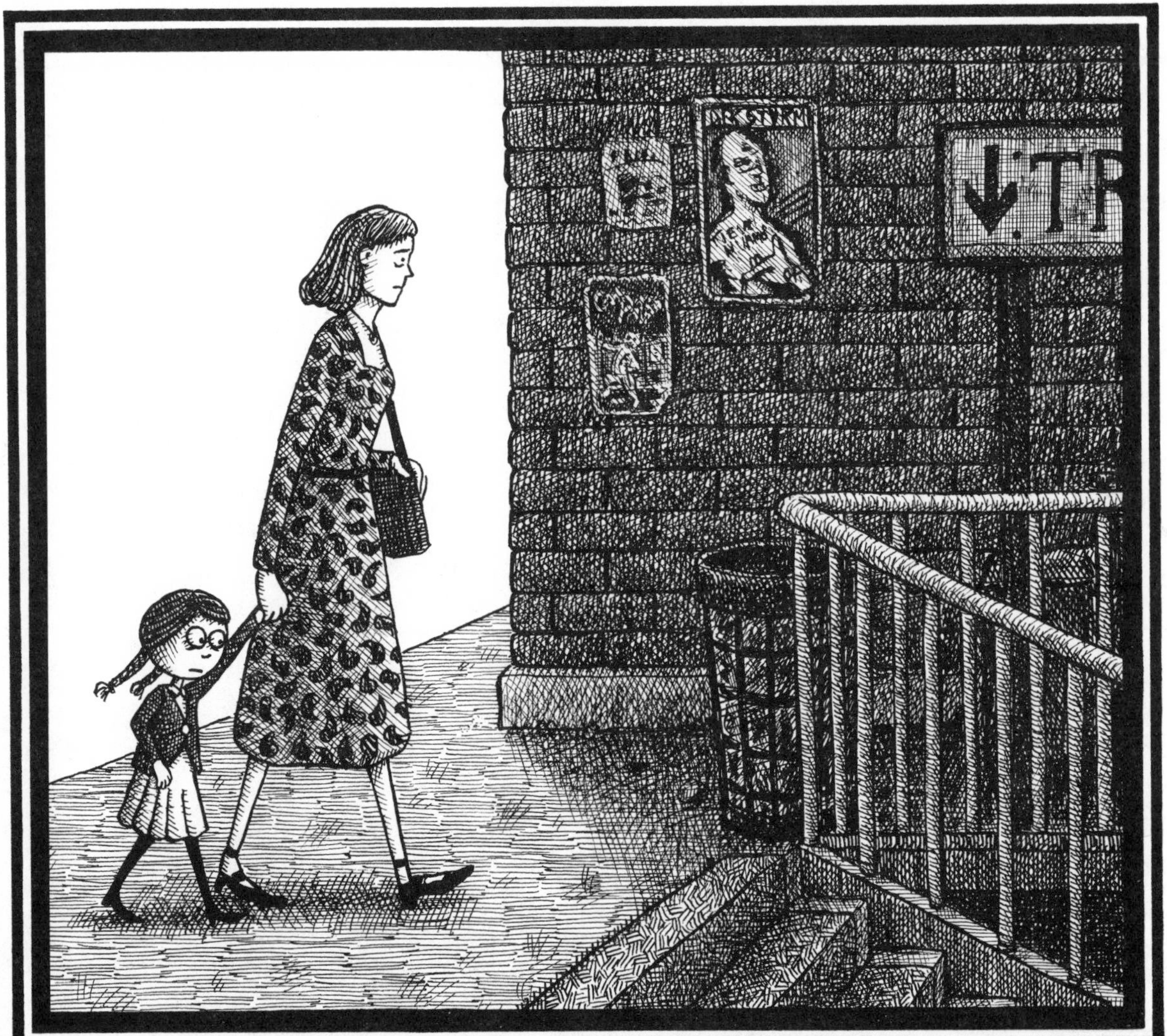
TR

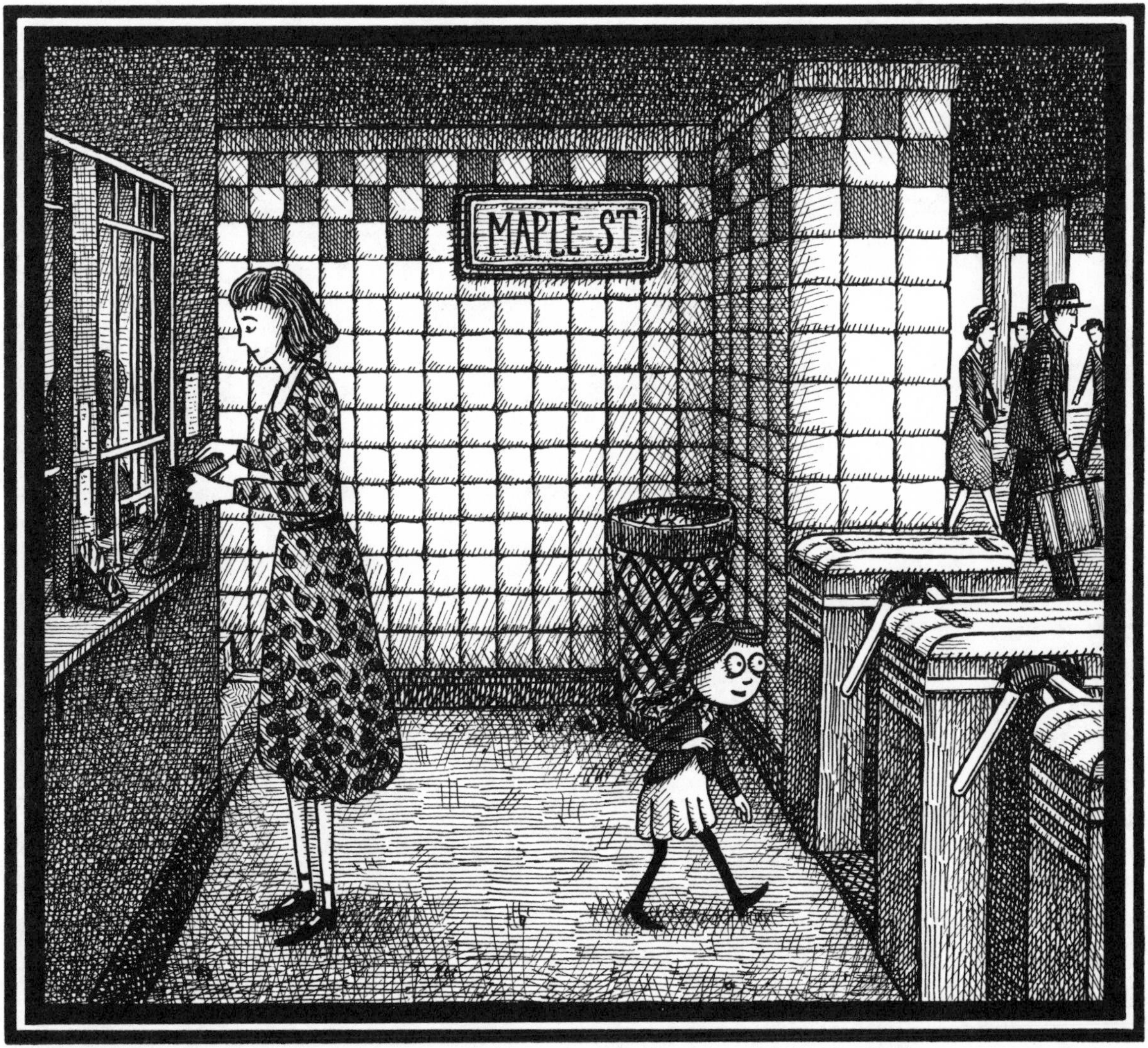
MAPLE ST.

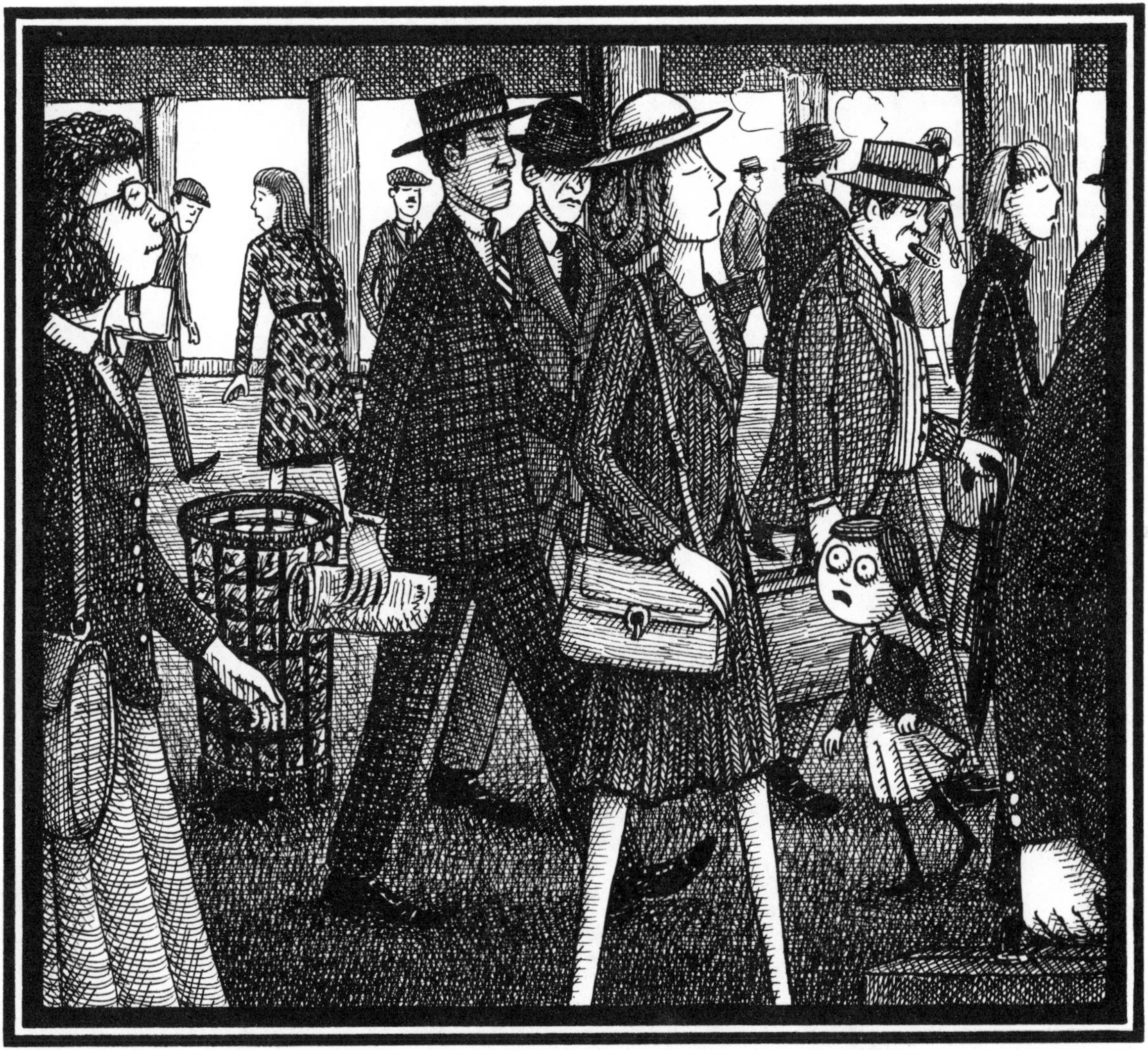

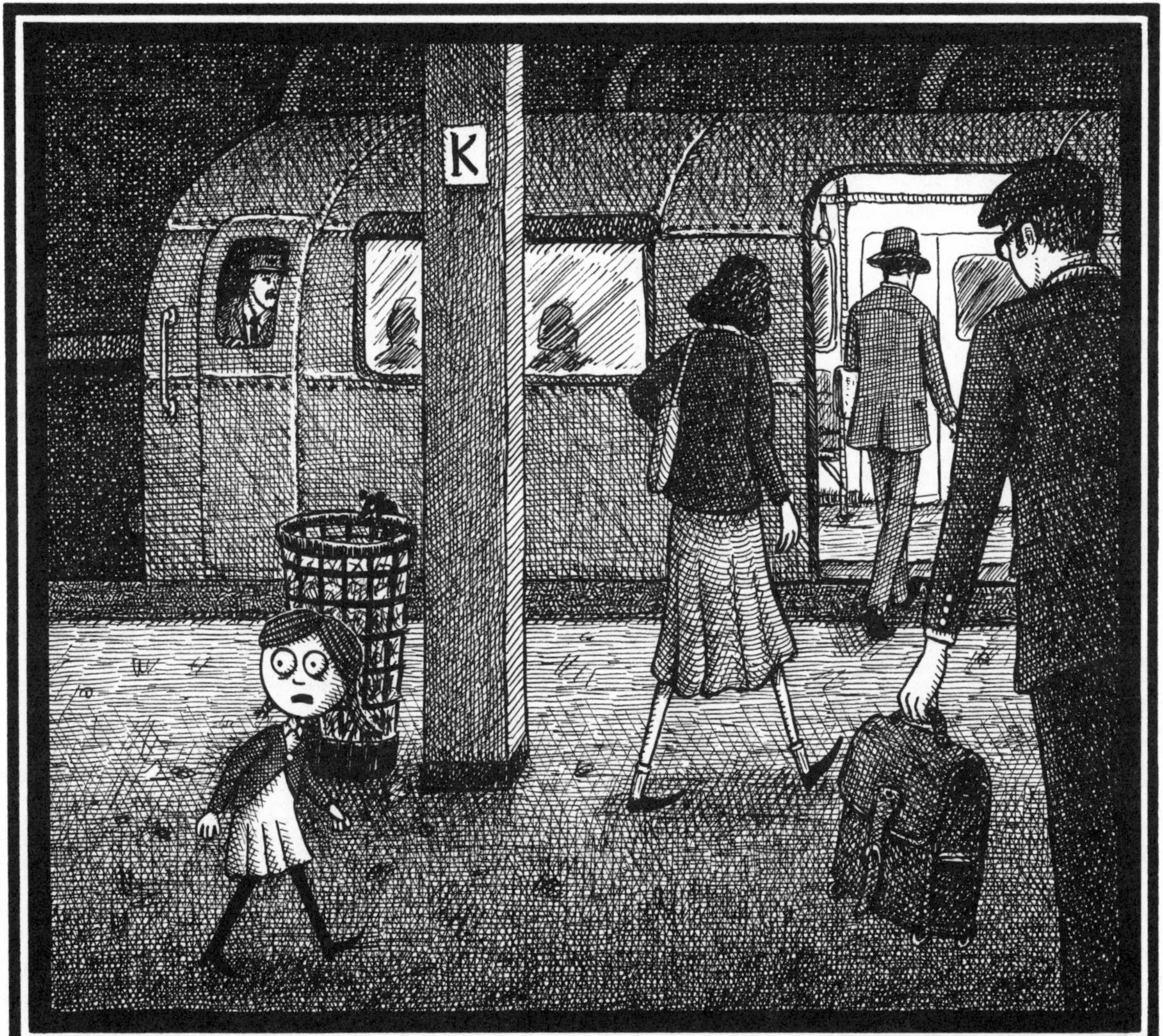
K

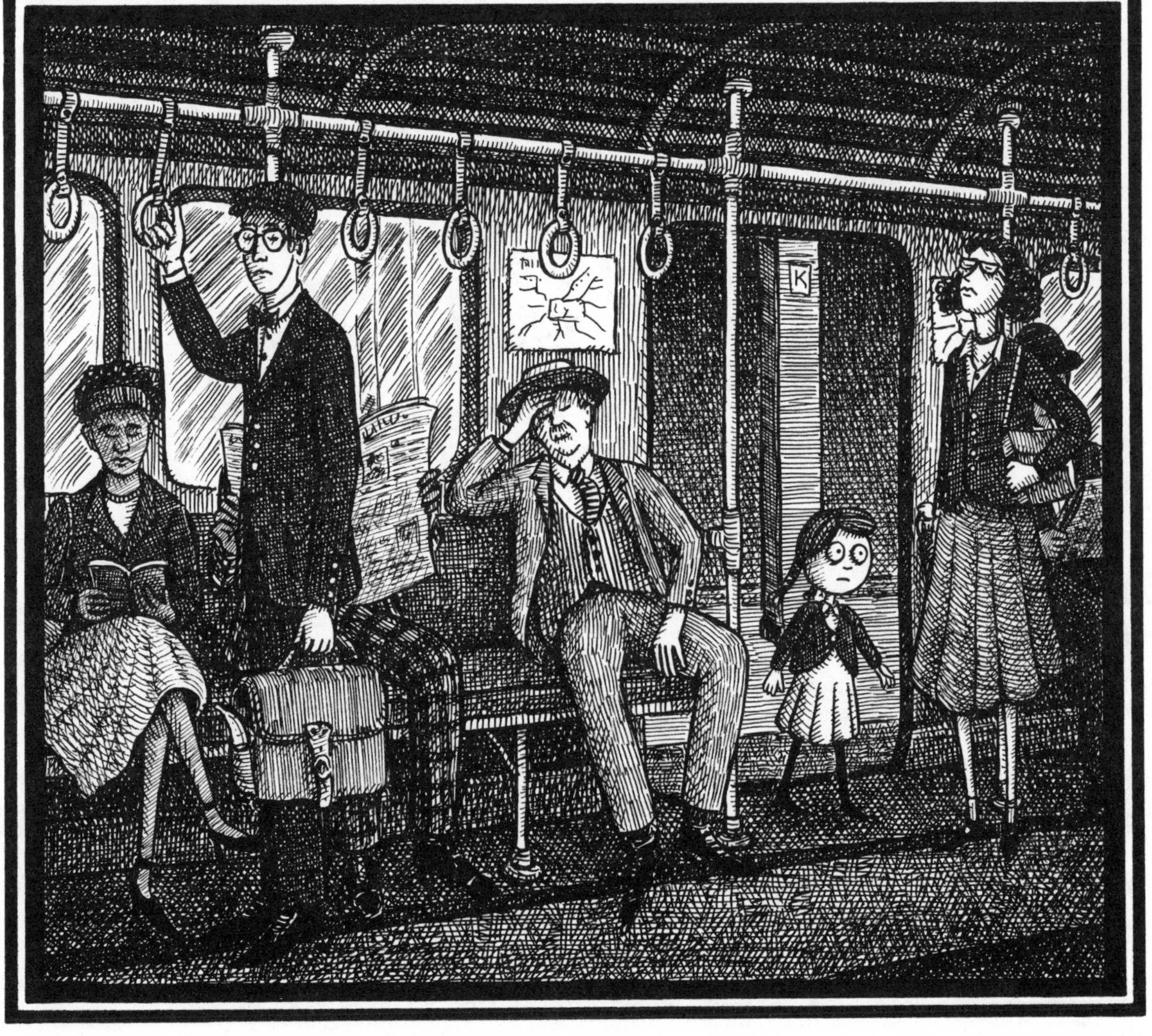
K

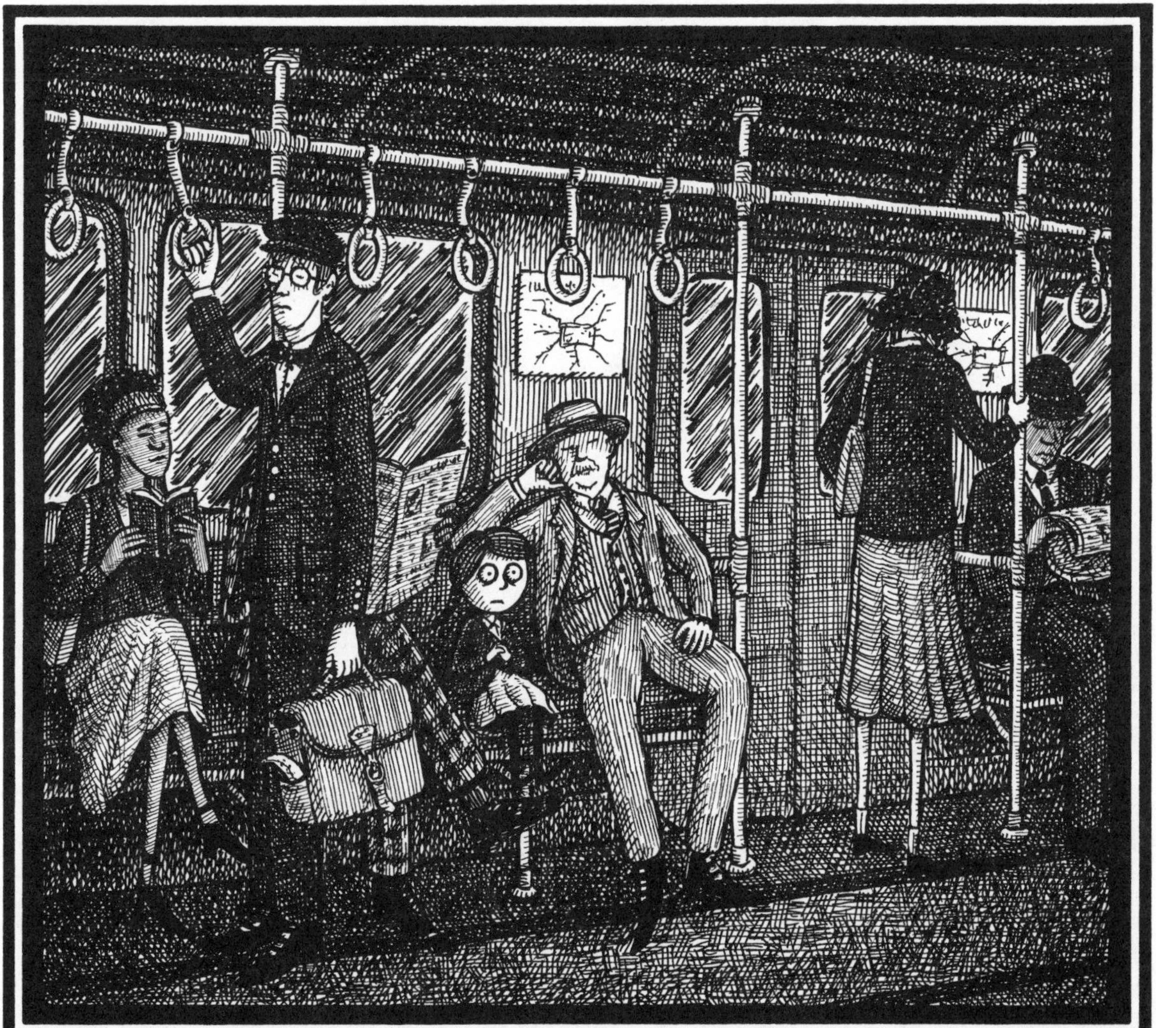

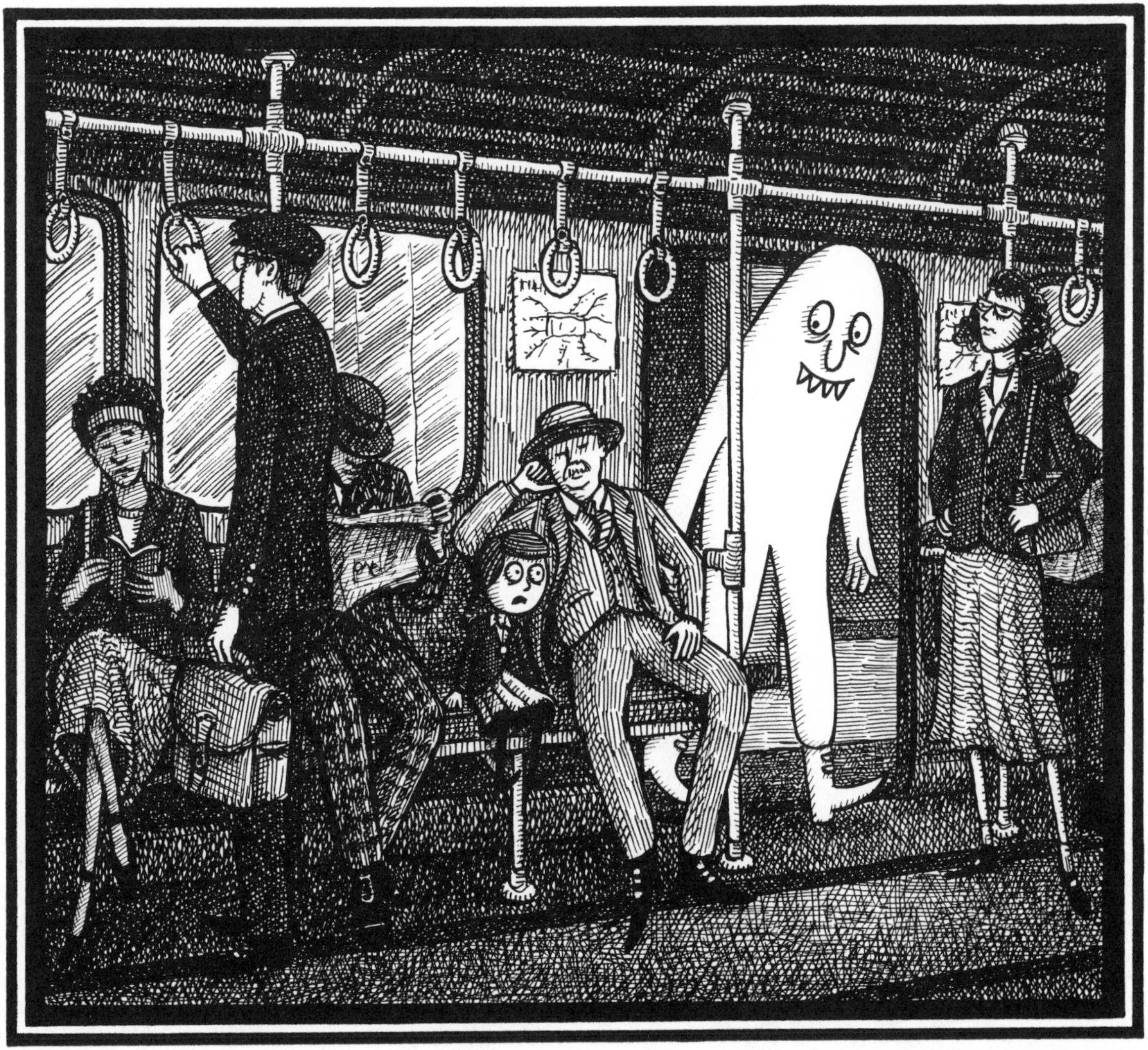

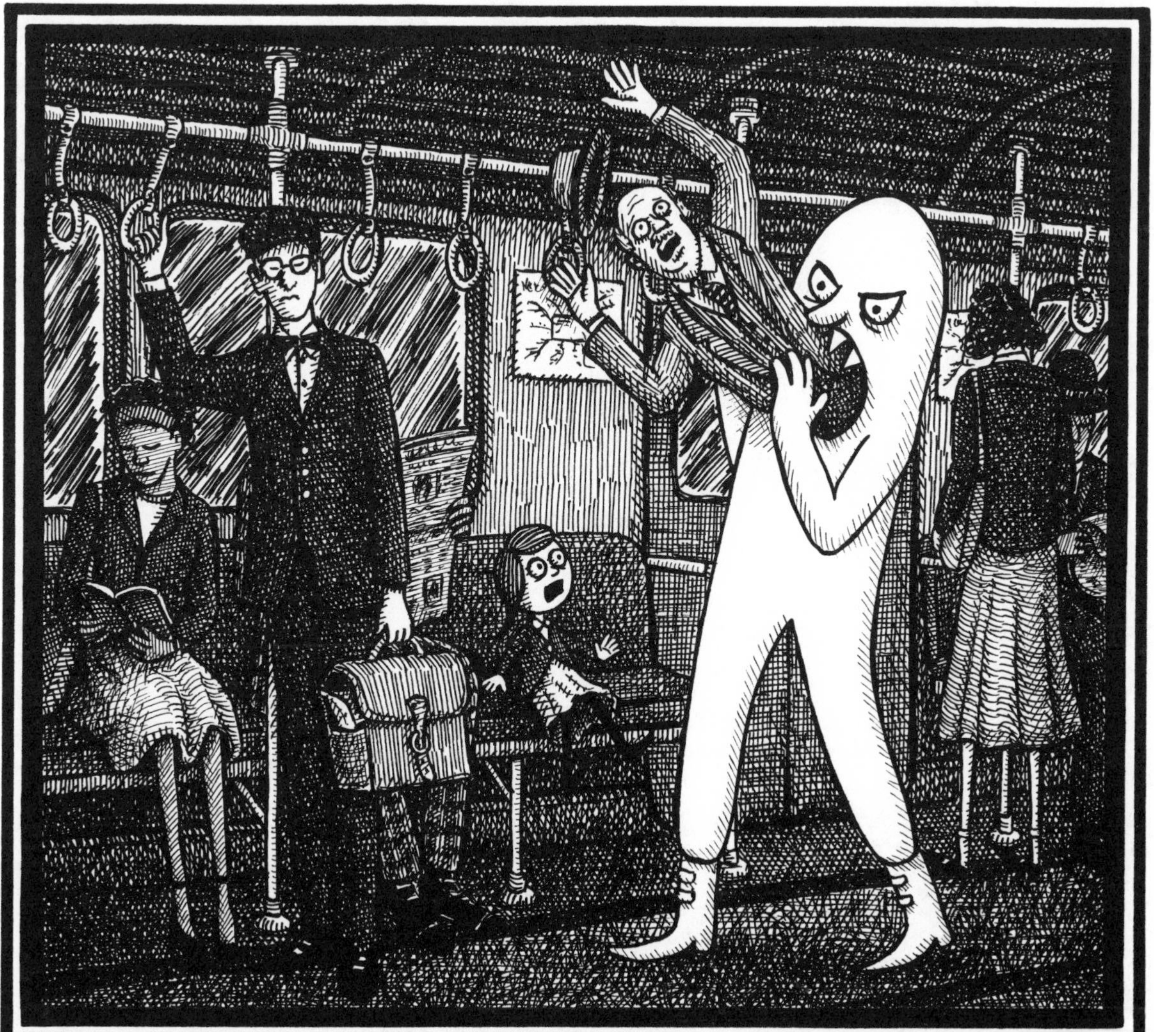

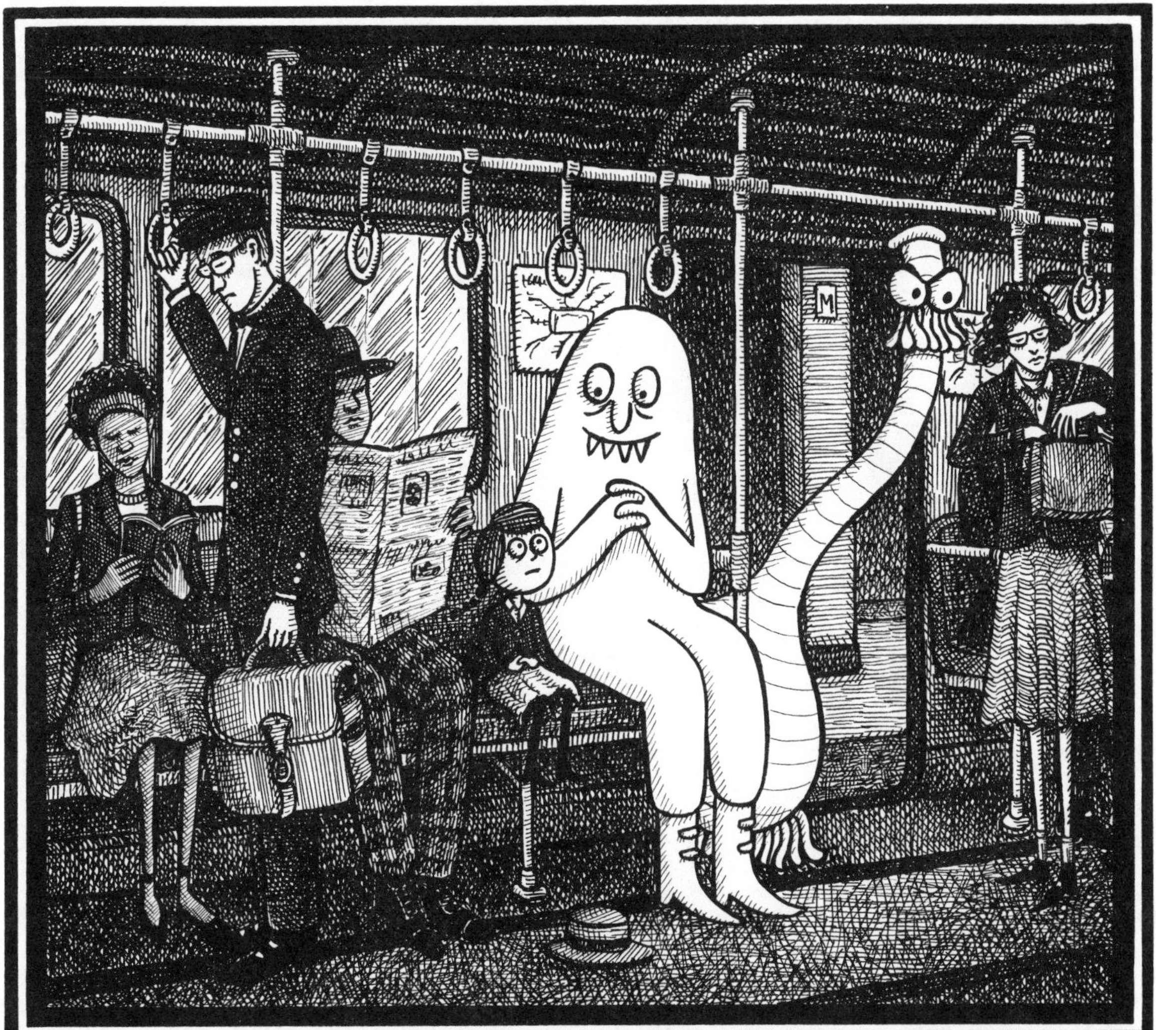
M

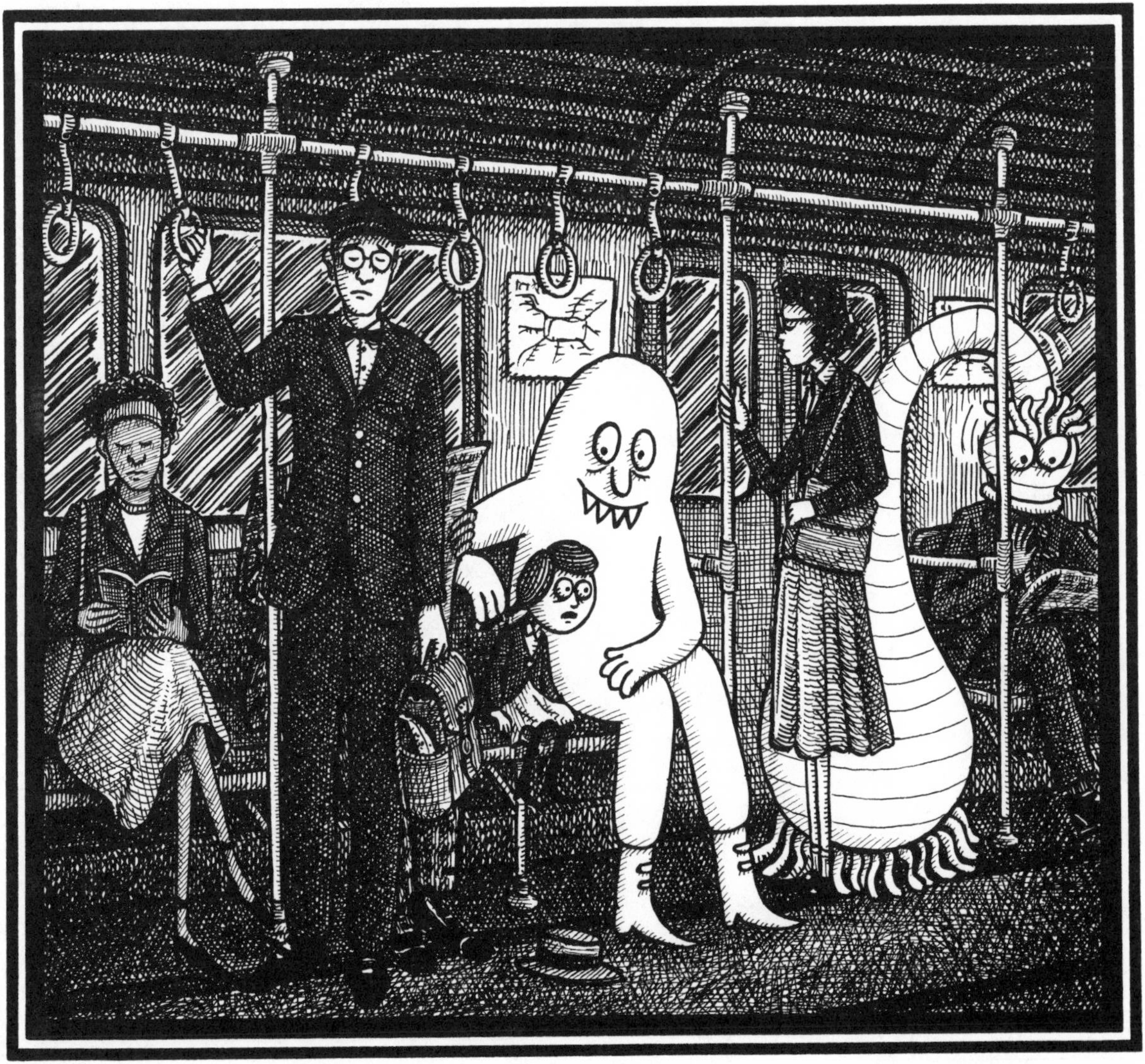

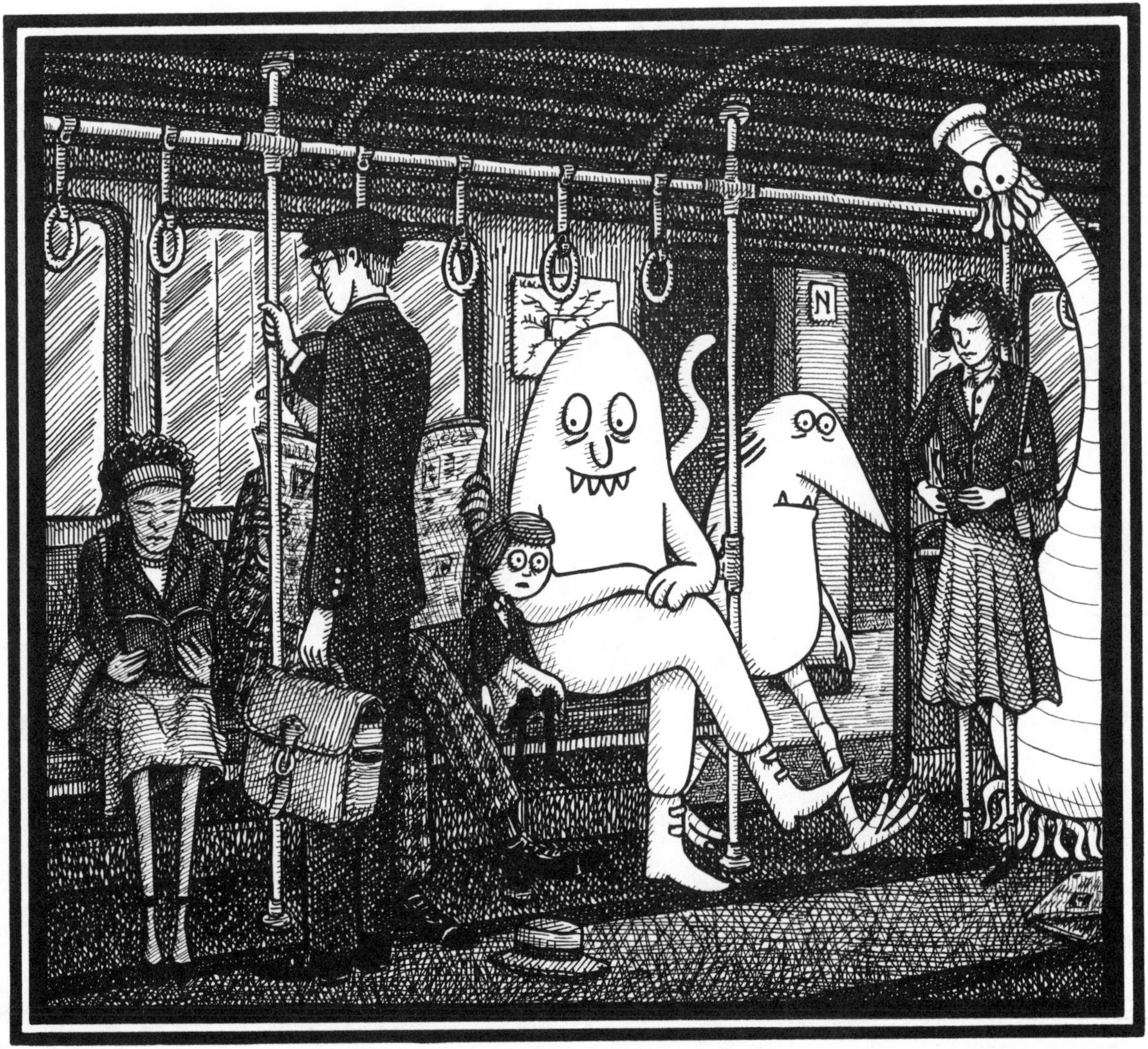
N

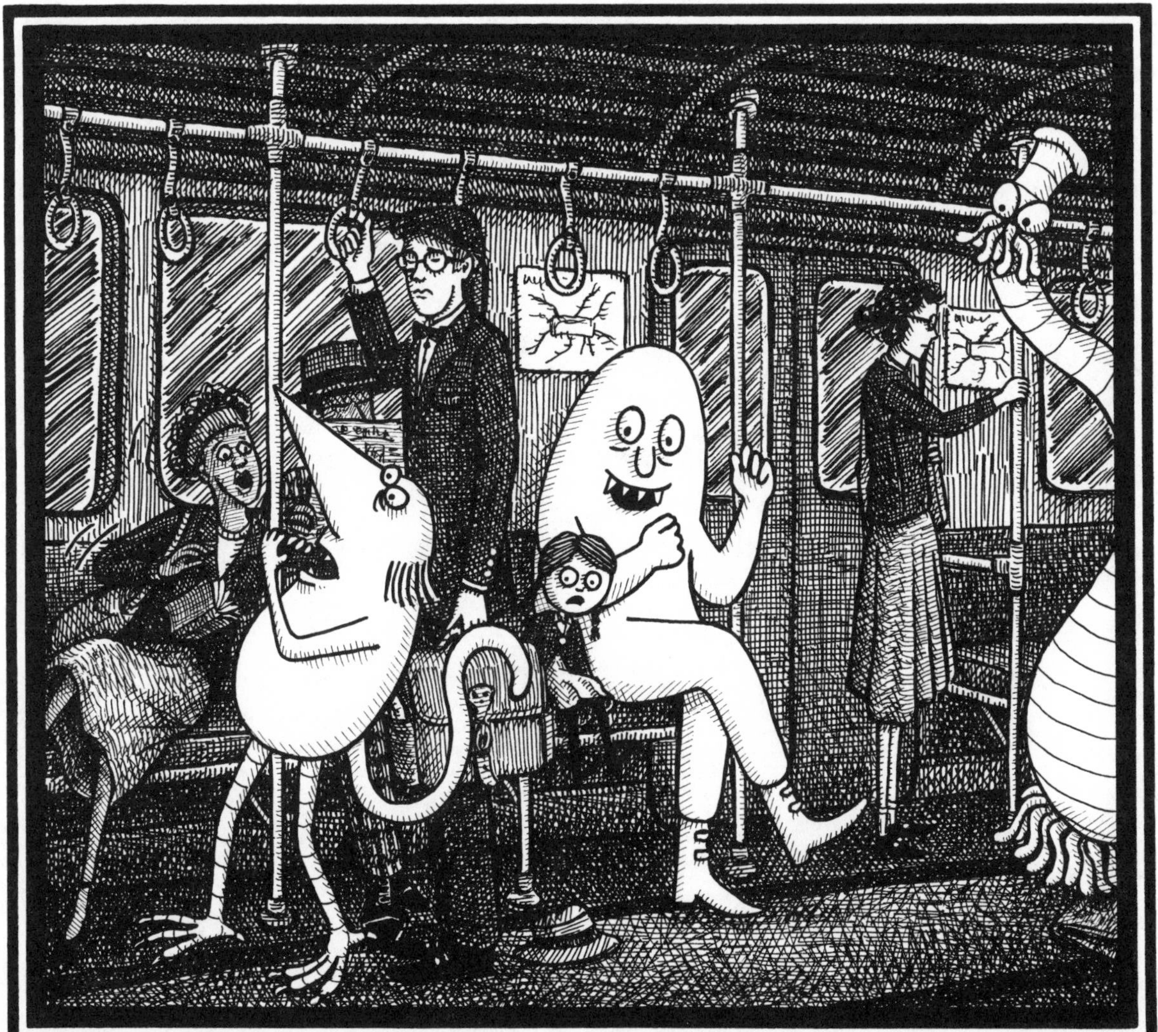

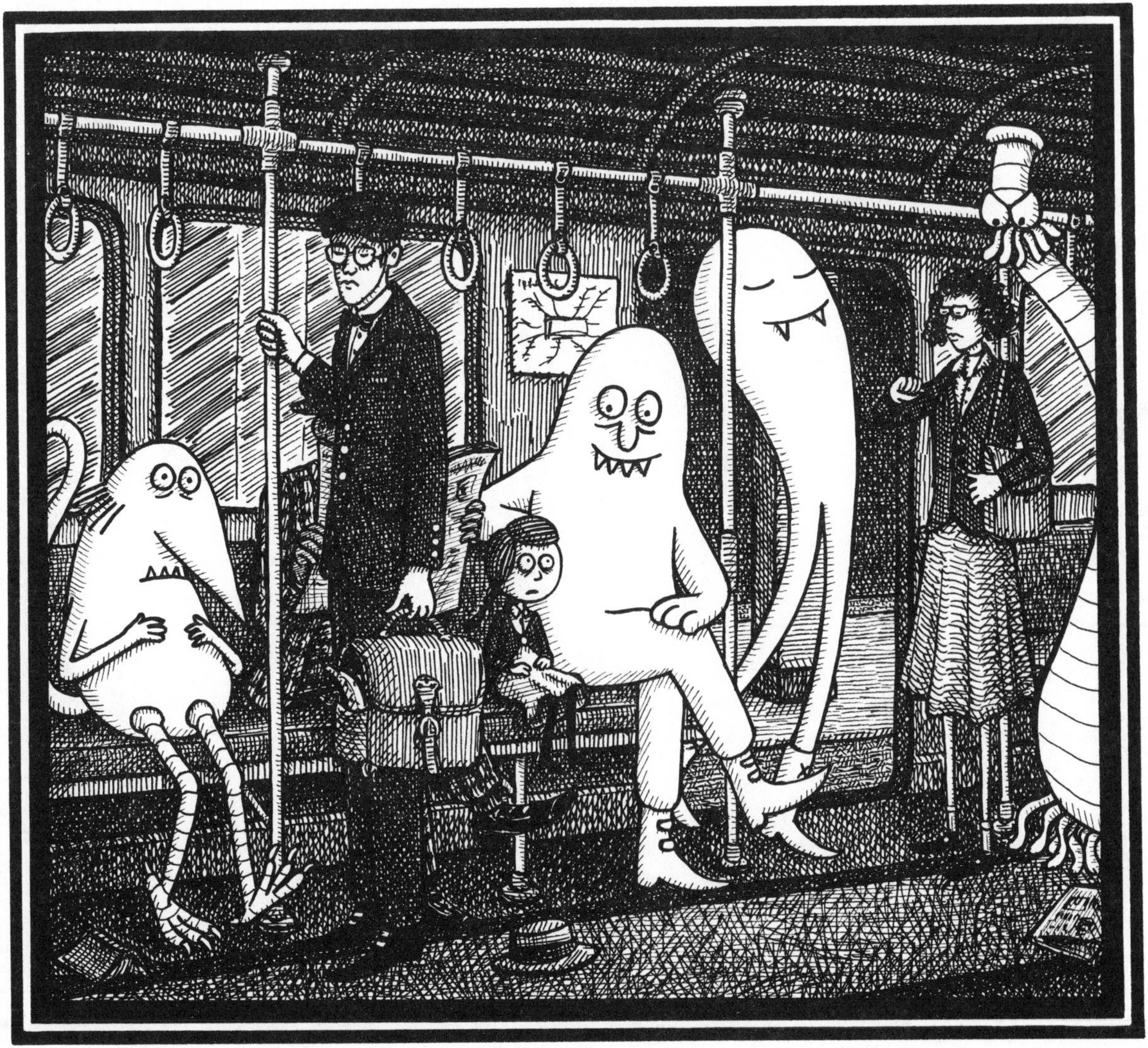

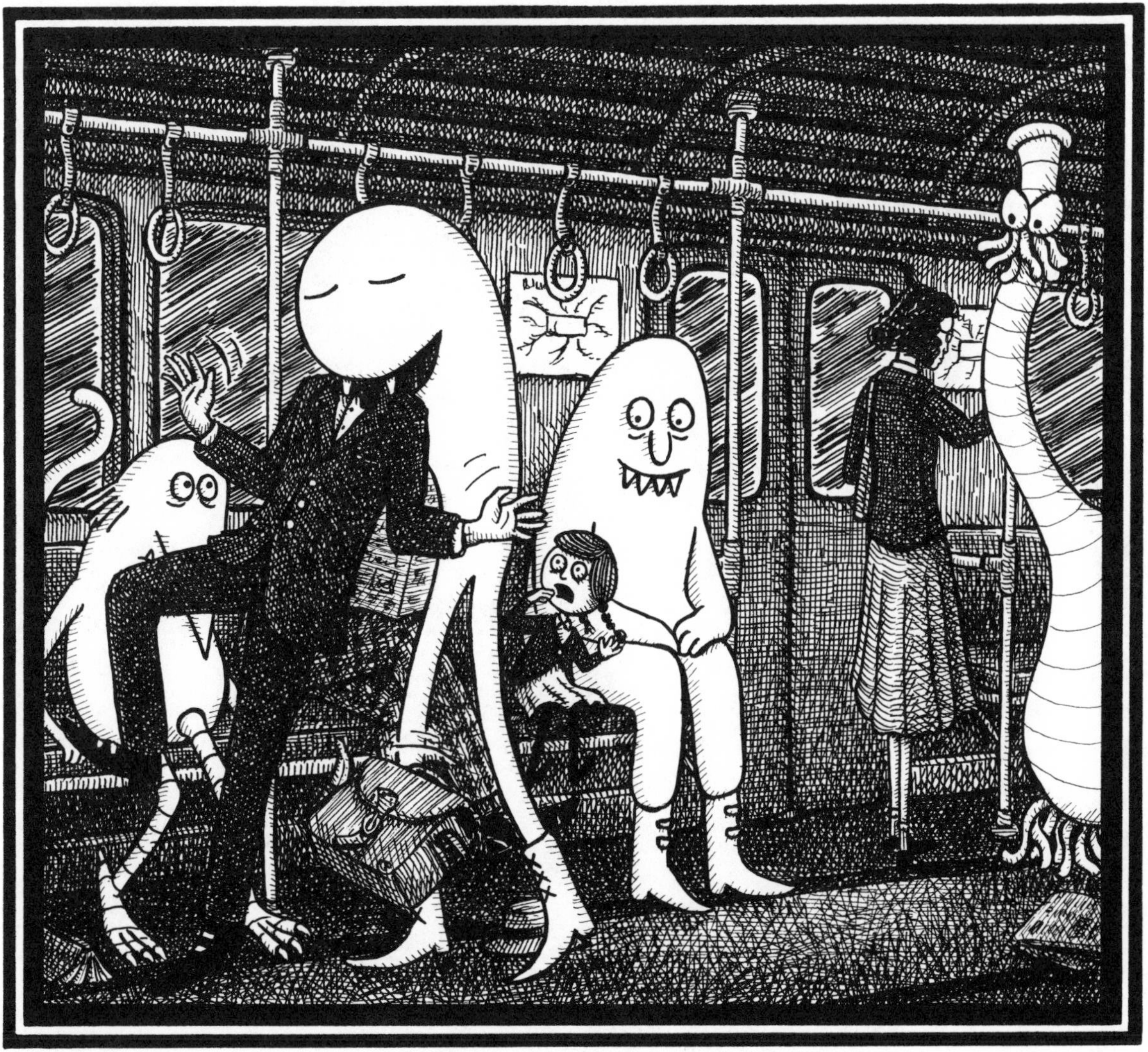

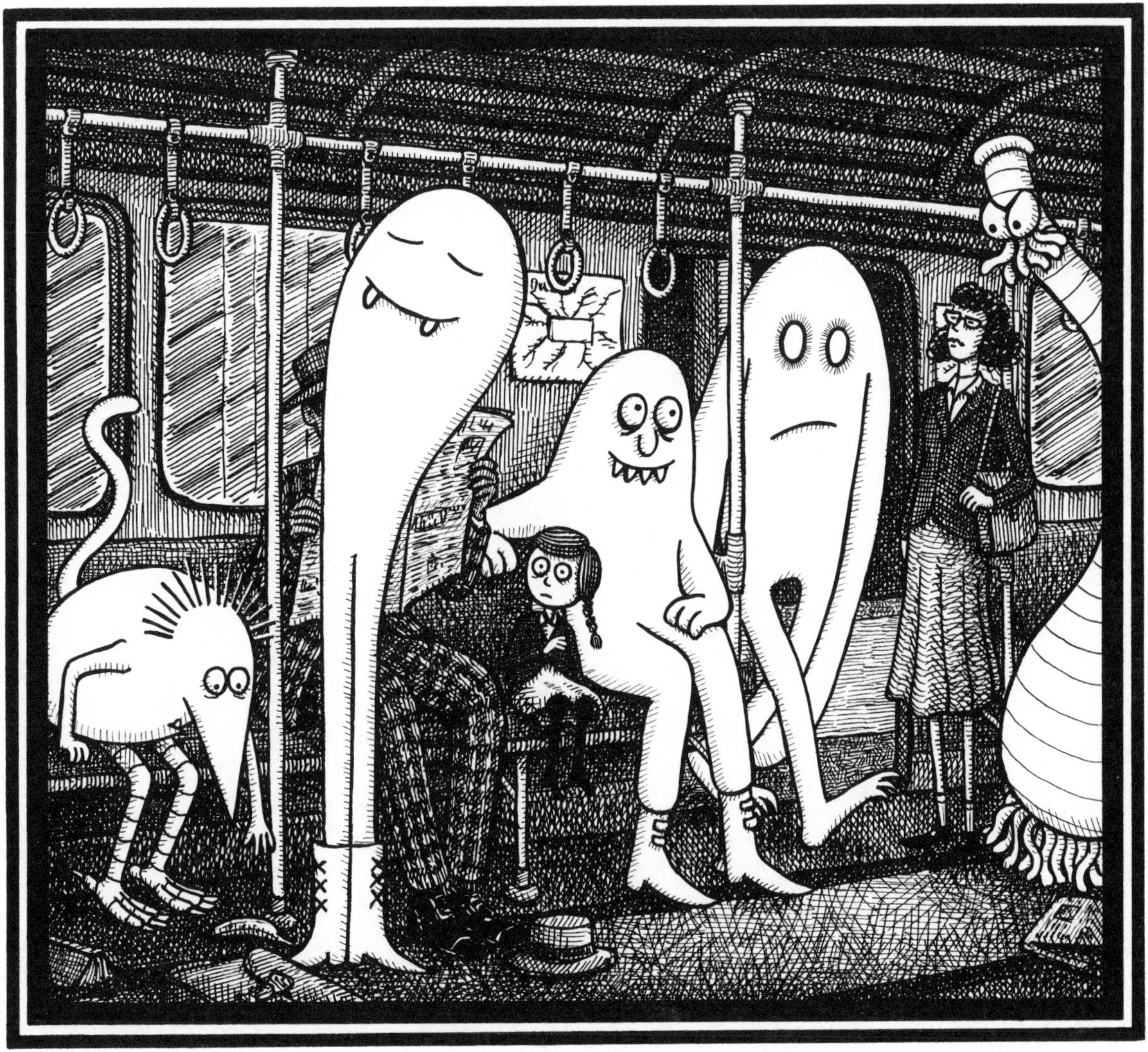

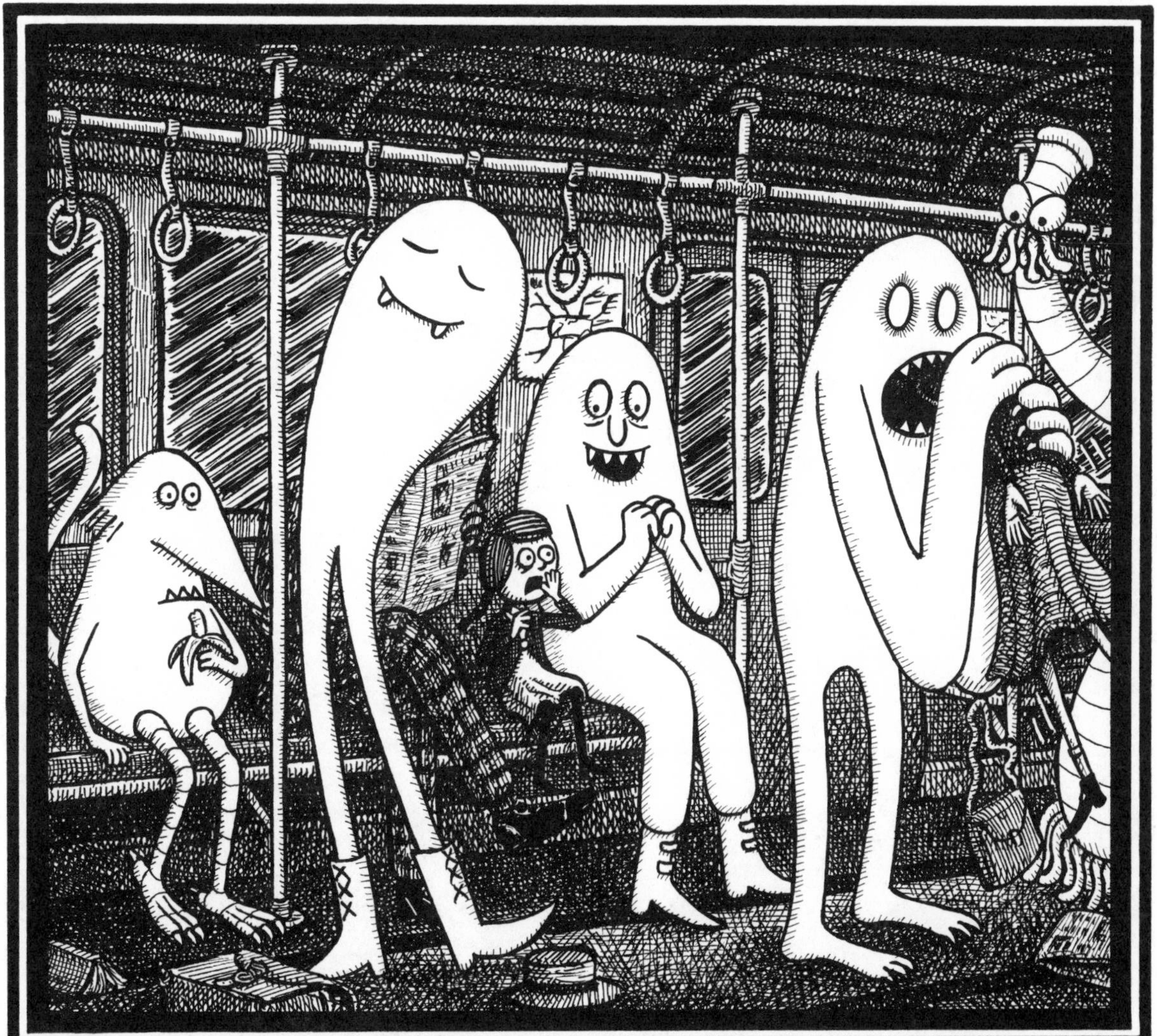

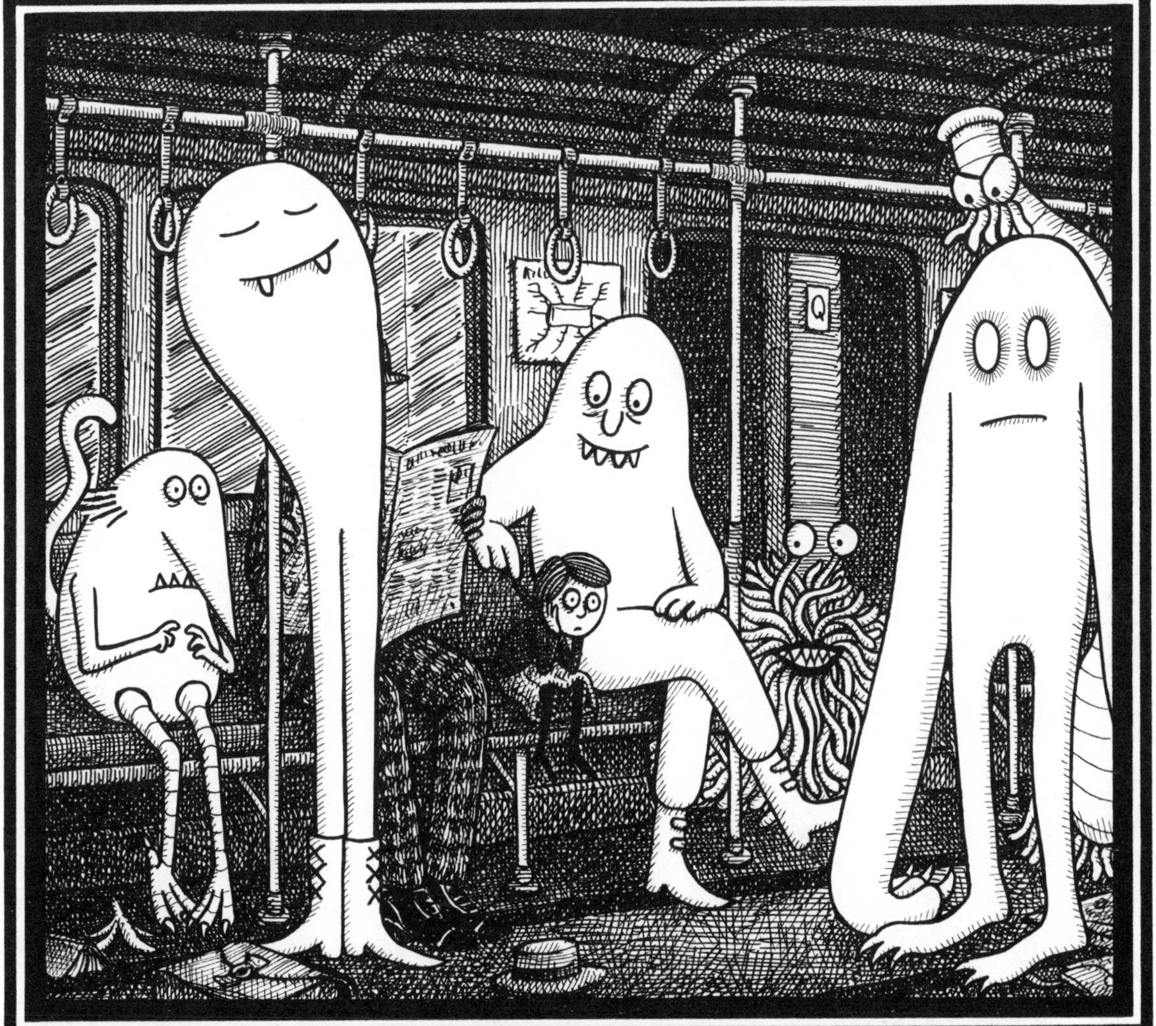
Q

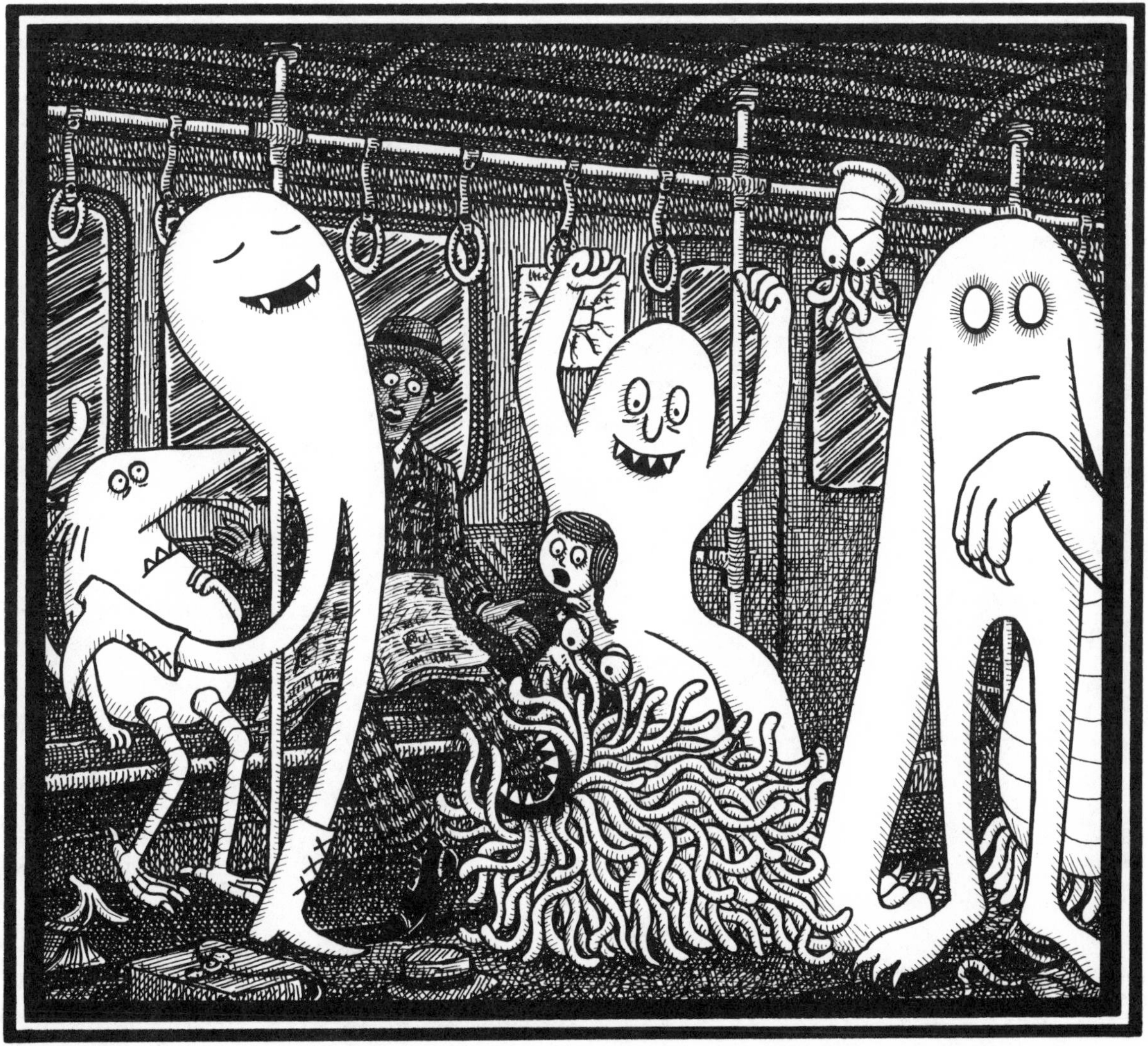

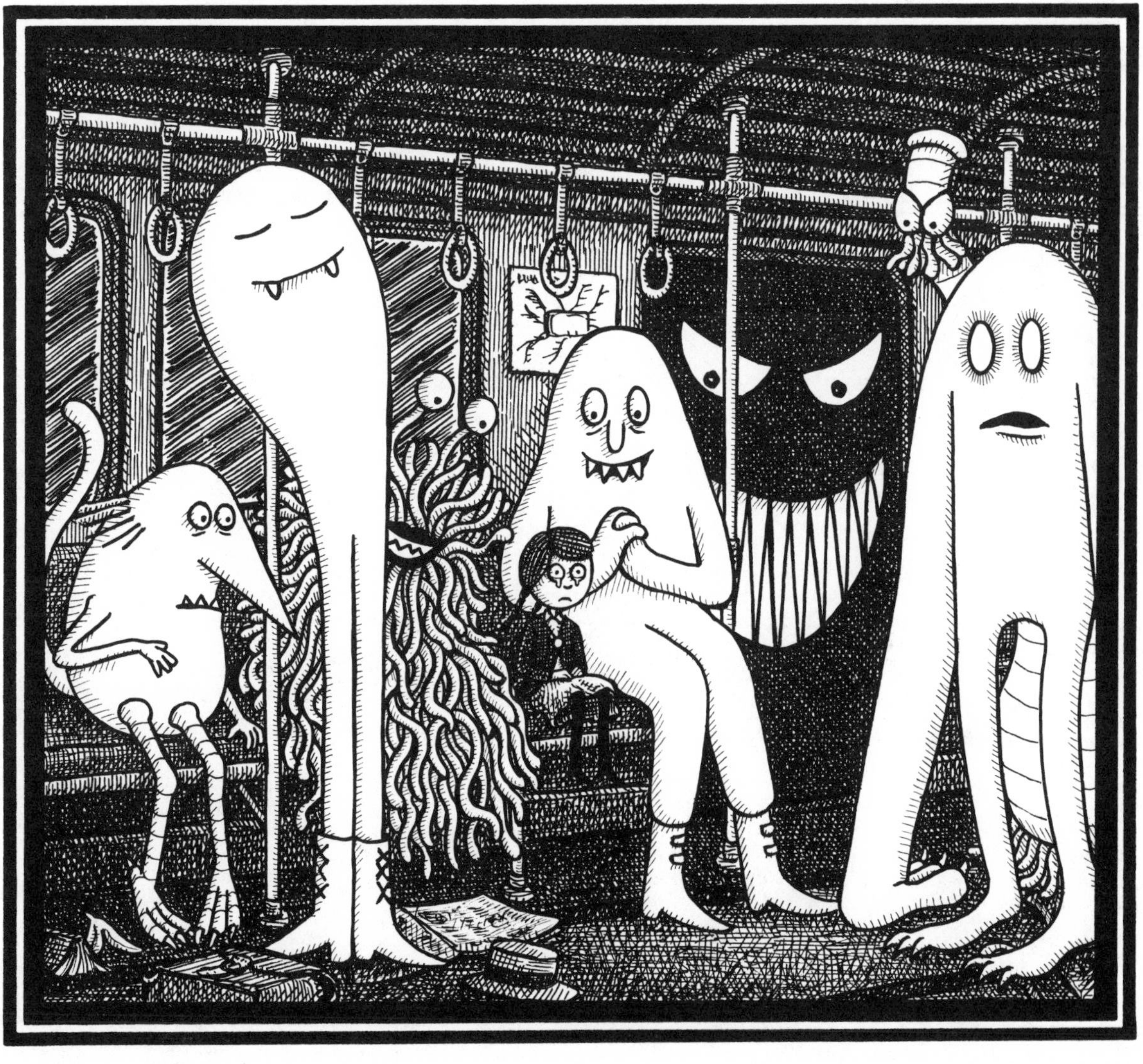

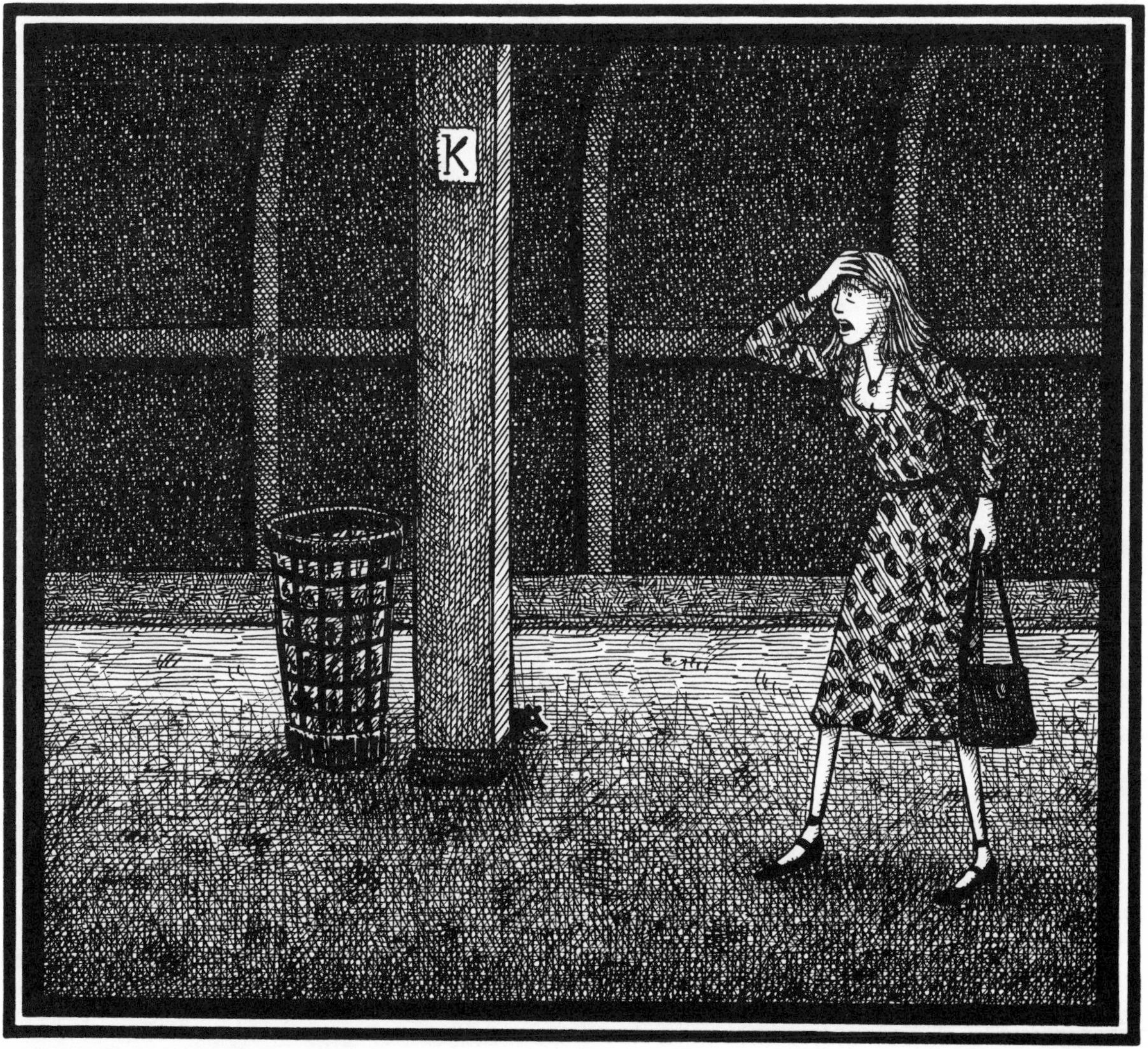
K

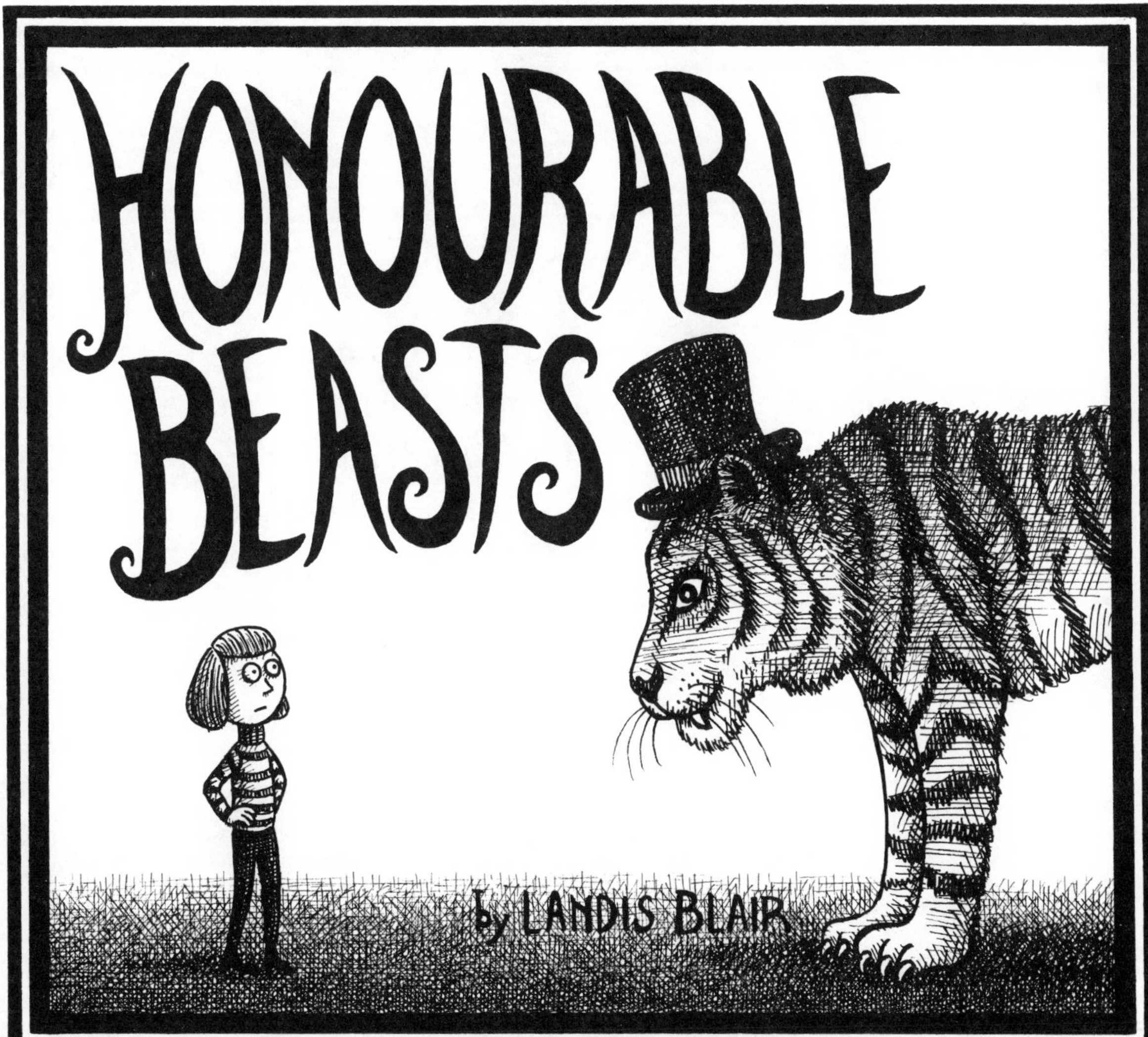
HONOURABLE
BEASTS
by LANDIS BLAIR

"Hester," said mother, "you're being a pest,
Go elsewhere till dinner and give me a rest."
"I hate you!" screamed Hester from deep in her chest,
Before stomping off at this hurtful request.

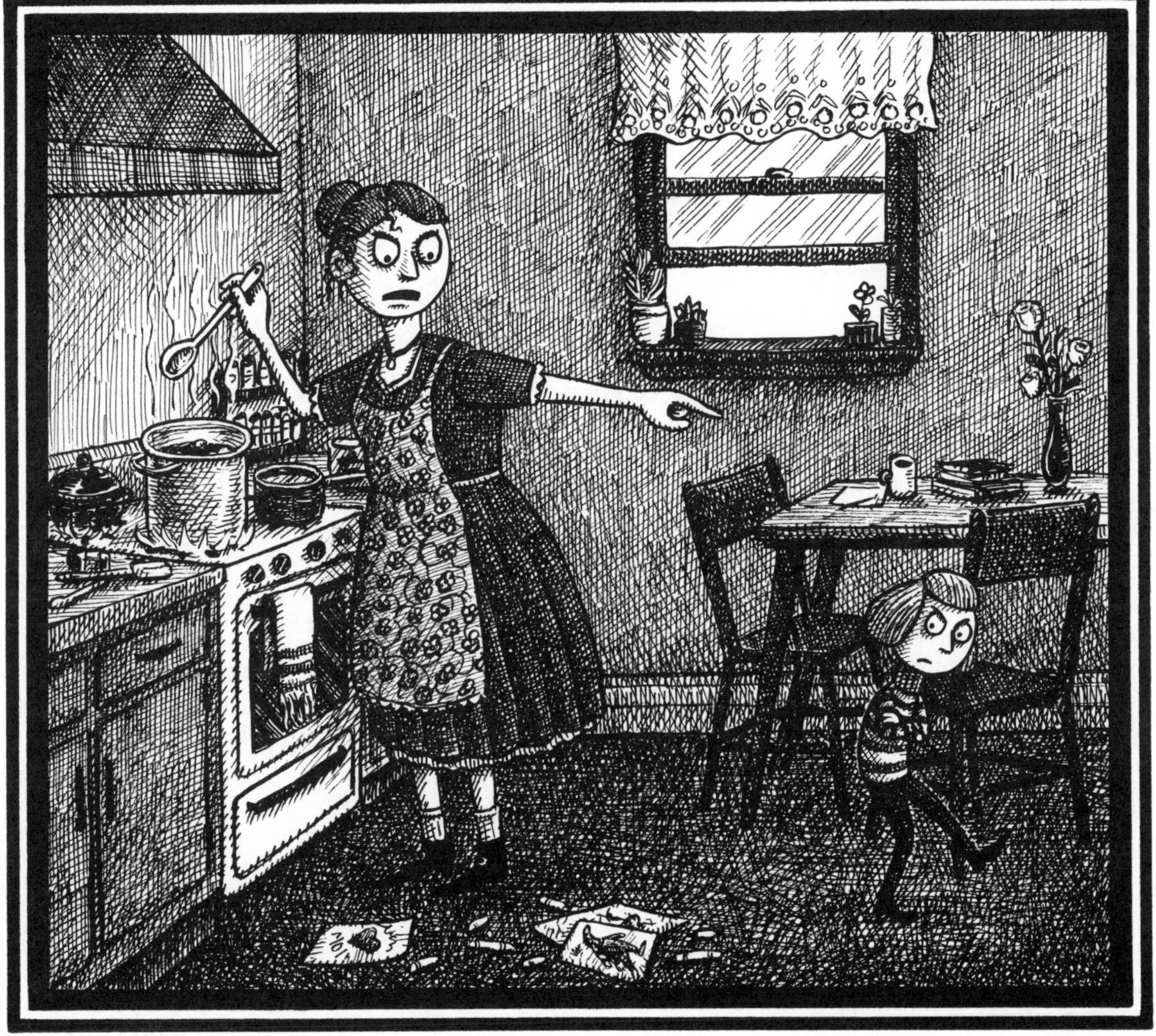

While crying with anger and some indignation,
Bemoaning her mother's imposed segregation,
She saw out her window with deep agitation
A tiger appearing without explanation.

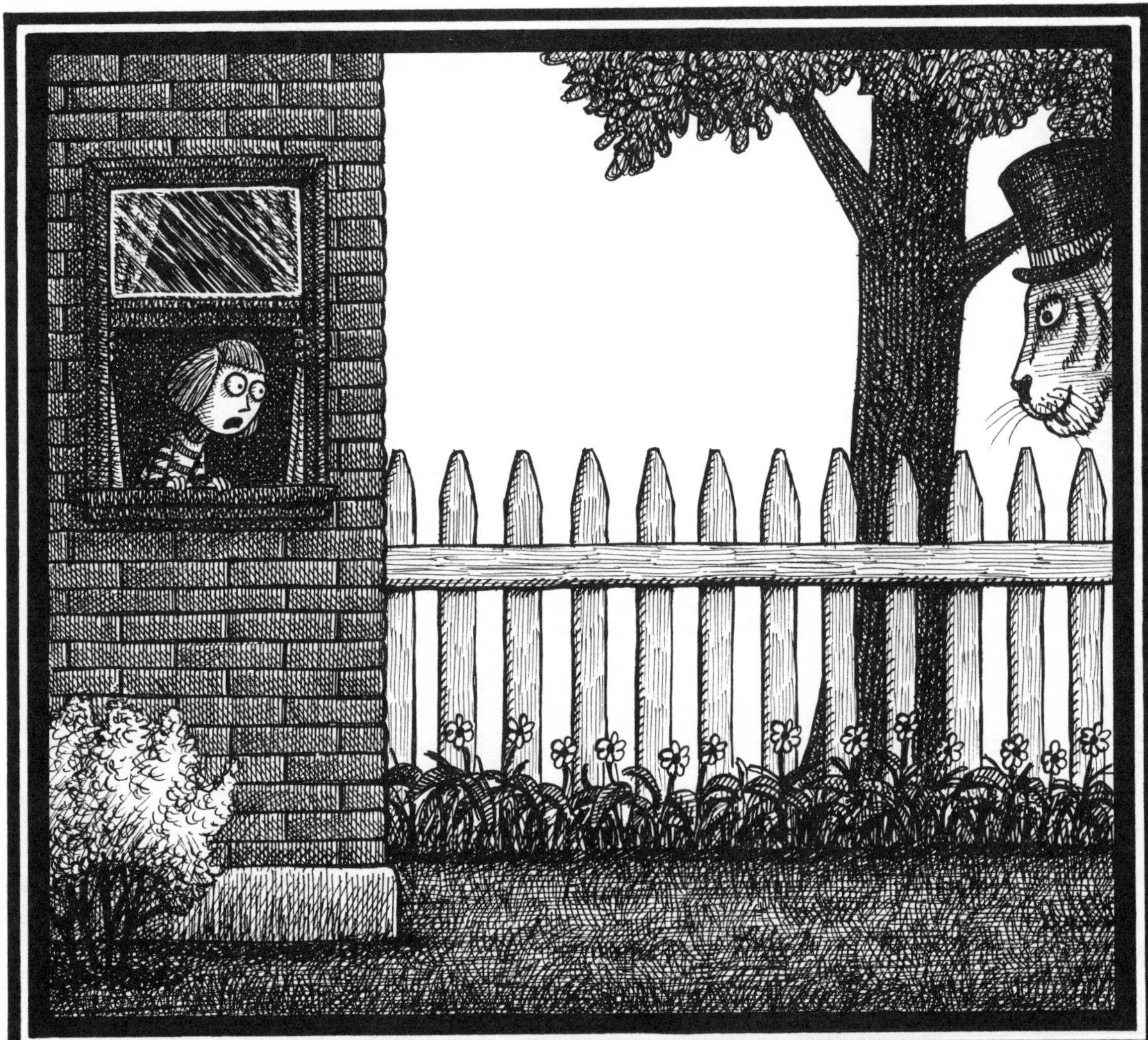

"Hello," said the tiger, "please join me outside."
Poor Hester just stared with her mouth open wide.
While pondering deeply before she replied,
"I thank you," she said, "but I'm too terrified."

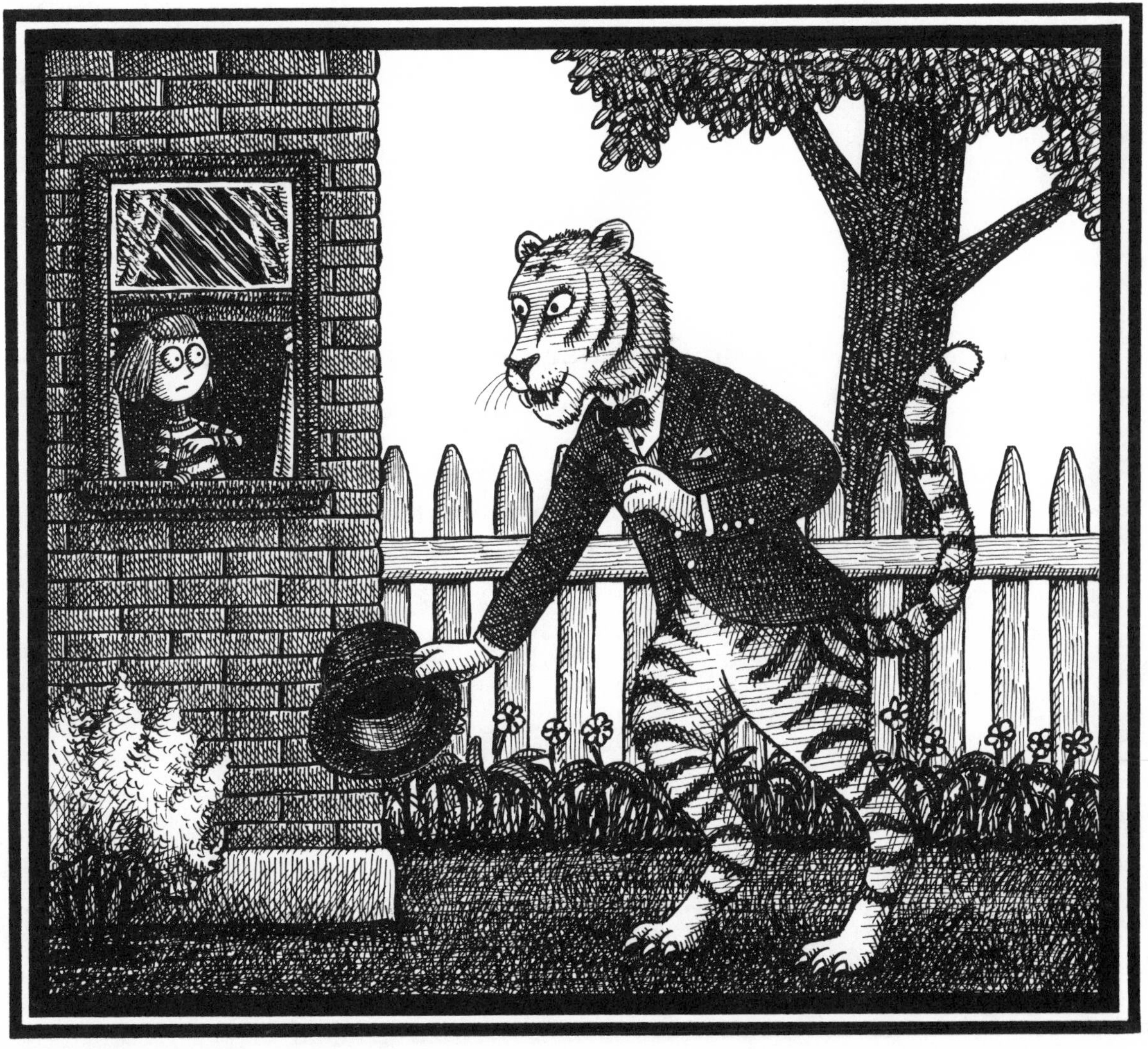

"Tut-tut," said the tiger, "your fear I can see,
And tigers are fierce, but I do guarantee
Your safety and merriment, if you agree
To come to my lair and have dinner with me."

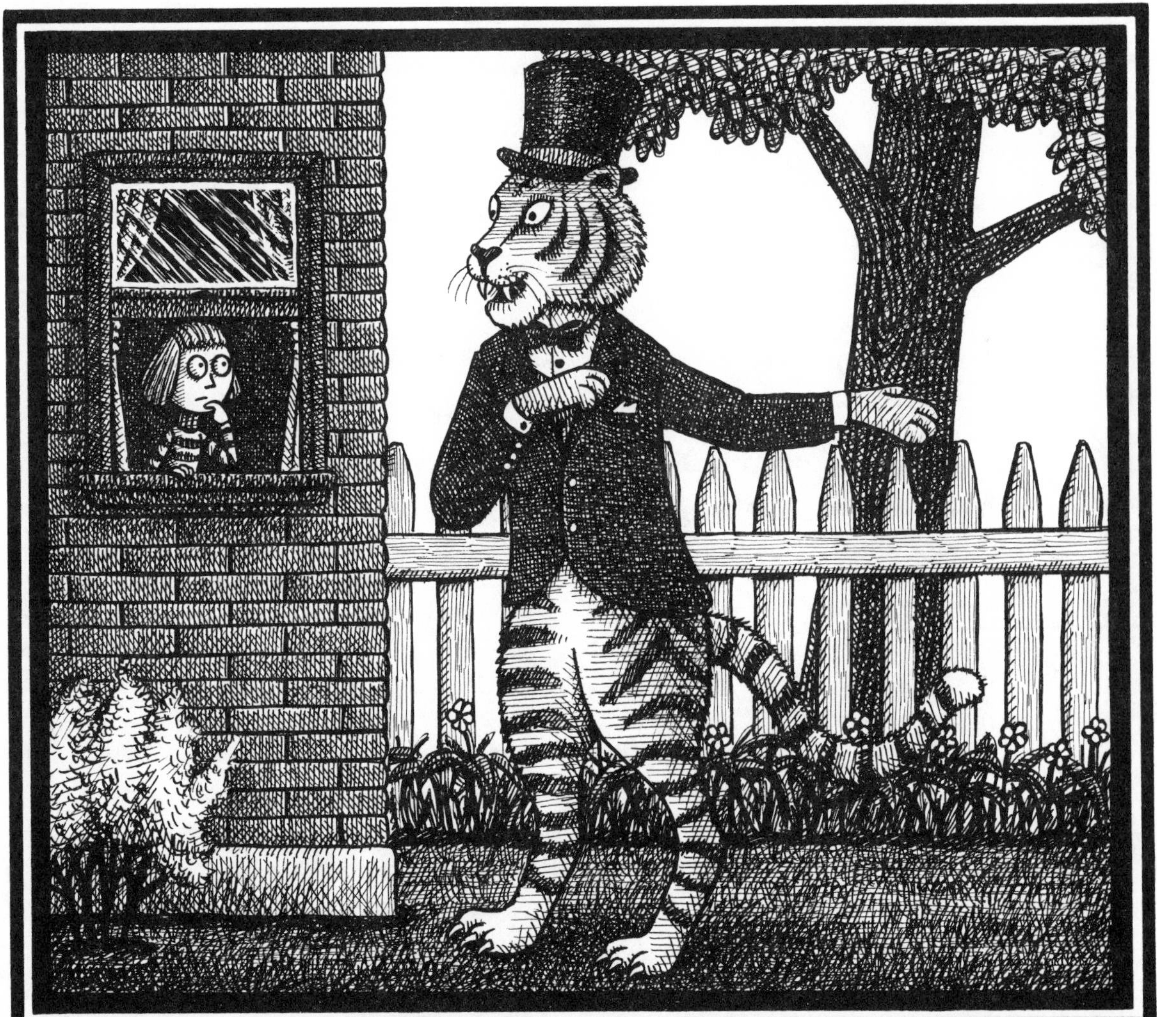

"Oh my," Hester said, "it sounds lovely, but no,
My mother won't like it and won't let me go."
"I see," said the tiger, "but I'm not your foe,
And you're not my only friend coming, you know."

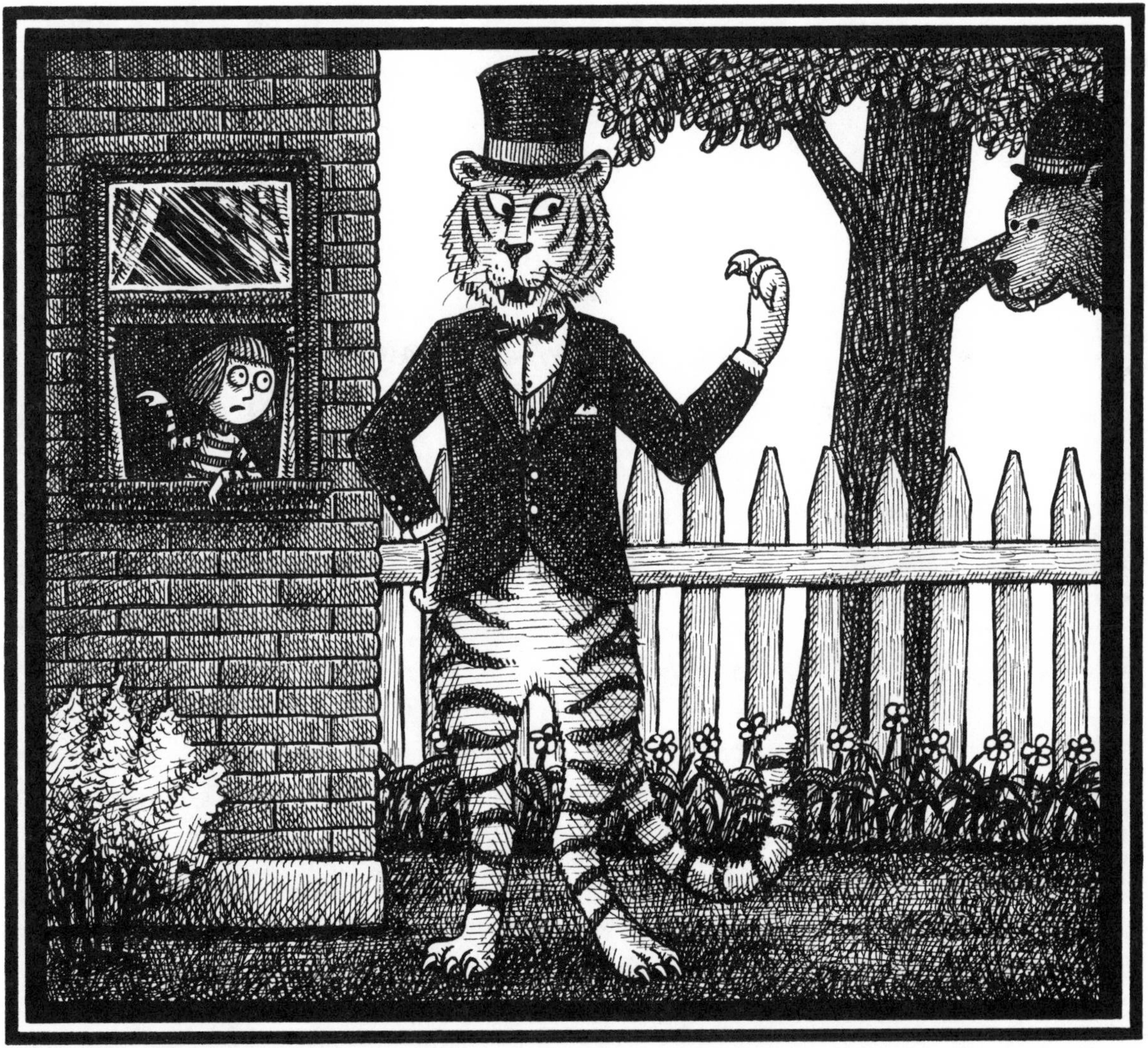

"Hello!" said a bear, "I am charmed, to be sure,
And dinner with you has a special allure,
With you as our guest we will put on our furs.
What a night we will have, what a feast will occur!"

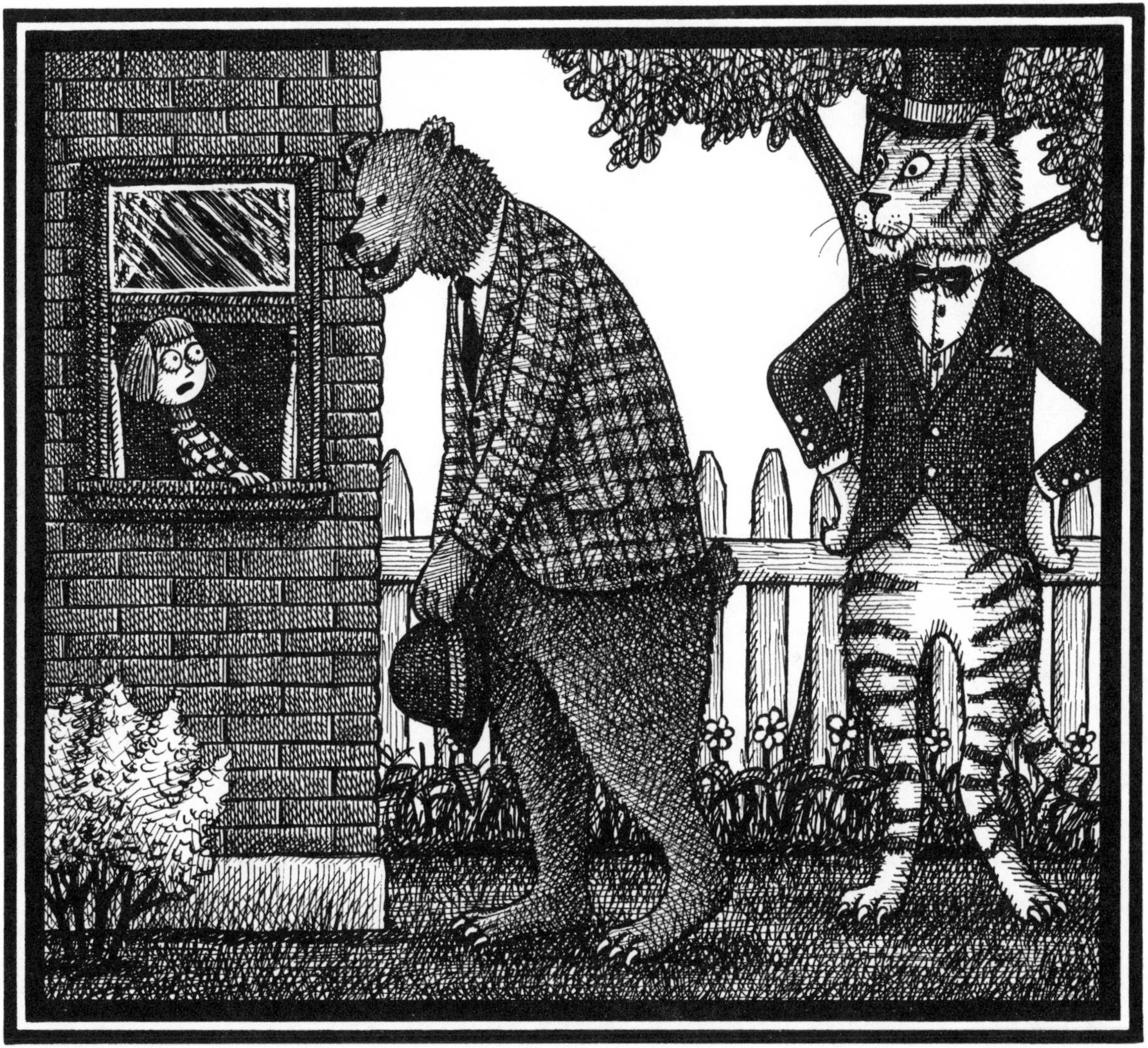

Then Hester let out a most pitiful sigh,
"My mother will yell at me until I cry,
For she's making dinner, expecting me nigh."
"Pish posh," said the tiger, "just look who's nearby!"

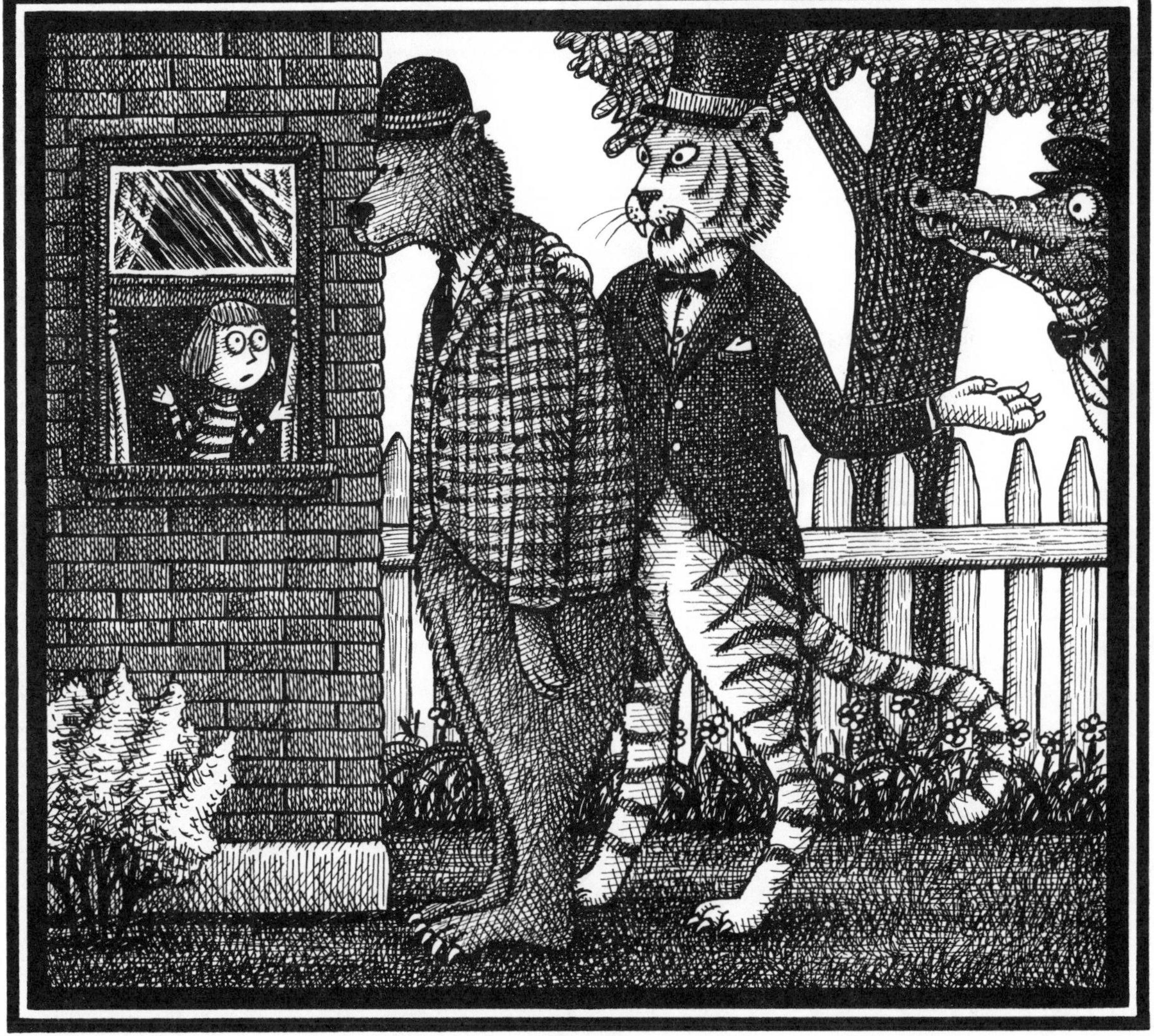

"Hello," said a gator, "how sumptuous you seem,
And you at our table? Oh my, what a dream.
I'm so excited I almost could scream!"
He said with a smile and teeth all agleam.

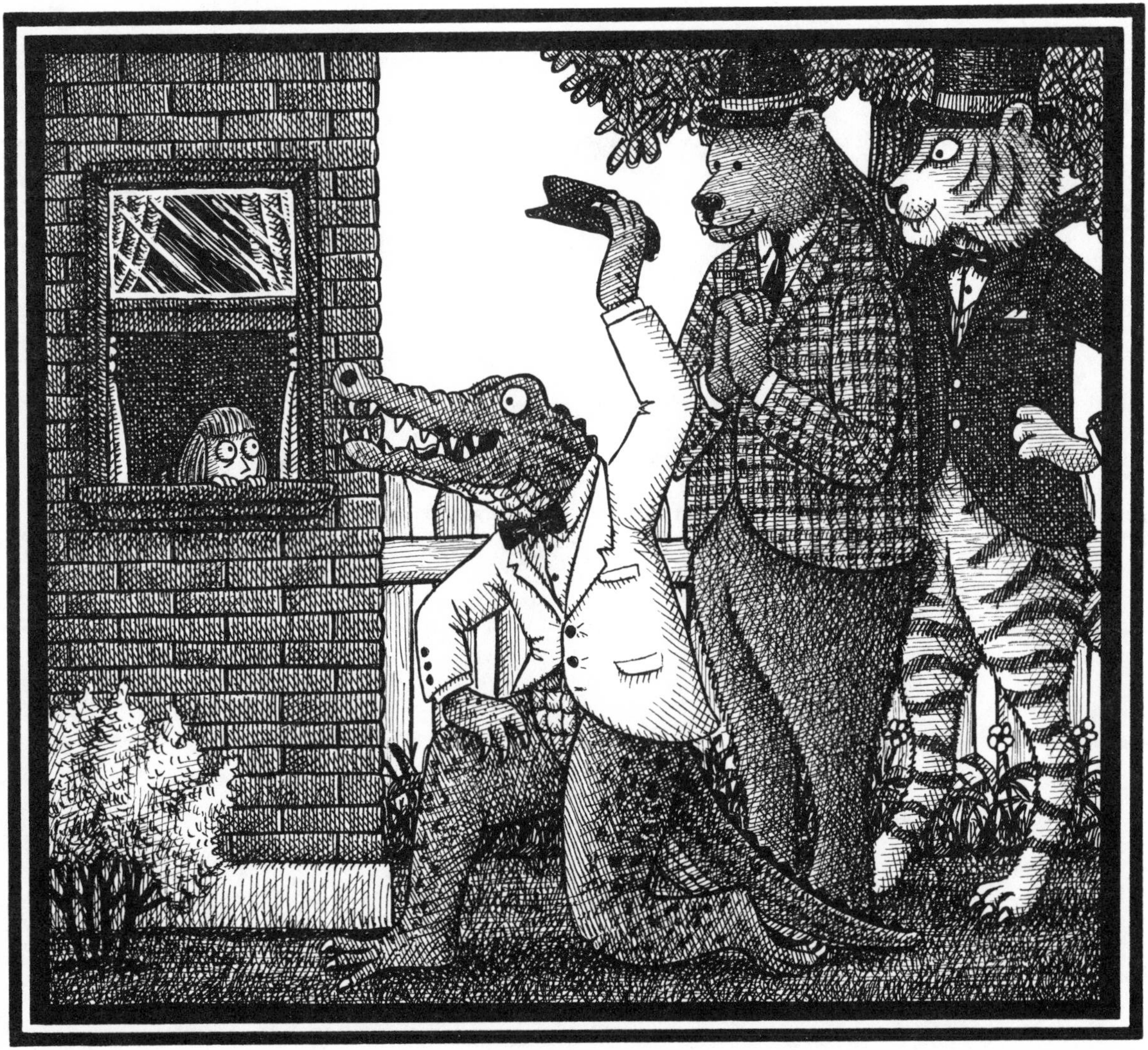

"How tempting," said Hester, "to join in your feast,
But if you knew mother, your welcome would cease.
She'd call you all wretched, dishonourable beasts,
And keep me inside for a year at the least!"

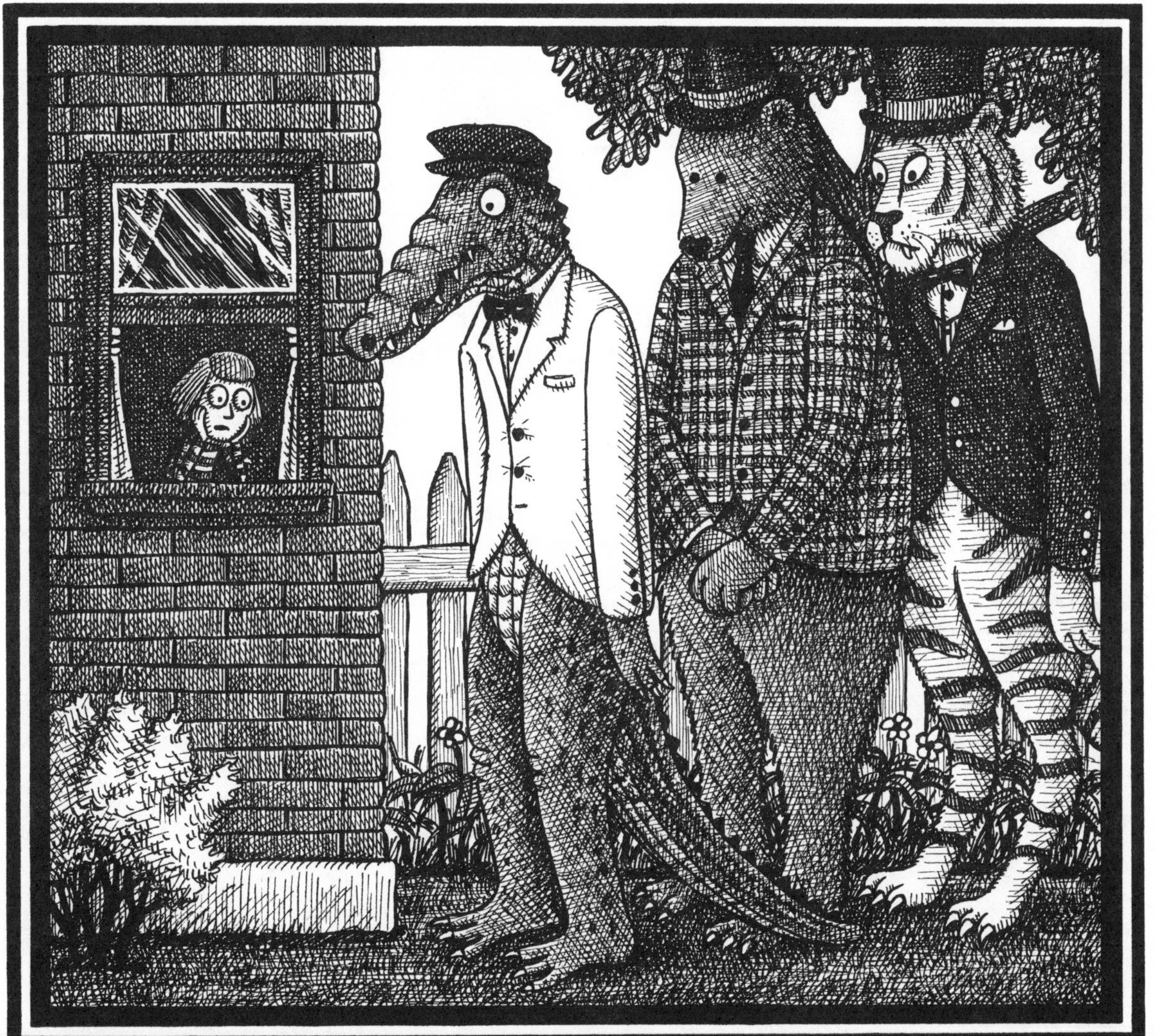

"How sad," said the gator, "your mother sounds horrid."
"And," said the bear, "her judgement's distorted."
"But," said the gator, "you will be supported,
For joining with us will ensure she is thwarted."

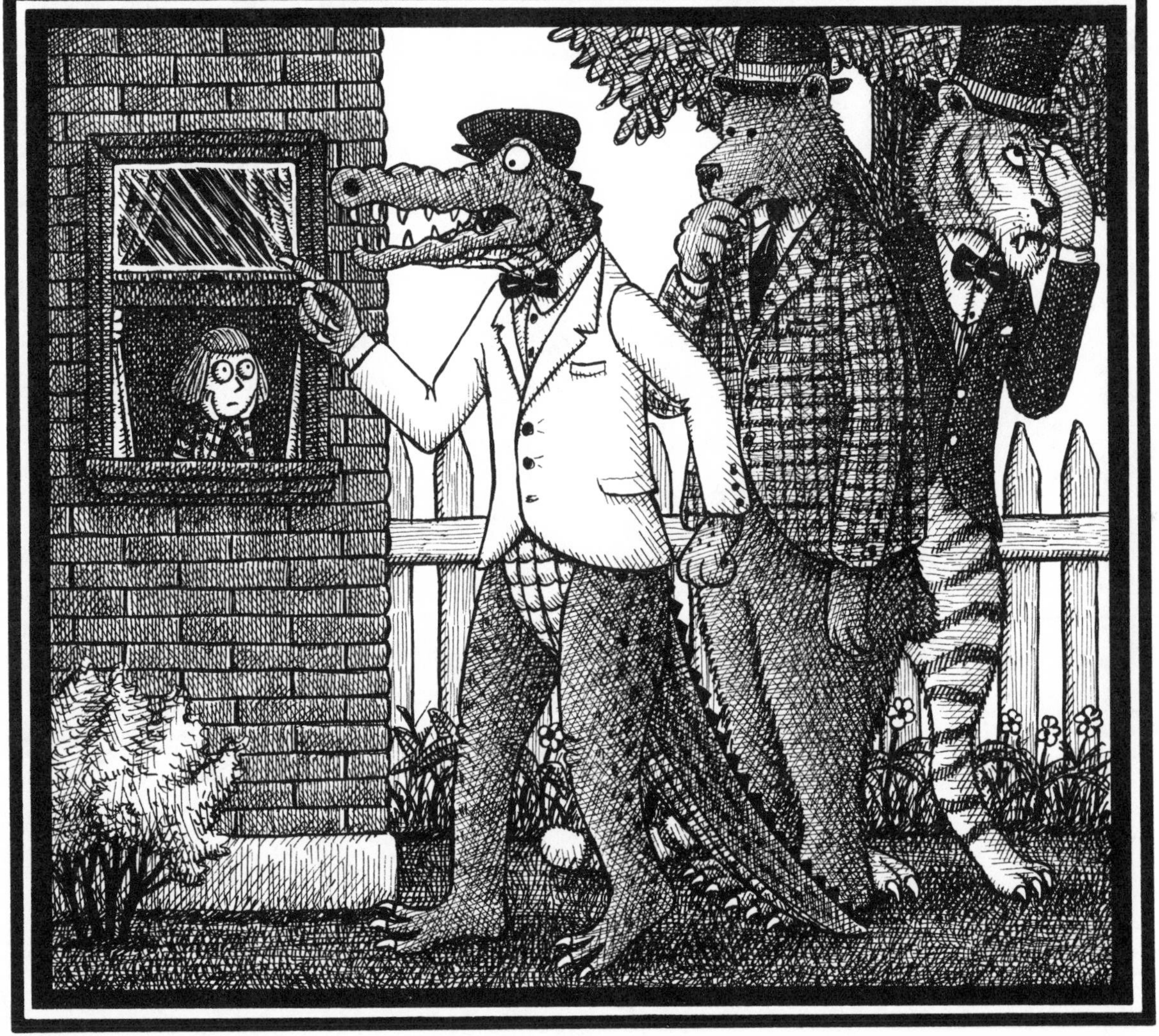

"It seems," said the tiger, "that I missed my cue,
In my excitement I failed to tell you,
Your mother will be at our fine dinner too."
And the bear and the gator responded, "It's true!"

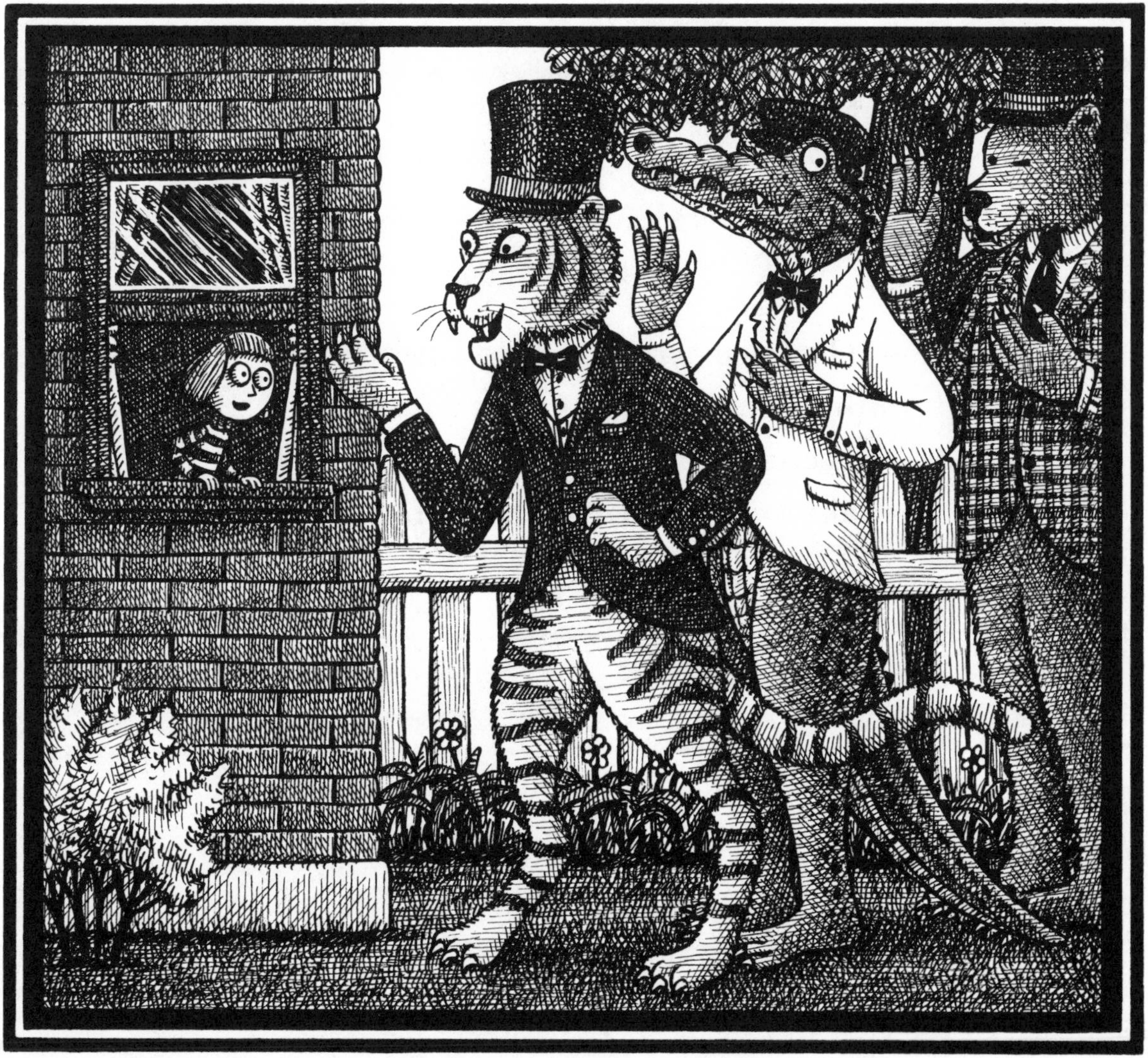

Then Hester cried out an ecstatic "Whoopee!"
And promptly climbed out of her window with glee.
"This changes everything, now I am free,
To make very merry with mother and thee."

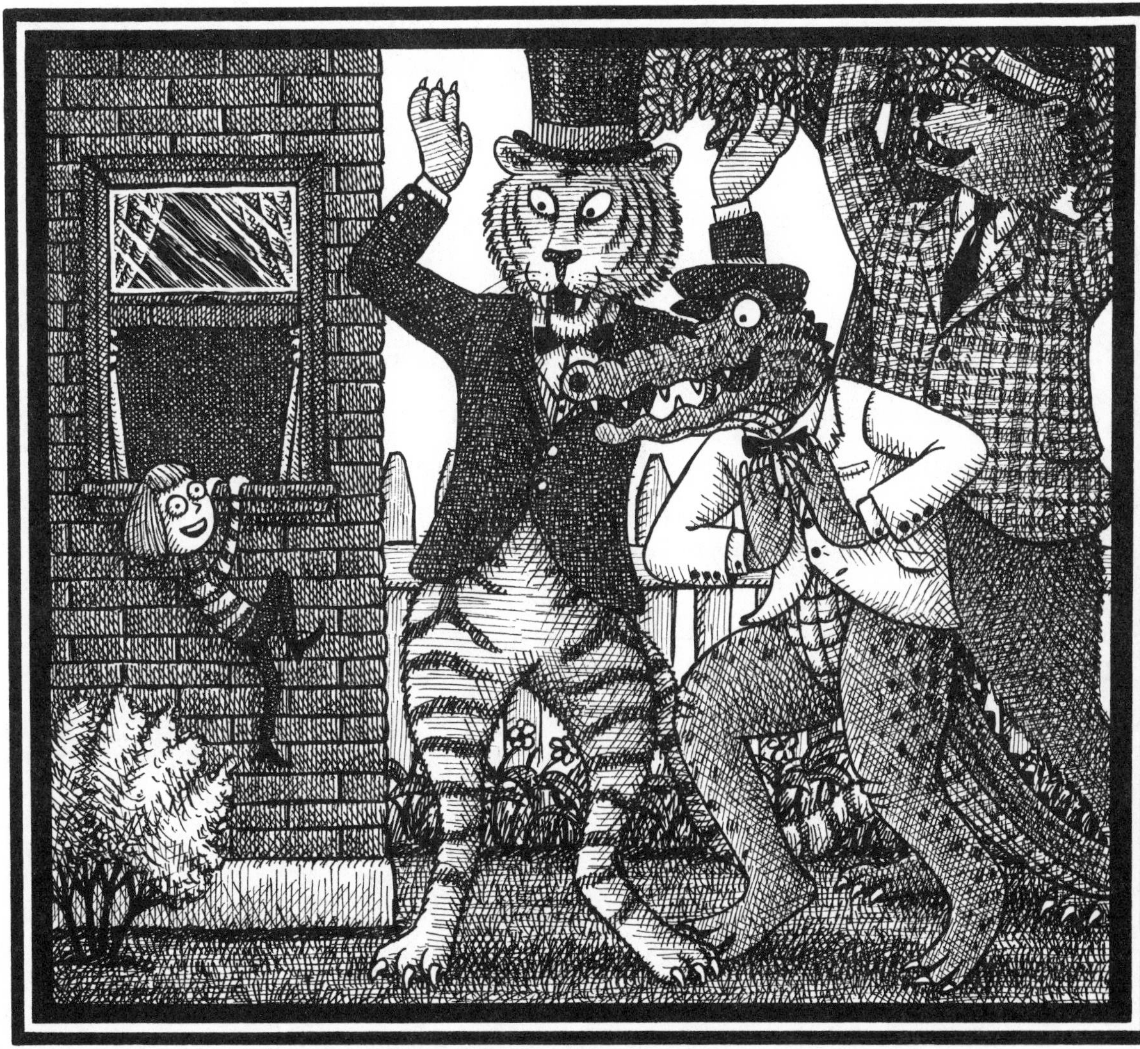

And what a fine picture the four of them made,
They danced and they sang as they marched through the glade,
They strutted and rollicked and never once strayed,
En route to the lair in their beastly parade.

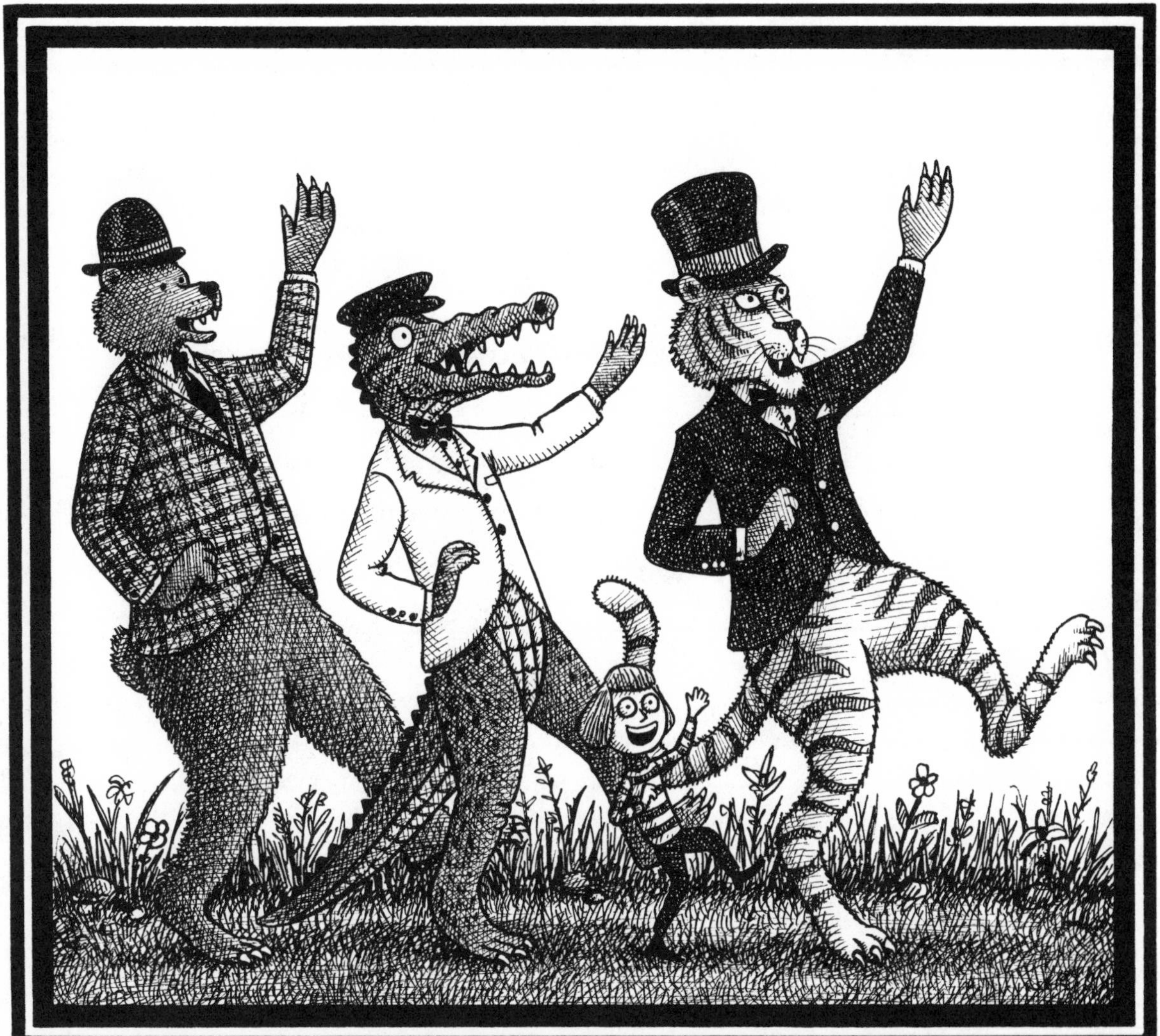

"At last," said the tiger, "now do step inside;
Discover what gaiety we can provide."
"Hurrah!" said the gator, "And how!" bear replied.
And Hester with gratitude promptly complied.

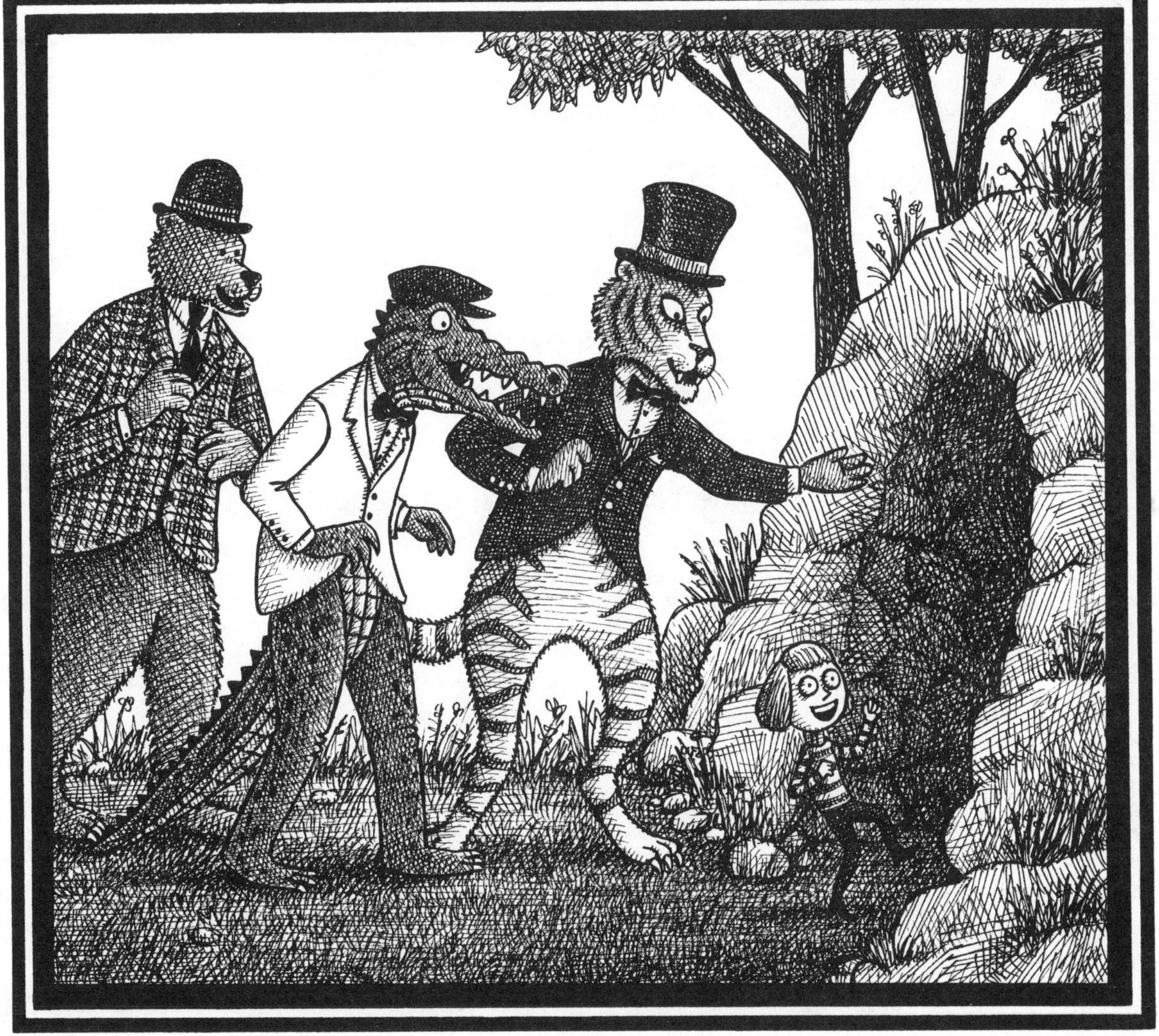

And lo, how the feast was displayed with great flair,
The best decorations, the best silverware,
And true to their word, Hester's mother was there,
Prepared on the table, plump and cooked rare.

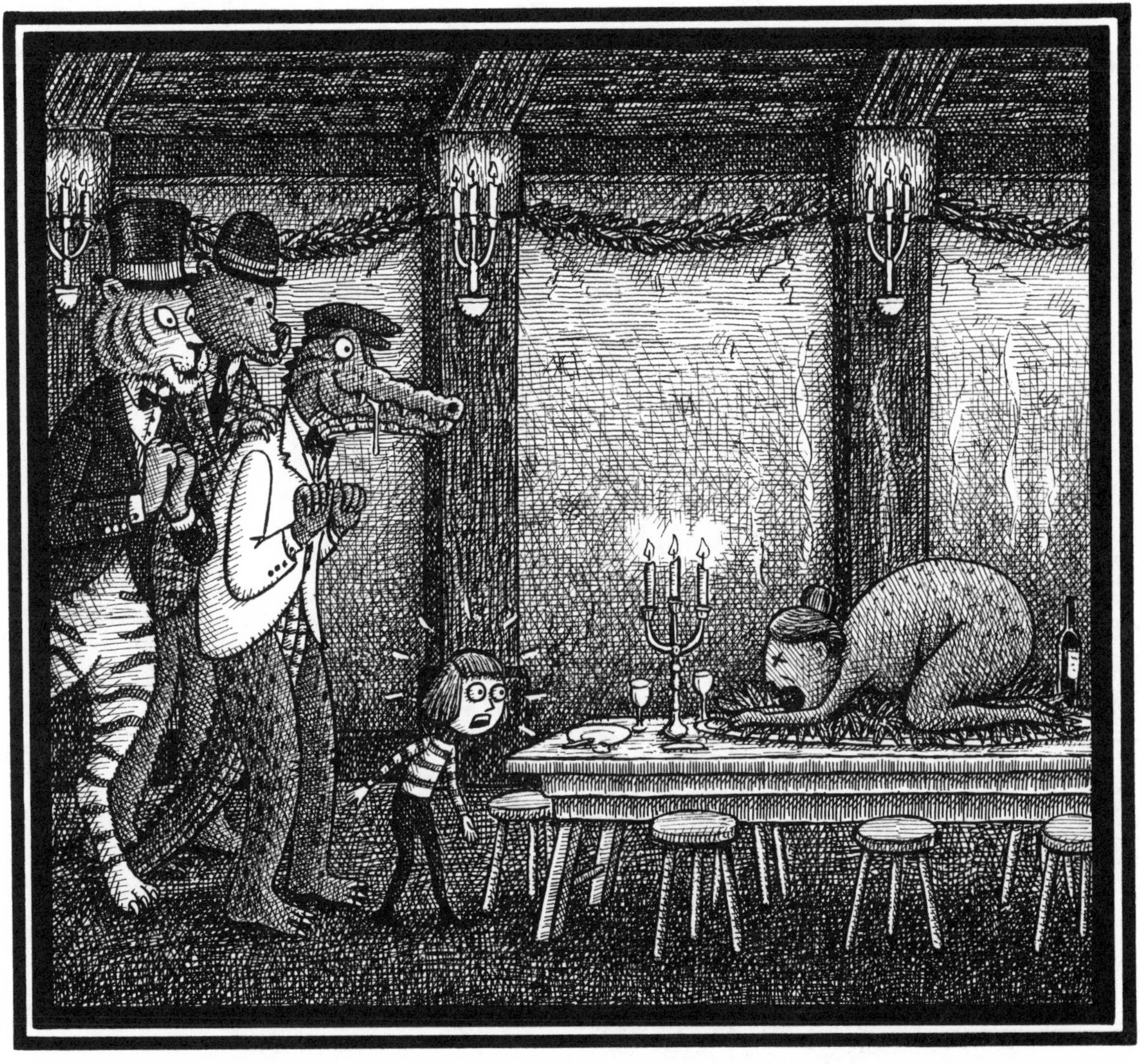

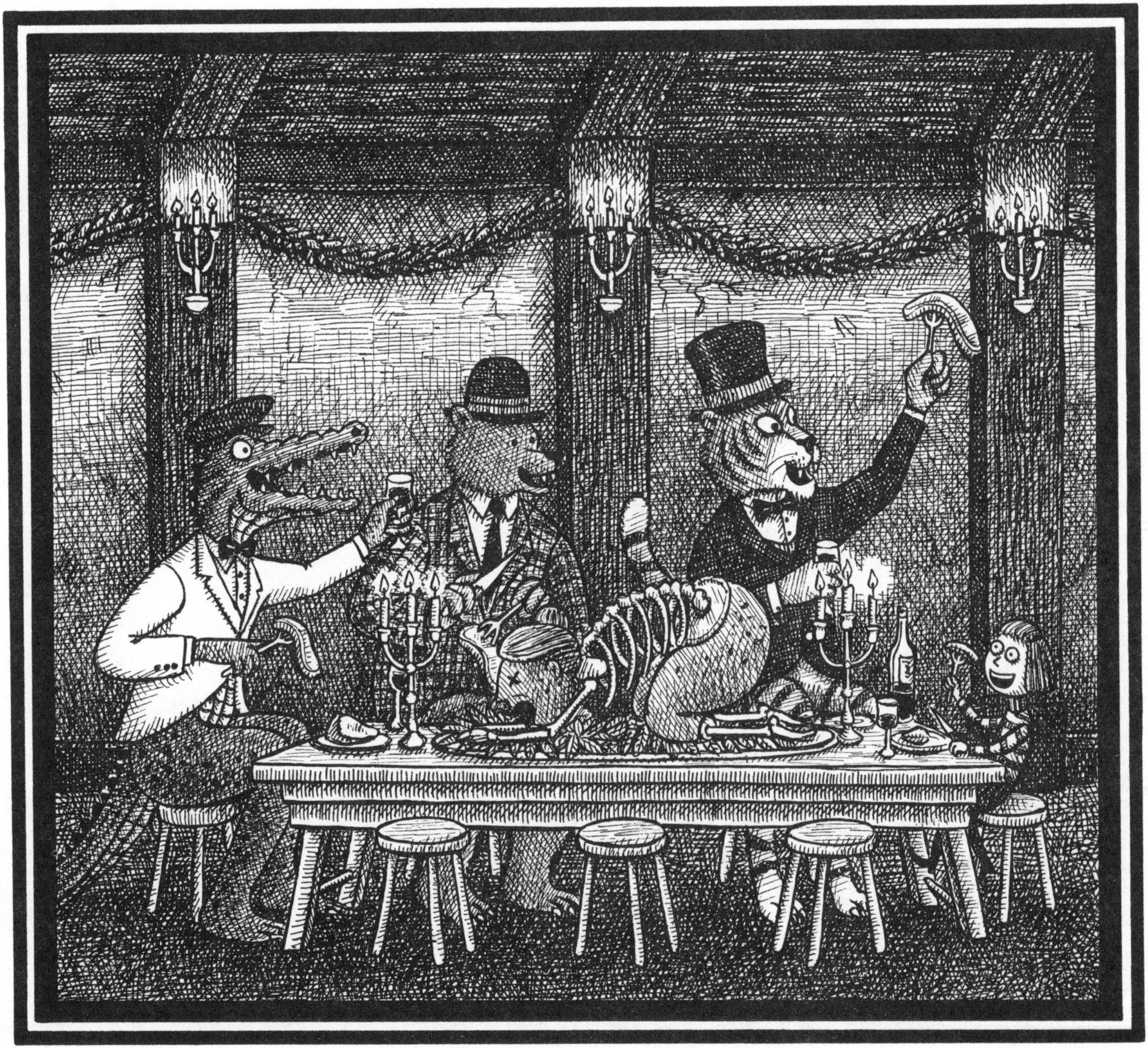

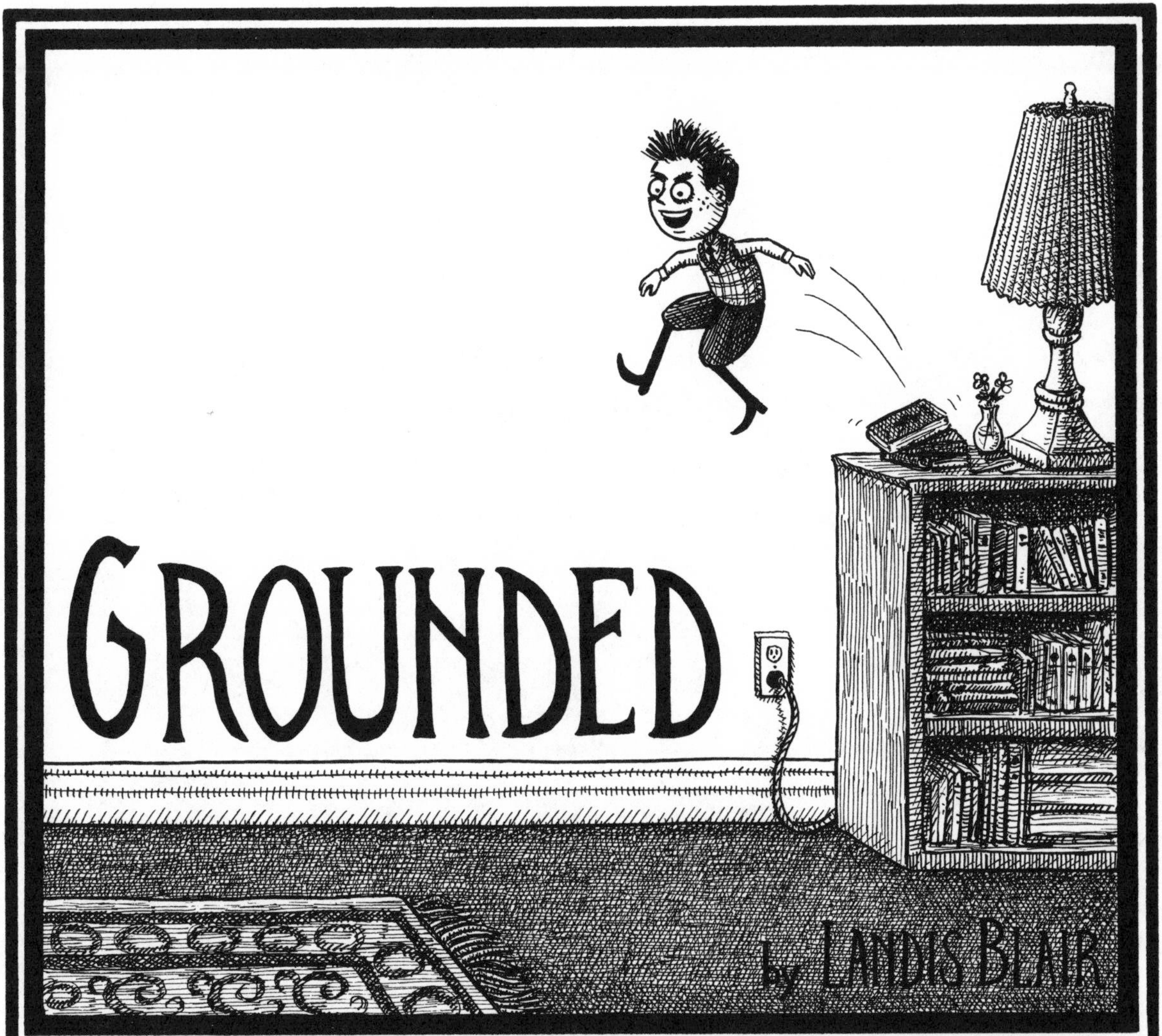
GROUNDED
by LANDIS BLAIR

William was jumping with boom after boom,
Submerging his mother into a deep gloom,
Rounding the corner while clutching her broom,
She bellowed repeatedly, "Go to your room!"

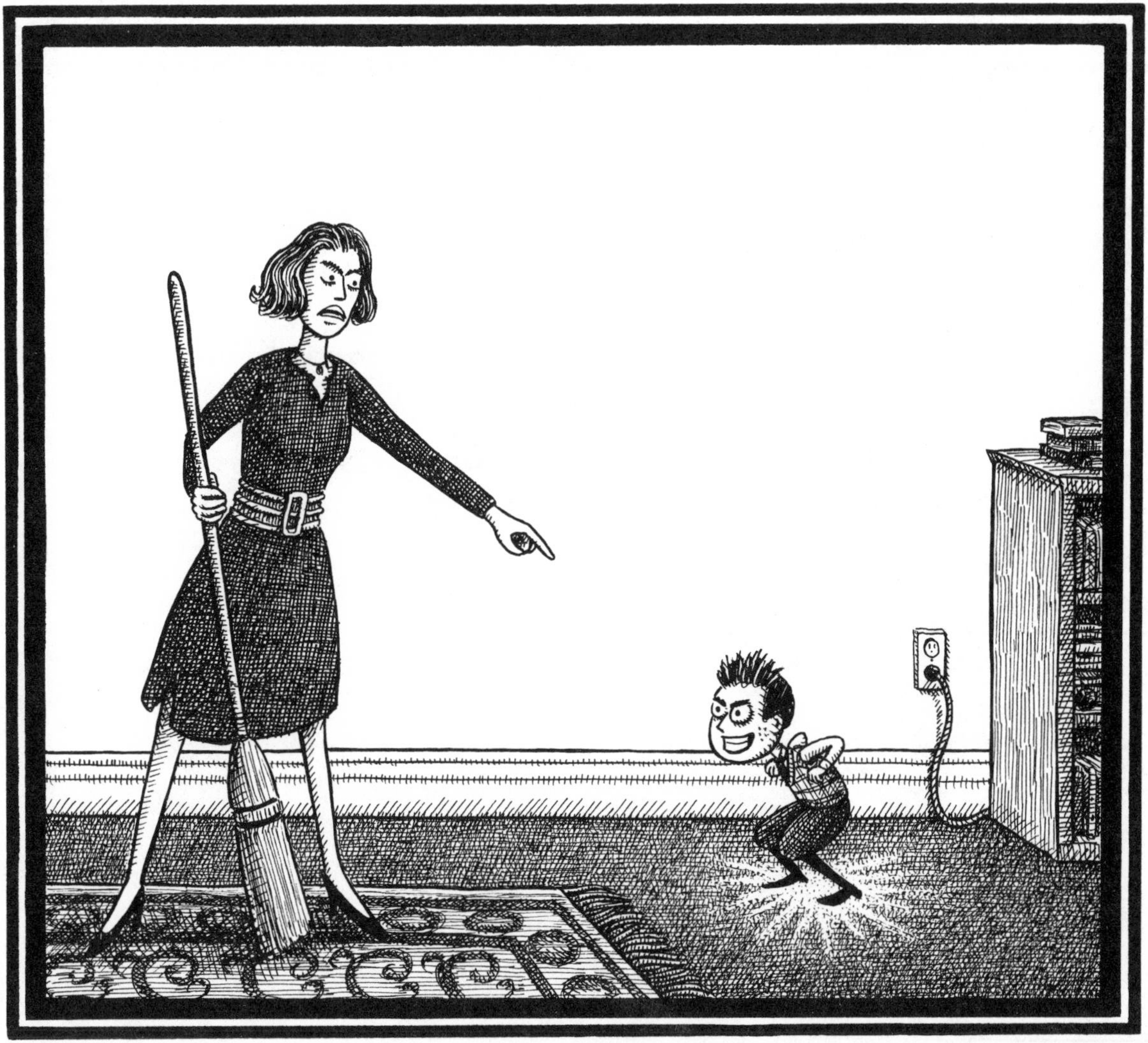

William ignored her and made such a din,
Renouncing the courtesy shown to one's kin.
Picking him up and erasing his grin,
She walked to his room and then threw him right in.

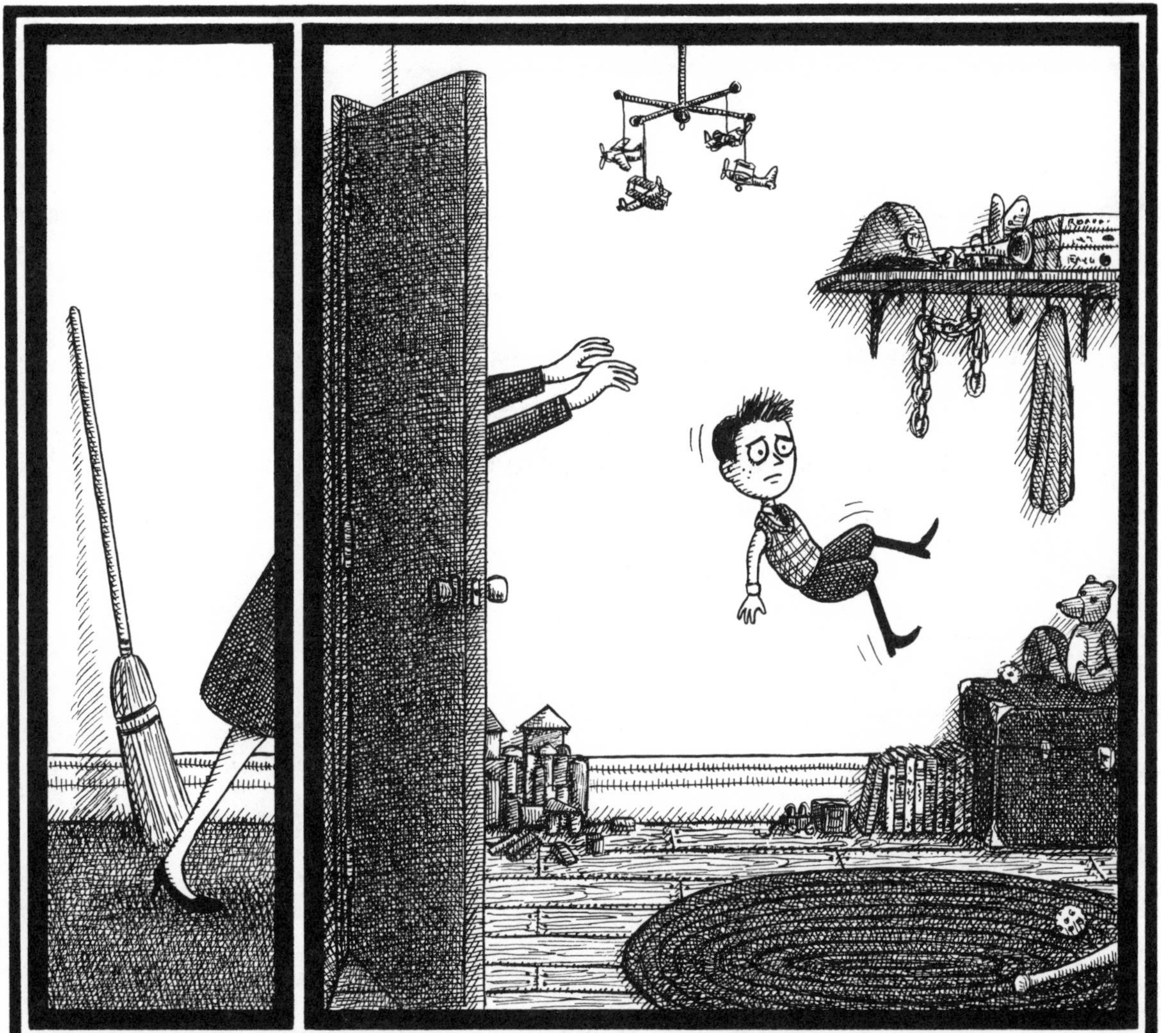

William he screamed and threw fits and made noise,
He chewed on the rug and he smashed all his toys.
Mom with her teacup remained full of poise,
And muttered indiff'rently, "Boys will be boys."

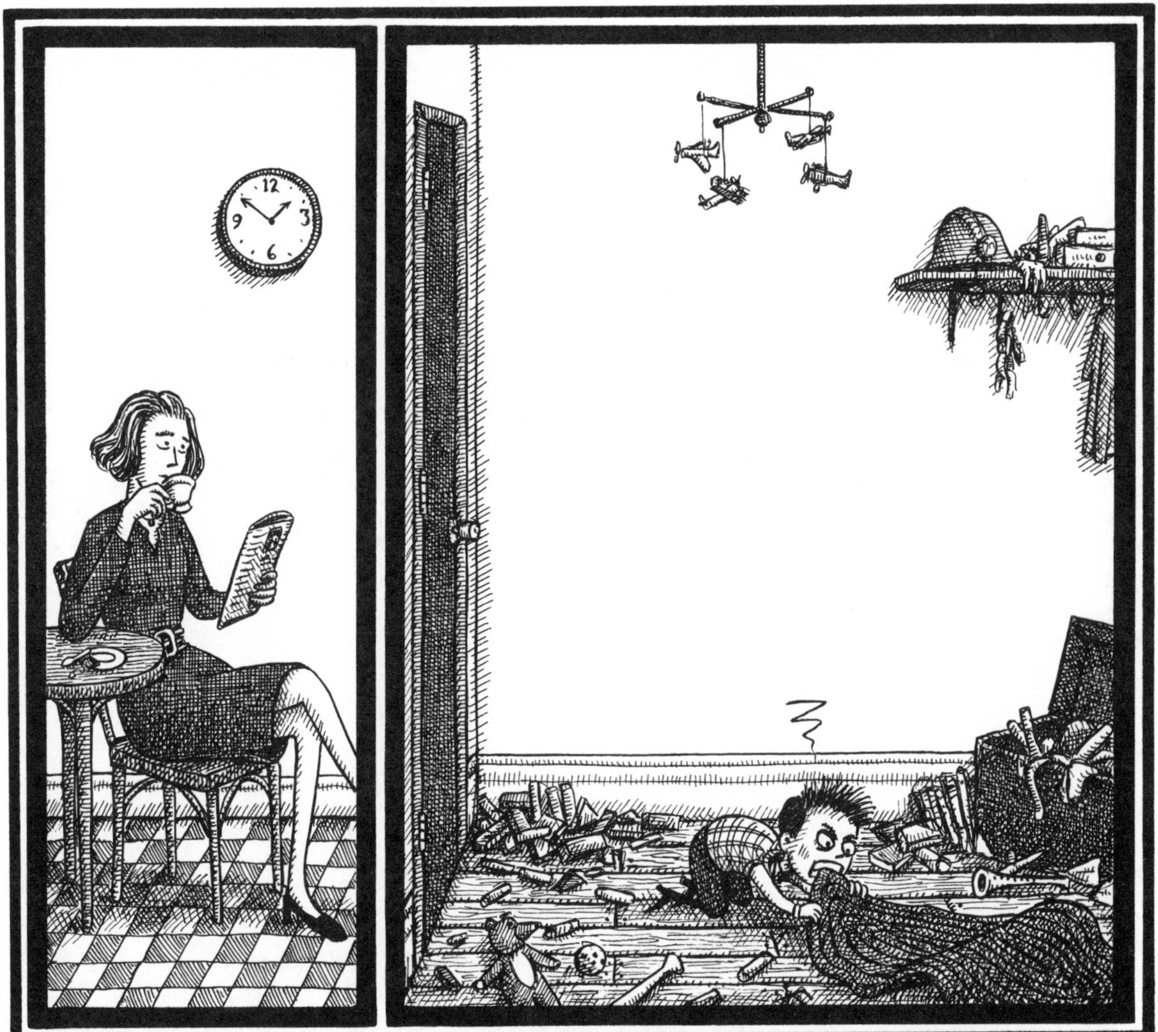

Father came home at a quarter past four,
First kissing his wife he then listened and swore,
Promptly discerning small William's uproar.
She sighed and replied, "He is hard to ignore."

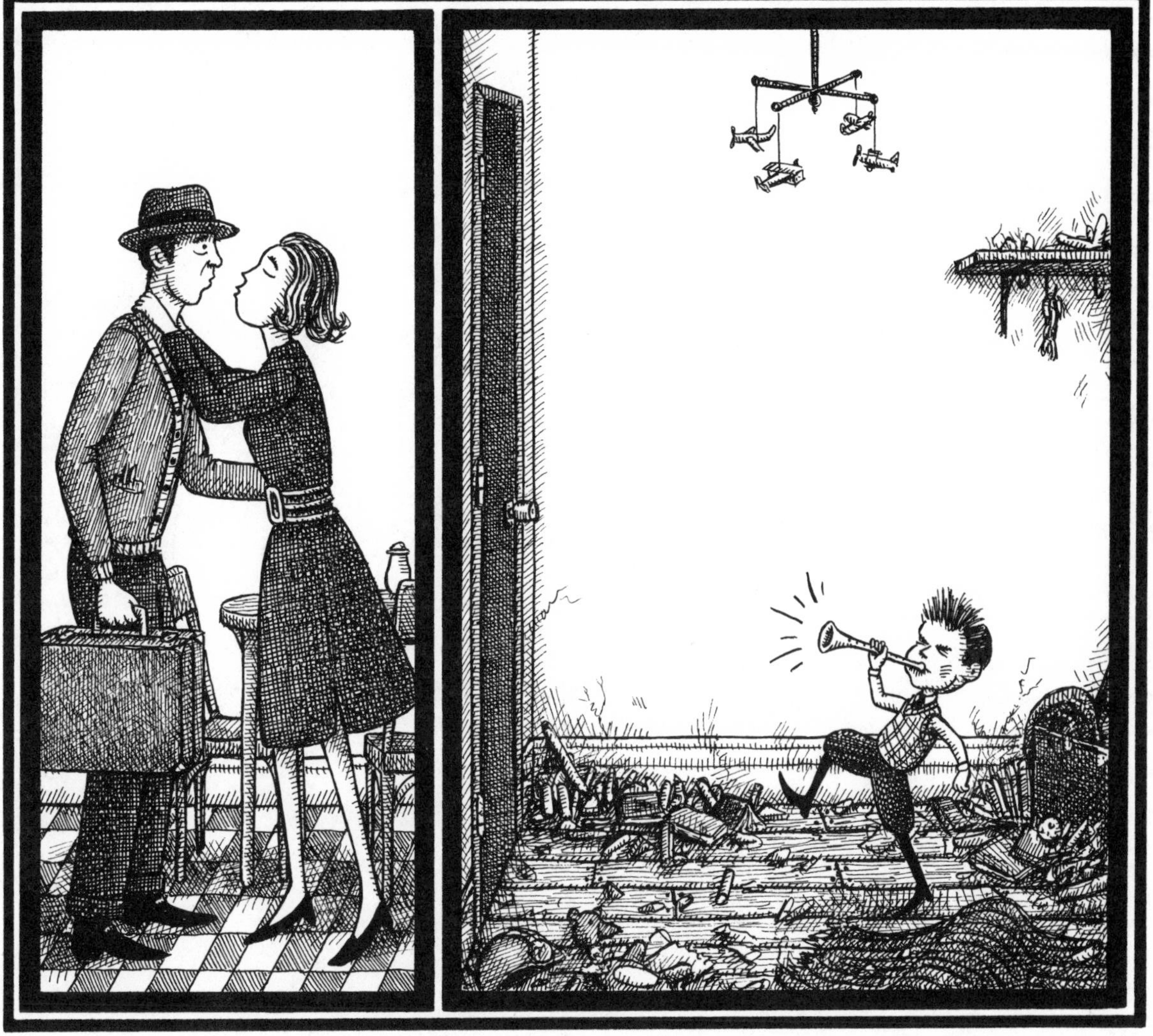

William proceeded with terrible clouts,
His father grew angry and started to shout,
"You settle down there what is this about?
Until you are quiet you'll never come out!"

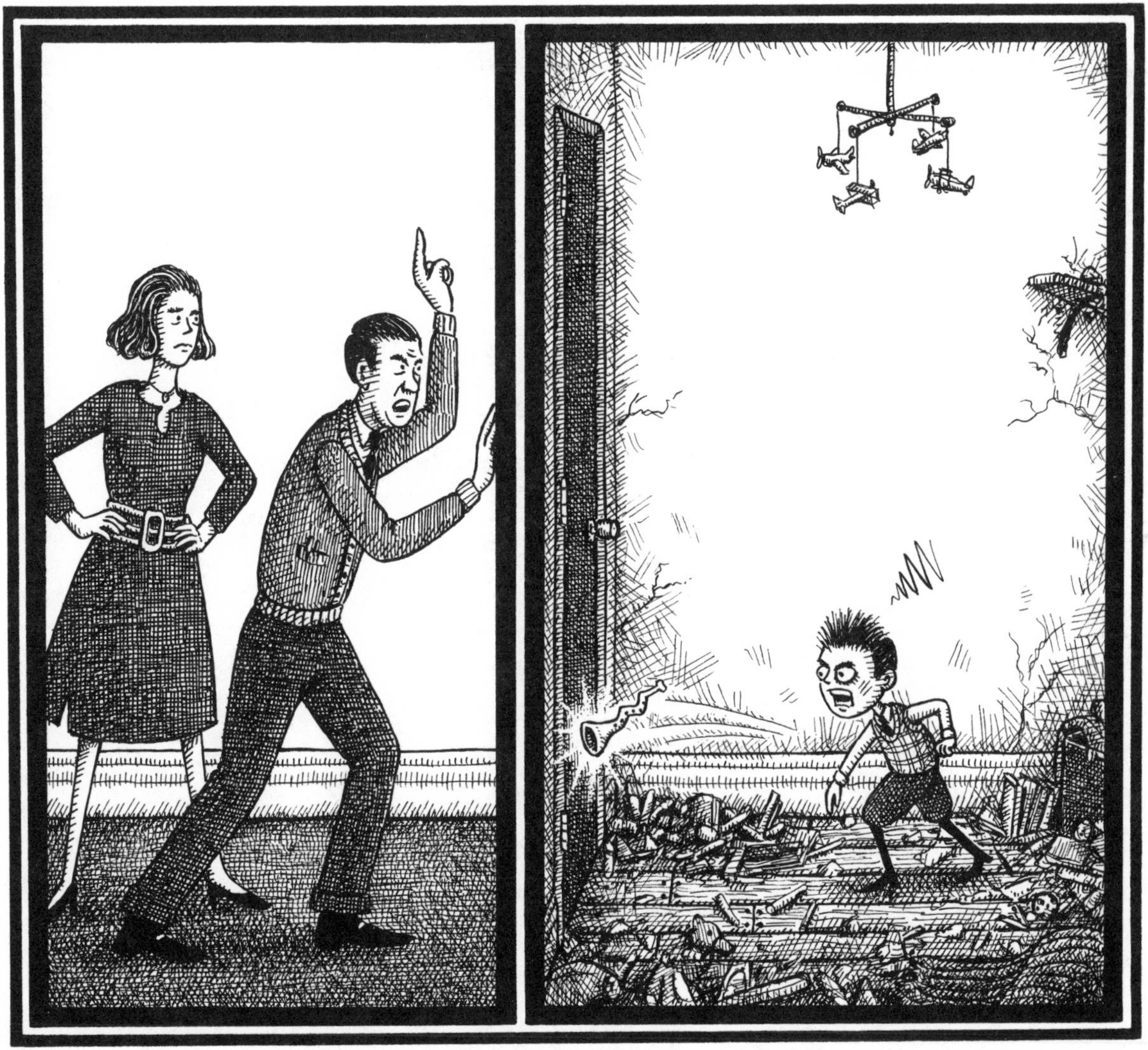

William he grunted, and grumbled, and groaned,
And made such a mess of his face while he moaned,
Telling his parents they'd just been disowned,
Insisting authorities must now be phoned.

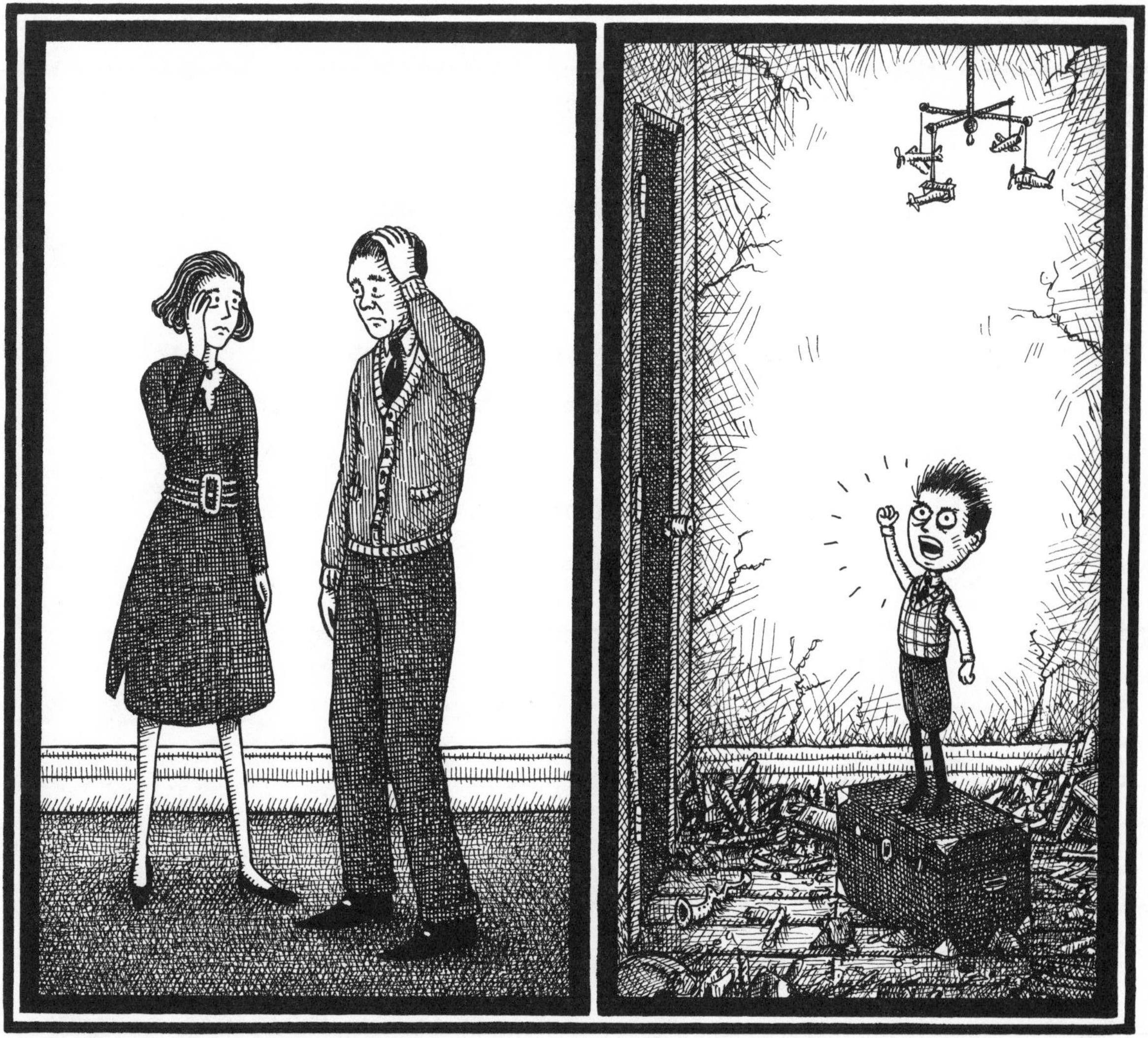

Mother and father sat down to roast beef,
As William grew hungry with anger and grief,
Doubling his tantrums denying relief;
He sensed that imprisonment would not be brief.

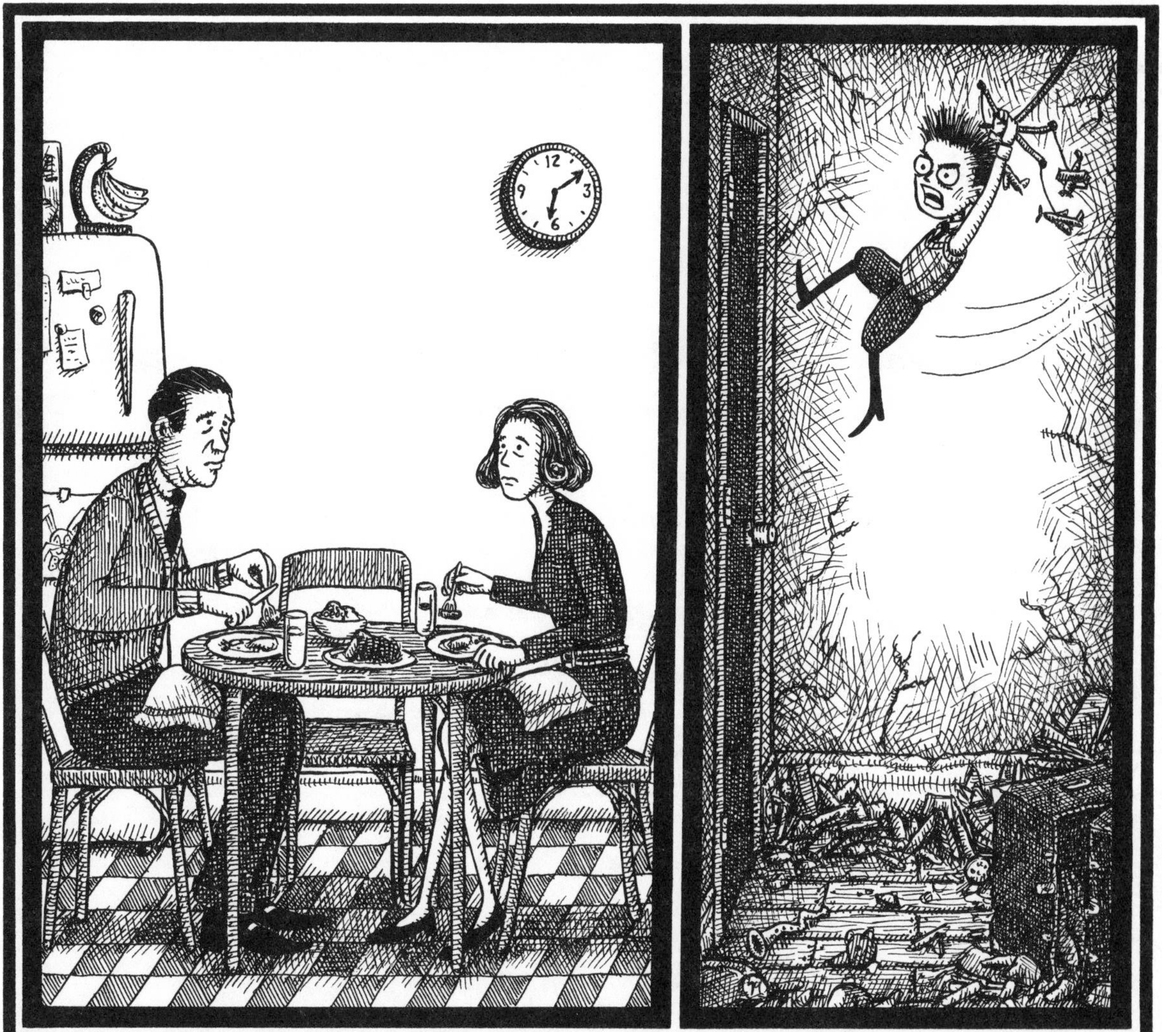

Mom tried to read and his dad tried to smoke,
And wondered if this might just all be a joke.
Having no priv'leges they could revoke,
Their William found ever new ways to provoke.

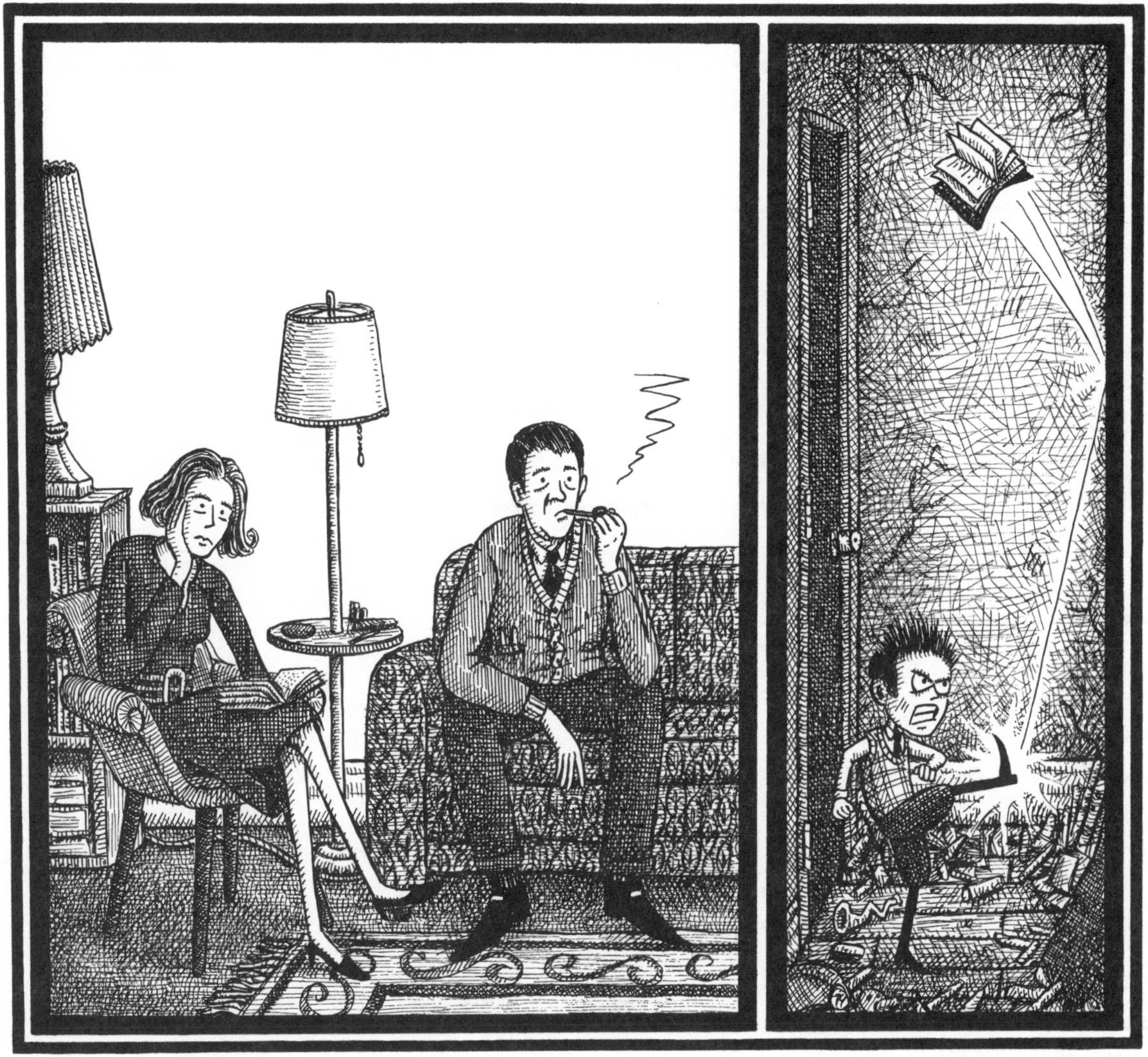

Later that even'ng when pushed to the brink,
His parents ignored him while having a drink.
Then did they wonder and hazard to think,
"To life without William," they said with a wink.

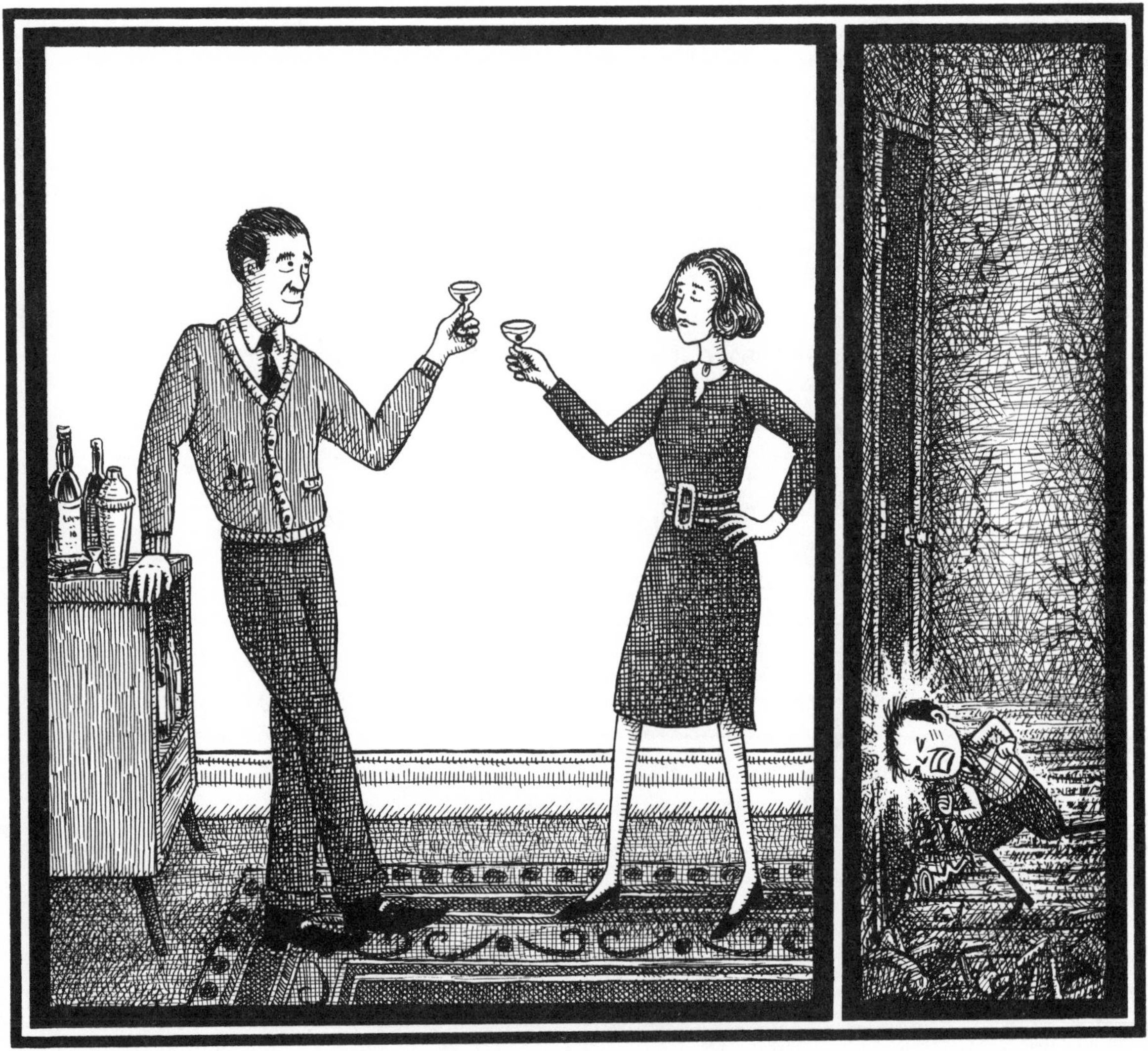

Mother and father both tried to forget,
And hoped that the morning would bring a reset.
William grew worse and made threat after threat,
Ensuring they knew he was no less upset.

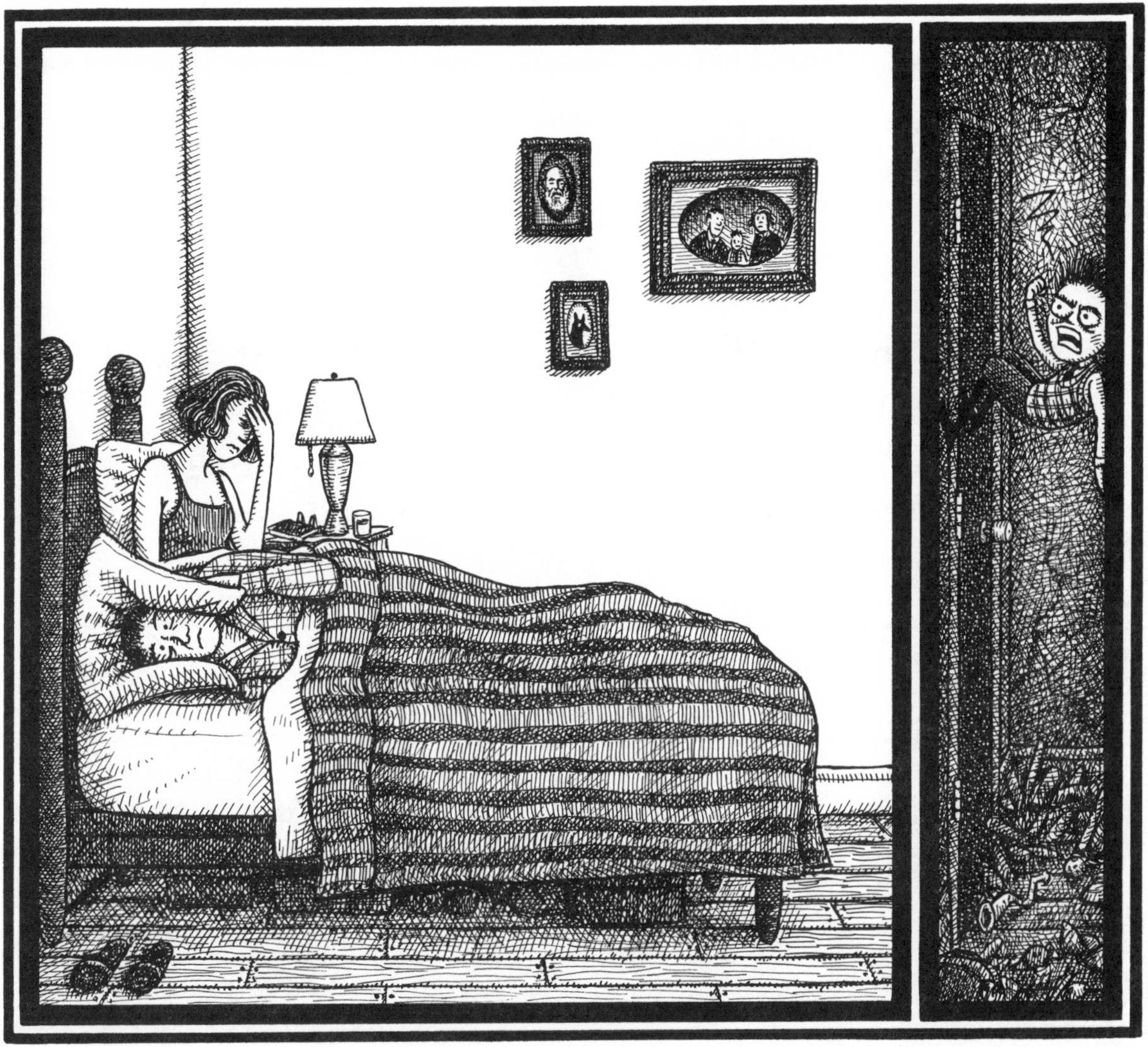

All through the night and then all the next day,
And all the next week and the first part of May,
William kept raging and would not give way,
Determined to deepen his parents' dismay.

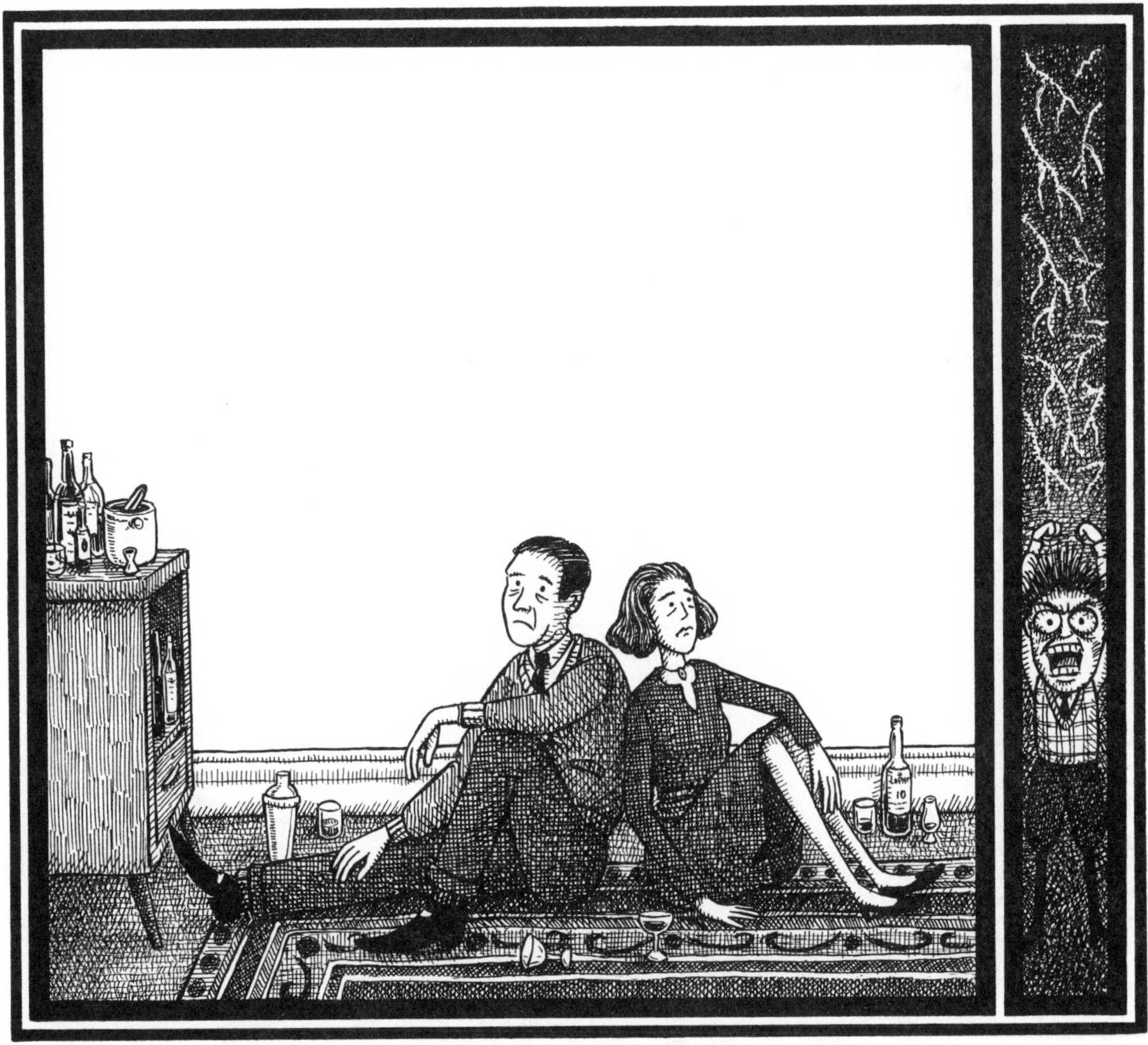

Finally one day the antics decreased,
And by six o'clockish entirely had ceased.
Mother and father were cautiously pleased,
And said, "Keep this up and you'll soon be released."

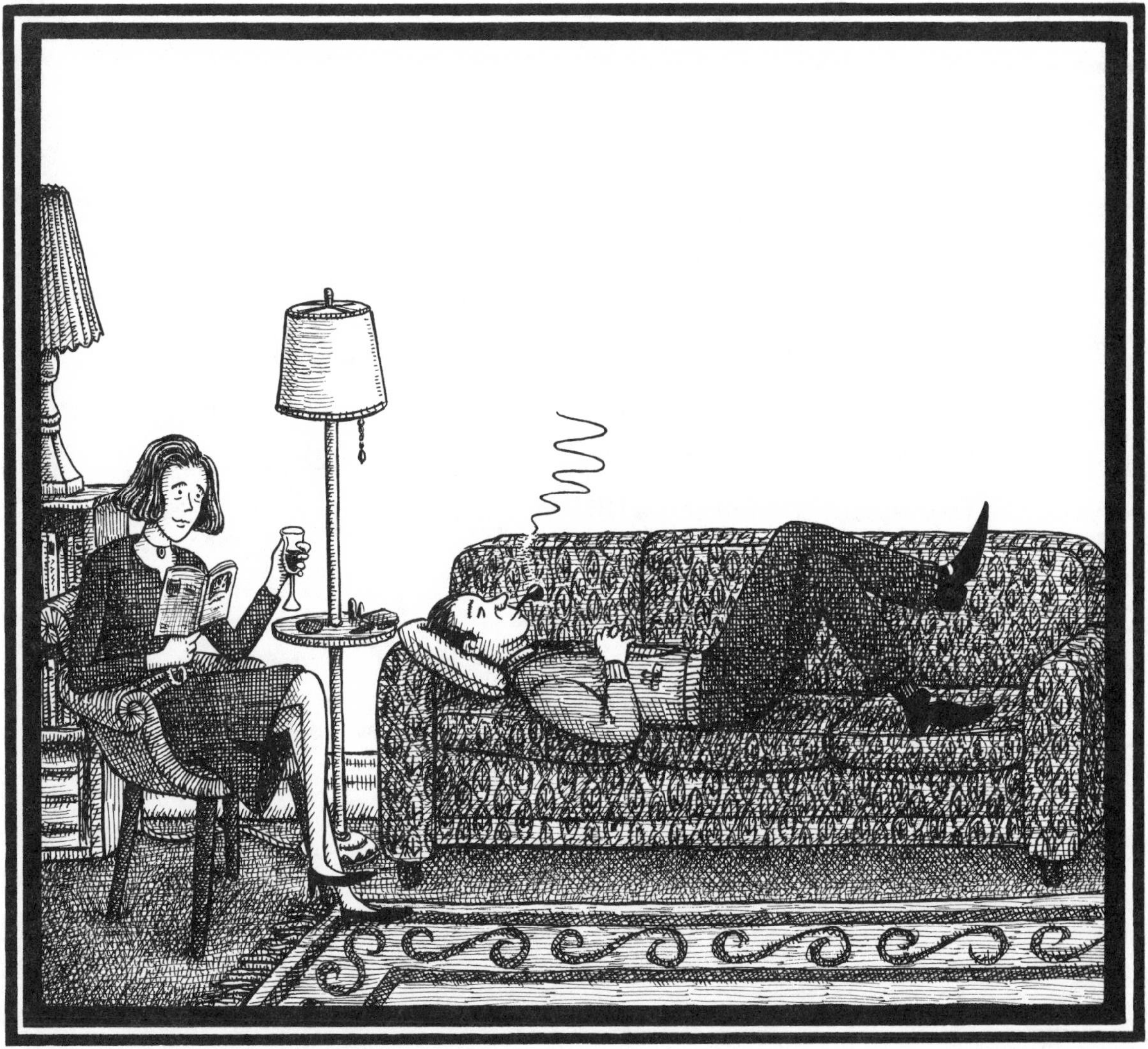

Sleeping so well since the house was so mild,
They woke full of joy at their son reconciled.
Reaching his door they then both gently smiled,
"Dear precious sweet William, you're such a good child."

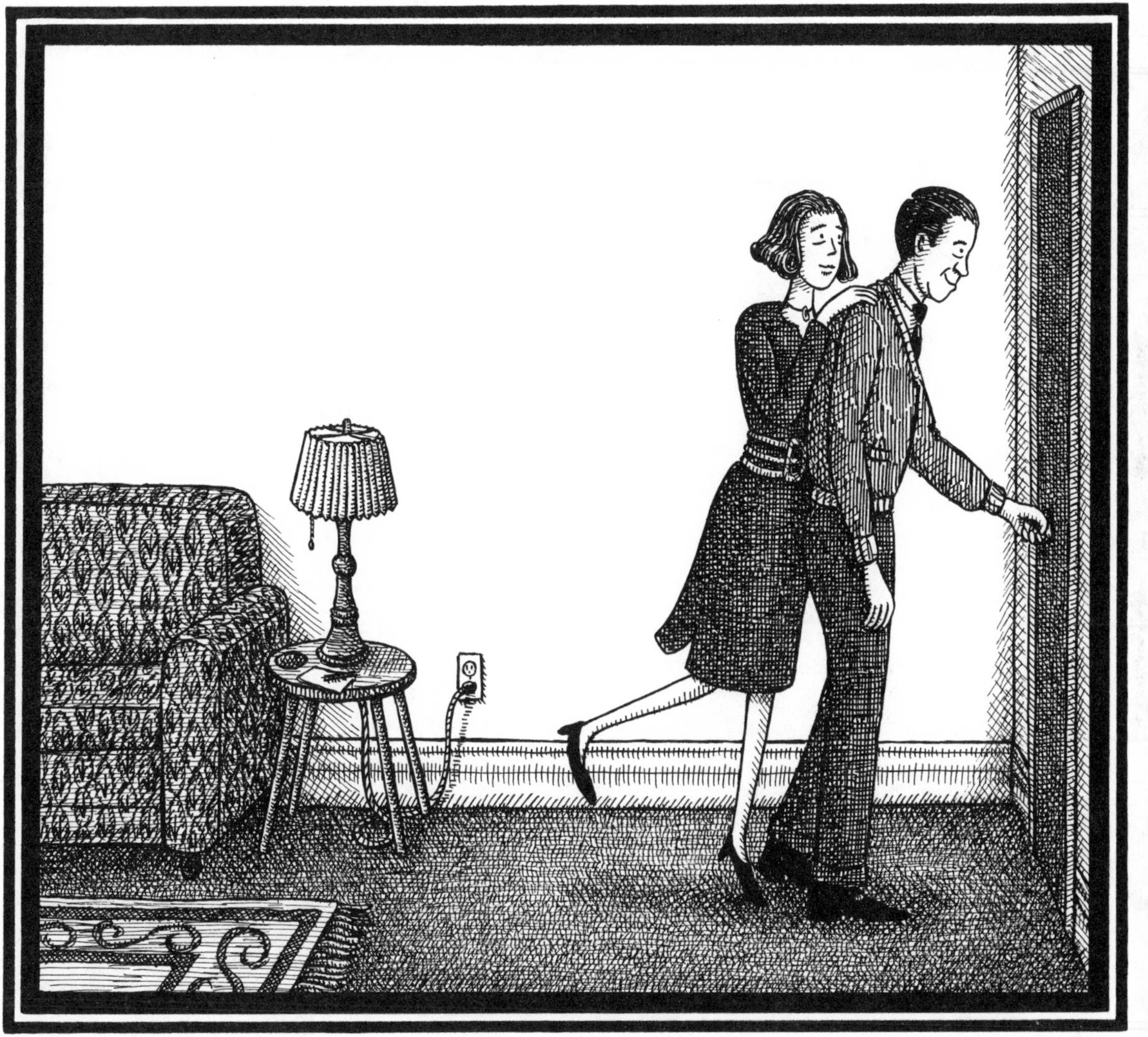

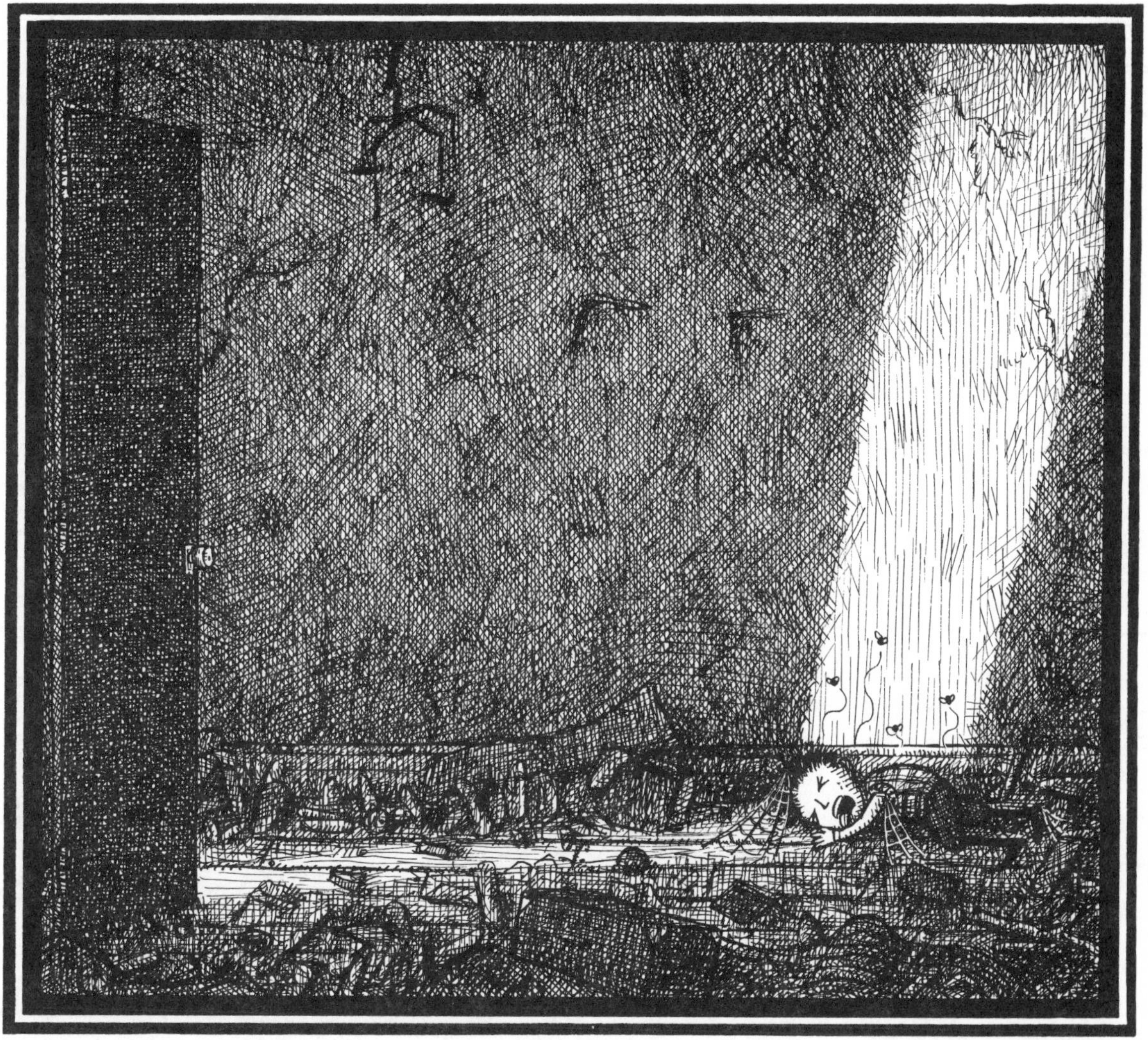

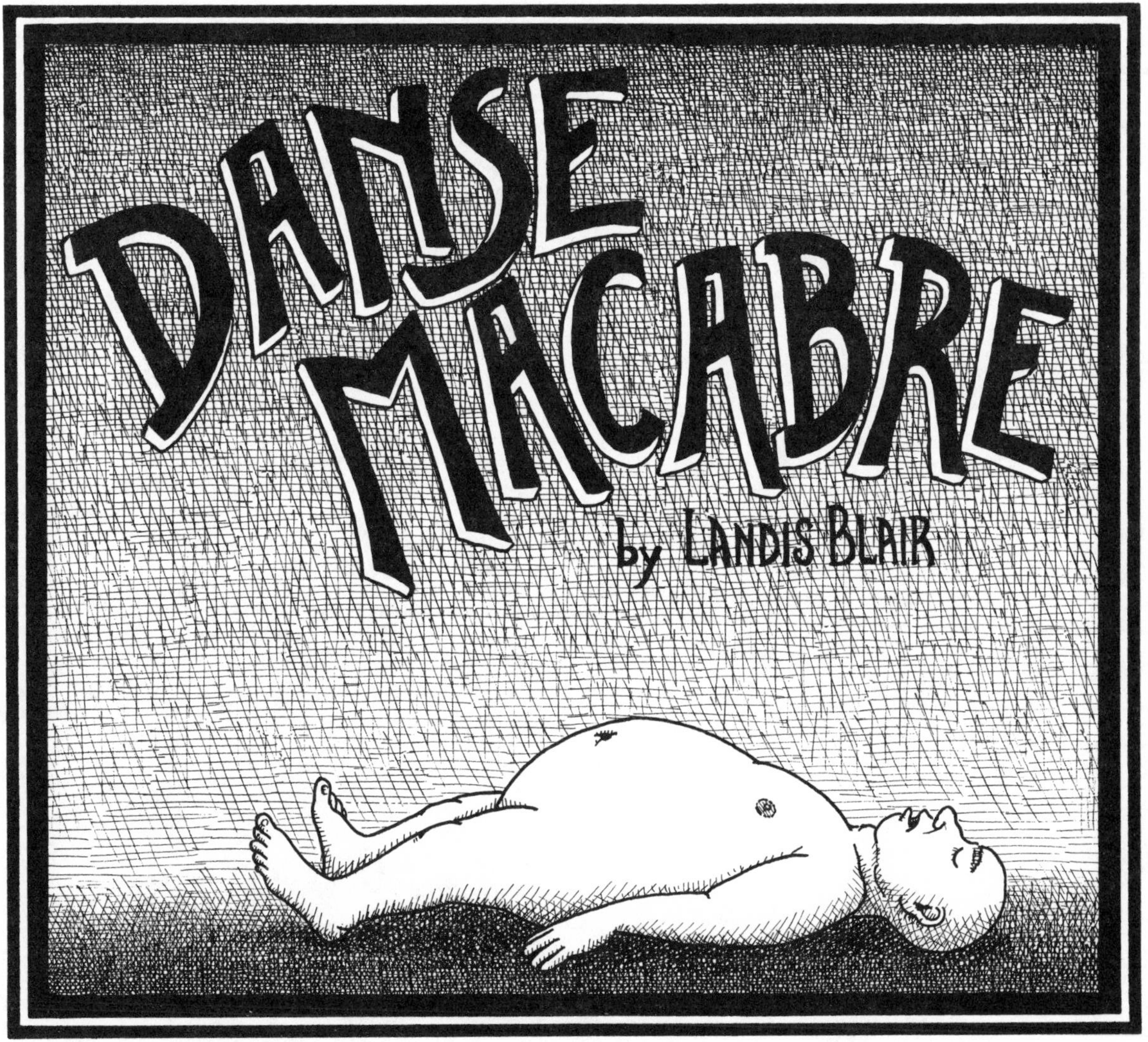
DANSE MACABRE
by LANDIS BLAIR

Hazoo huzzay! We dance today,
For death has come, hip hip hooray!

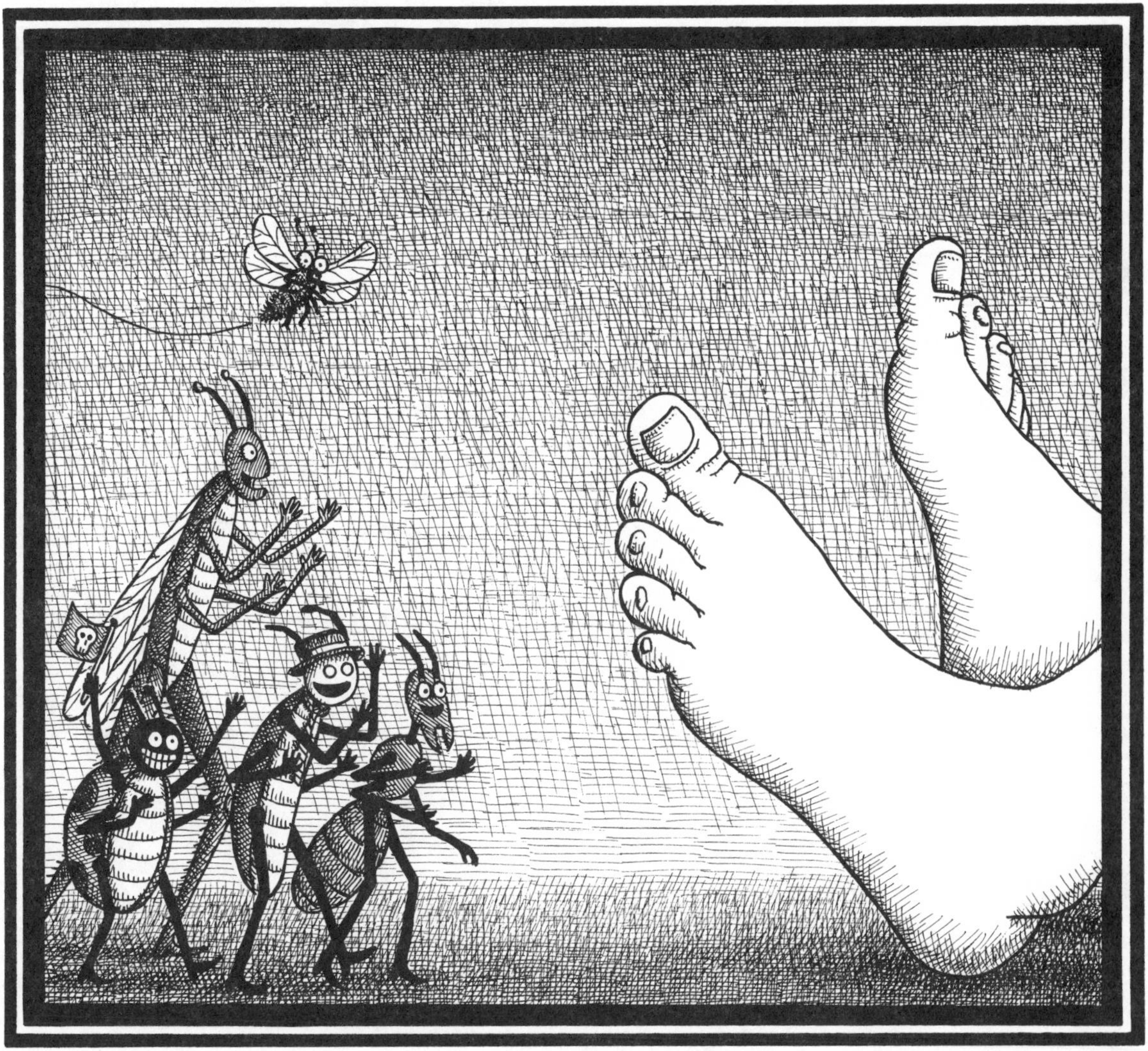

Our fav'rite chance and circumstance
Is finding death on which to prance.

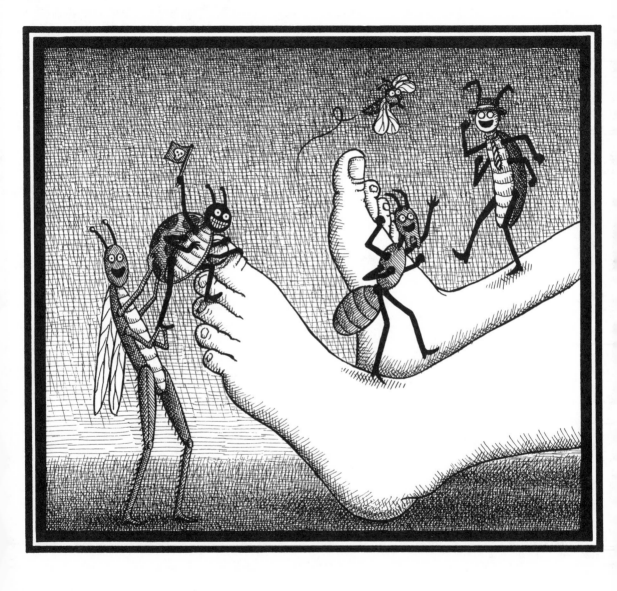

It's hard to wait when death is late,
But when it comes, the party's great.

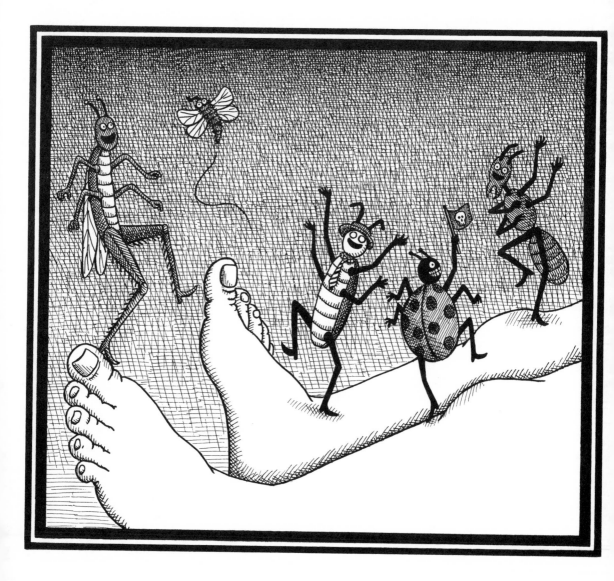

A floor of meat cannot be beat,
We love a corpse beneath our feet.

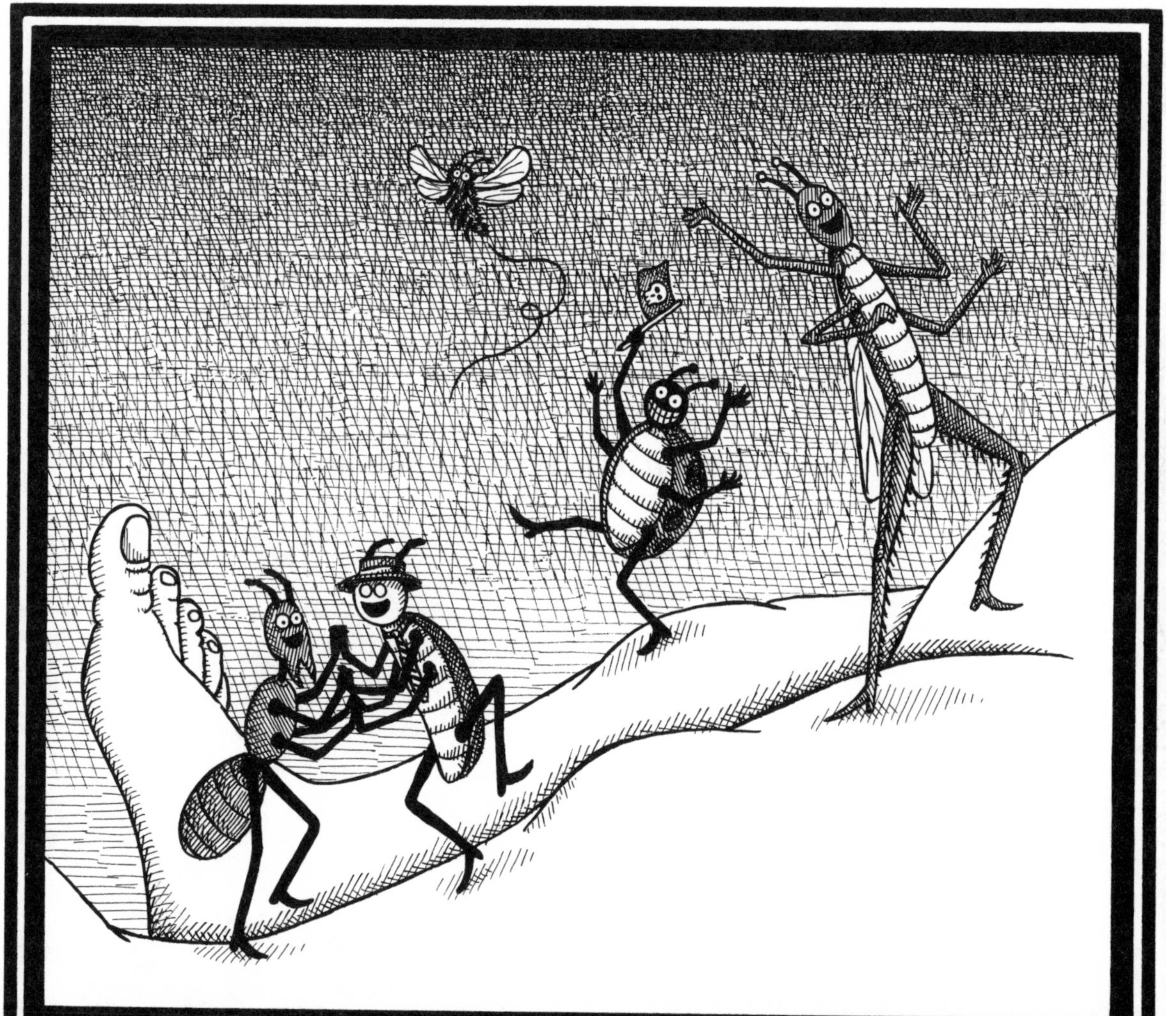

Without delay our feet obey,
We're coaxing odors of decay.

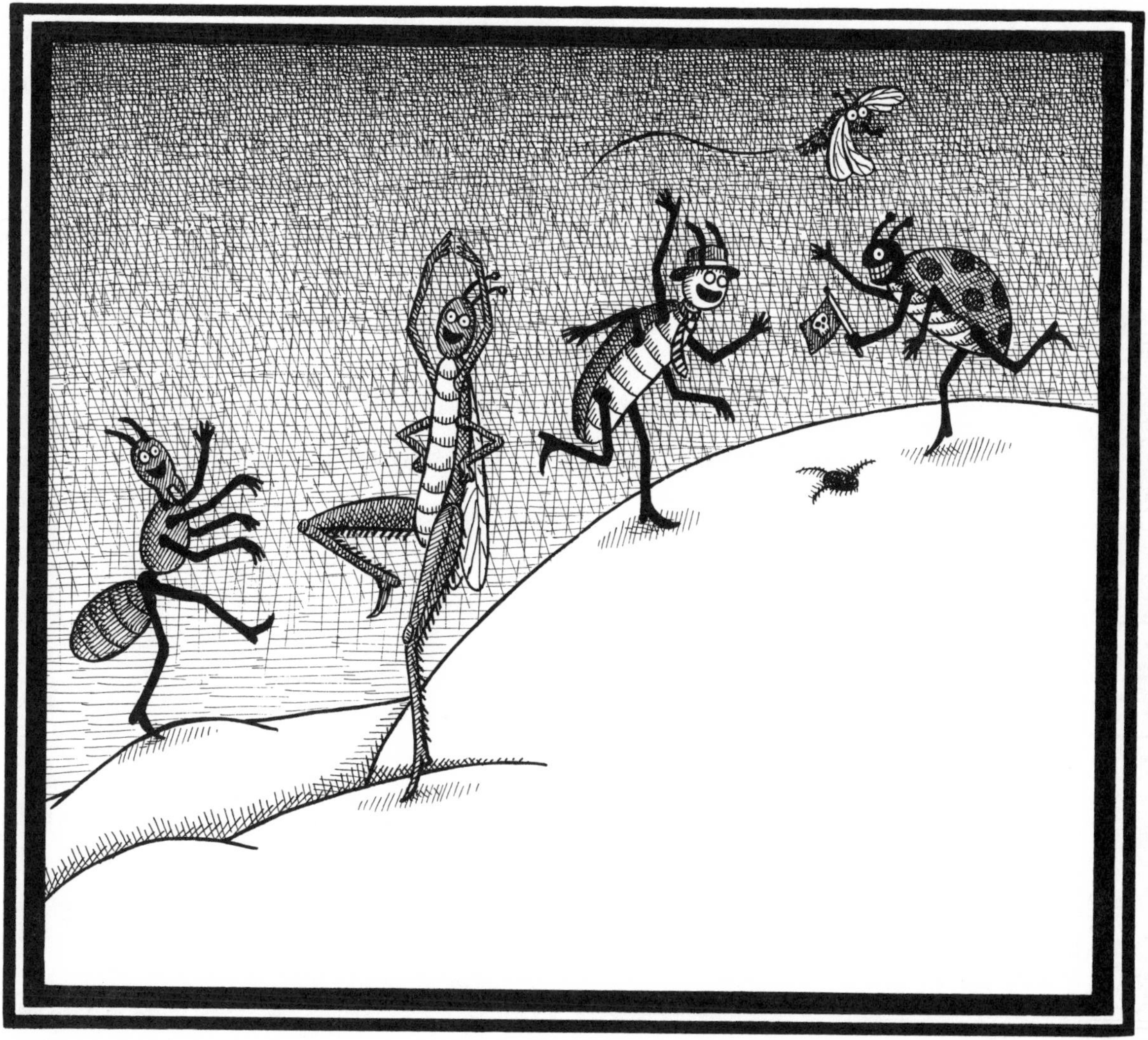

Oh what a sight! We'll dance all night,
On clammy flesh in cold moonlight.

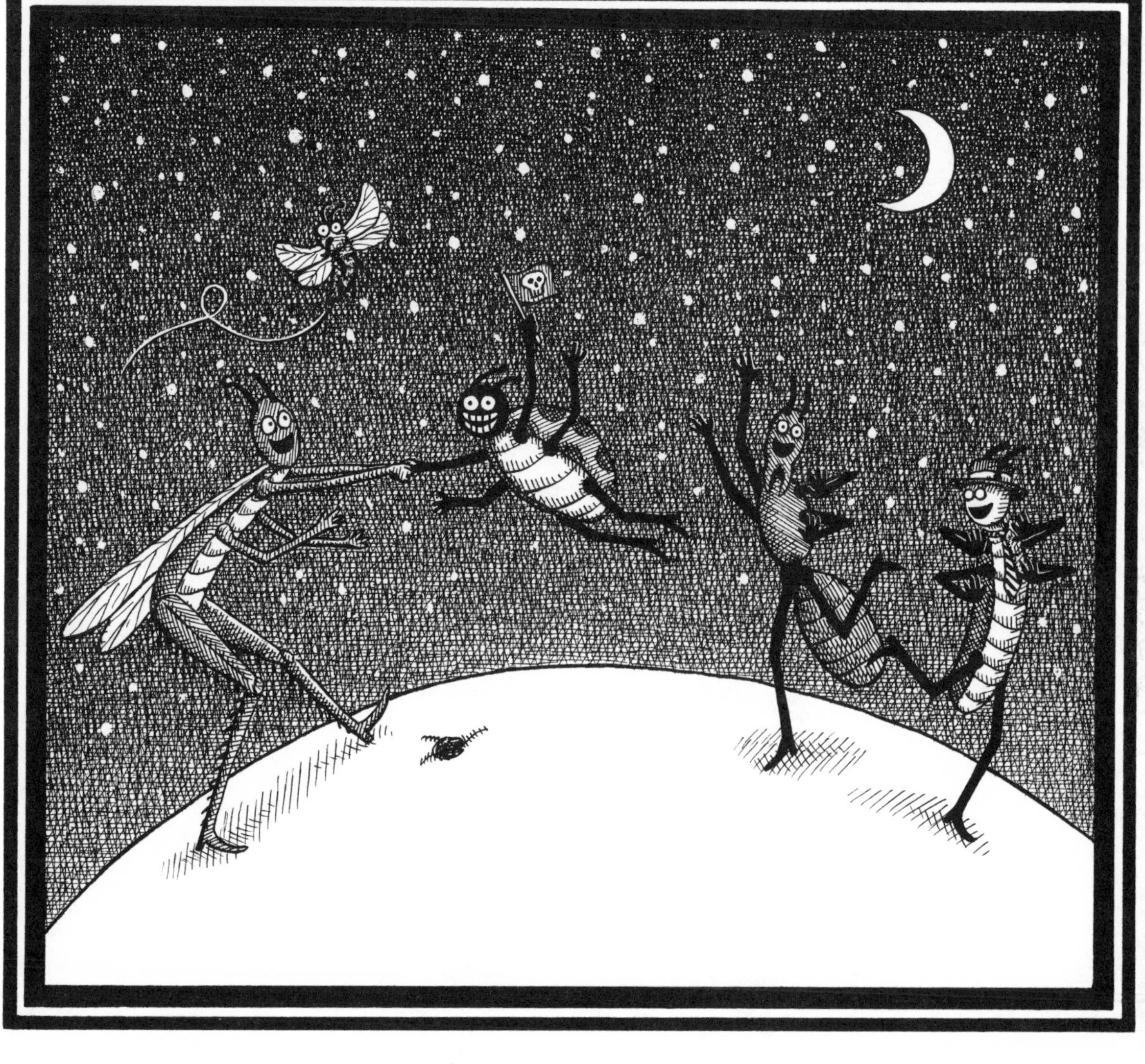

We dance for fun since life is done,
This body's spark has gone and run.

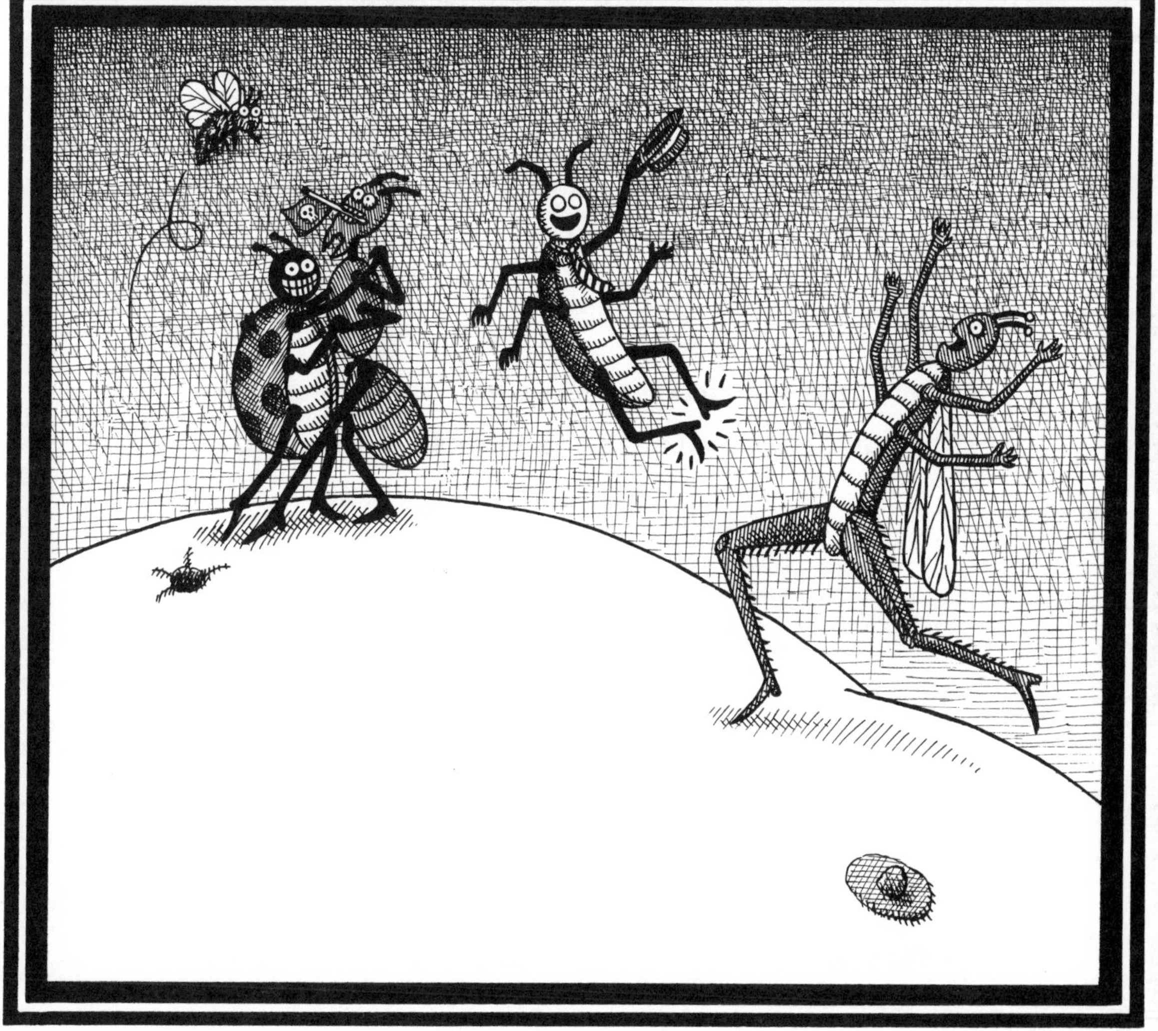

As we progress, we are obsessed,
For death with dance is best expressed.

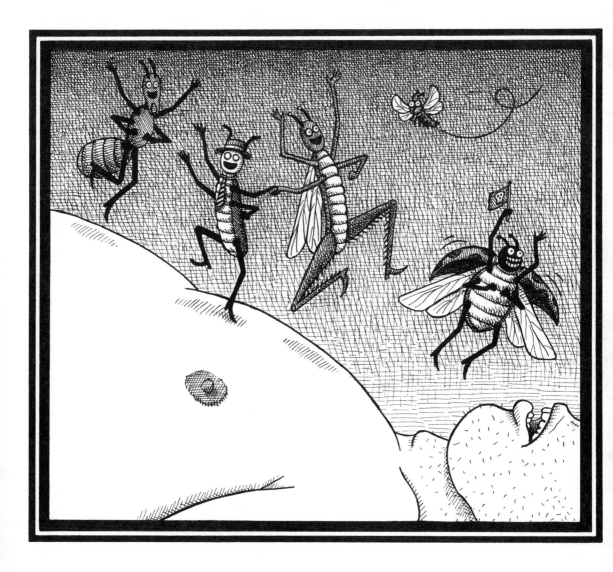

Get off my head! What's that you said?
You all are daft, I am not dead!

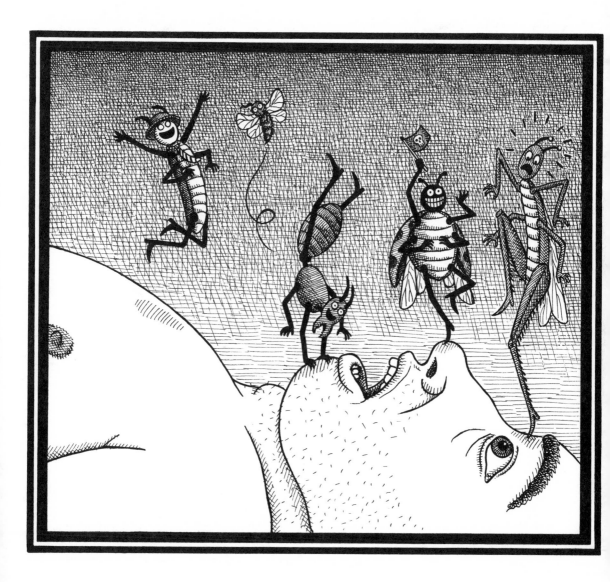

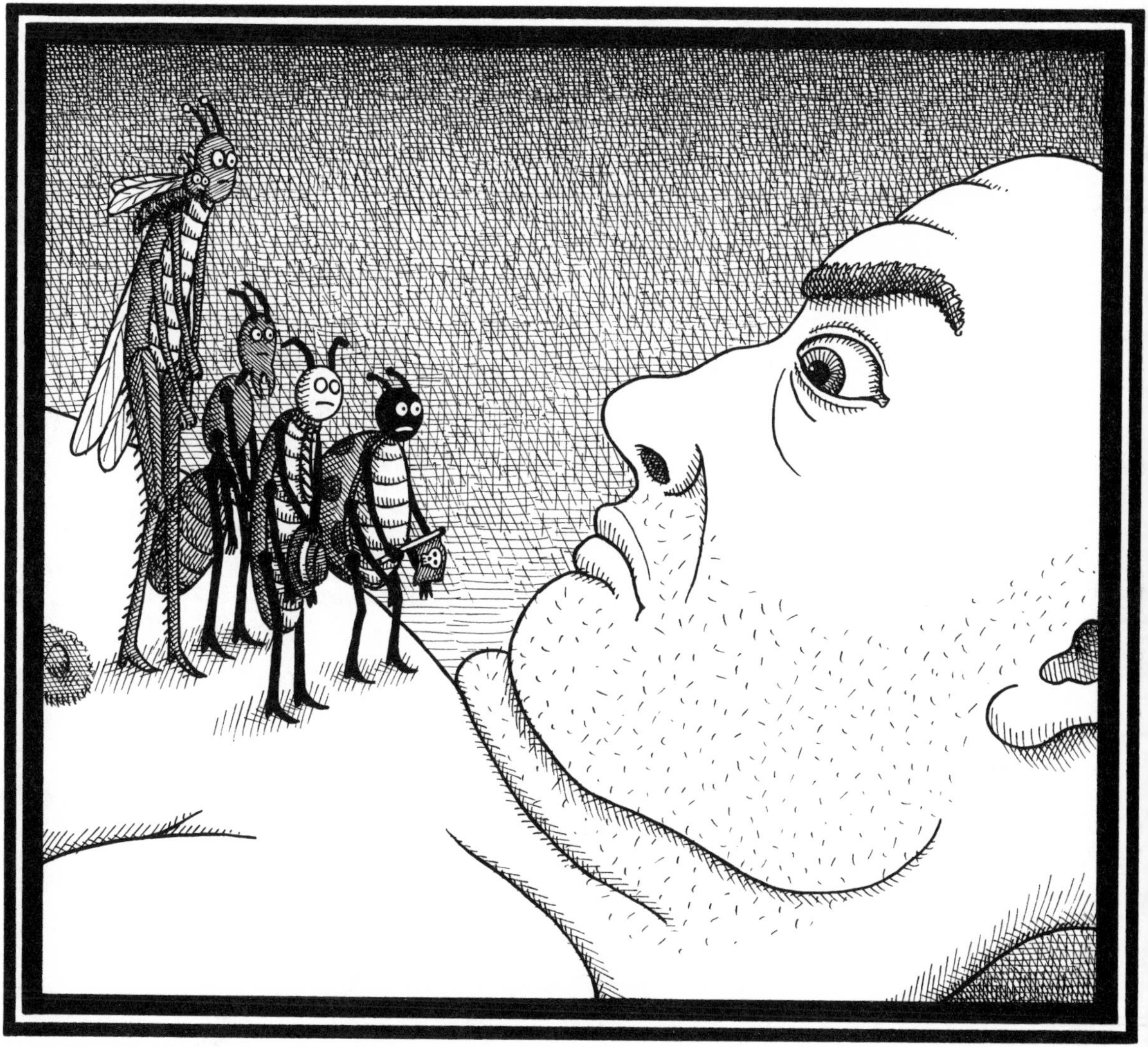

Hazoo huzzay! I dance today,
For death has come, hip hip hooray!

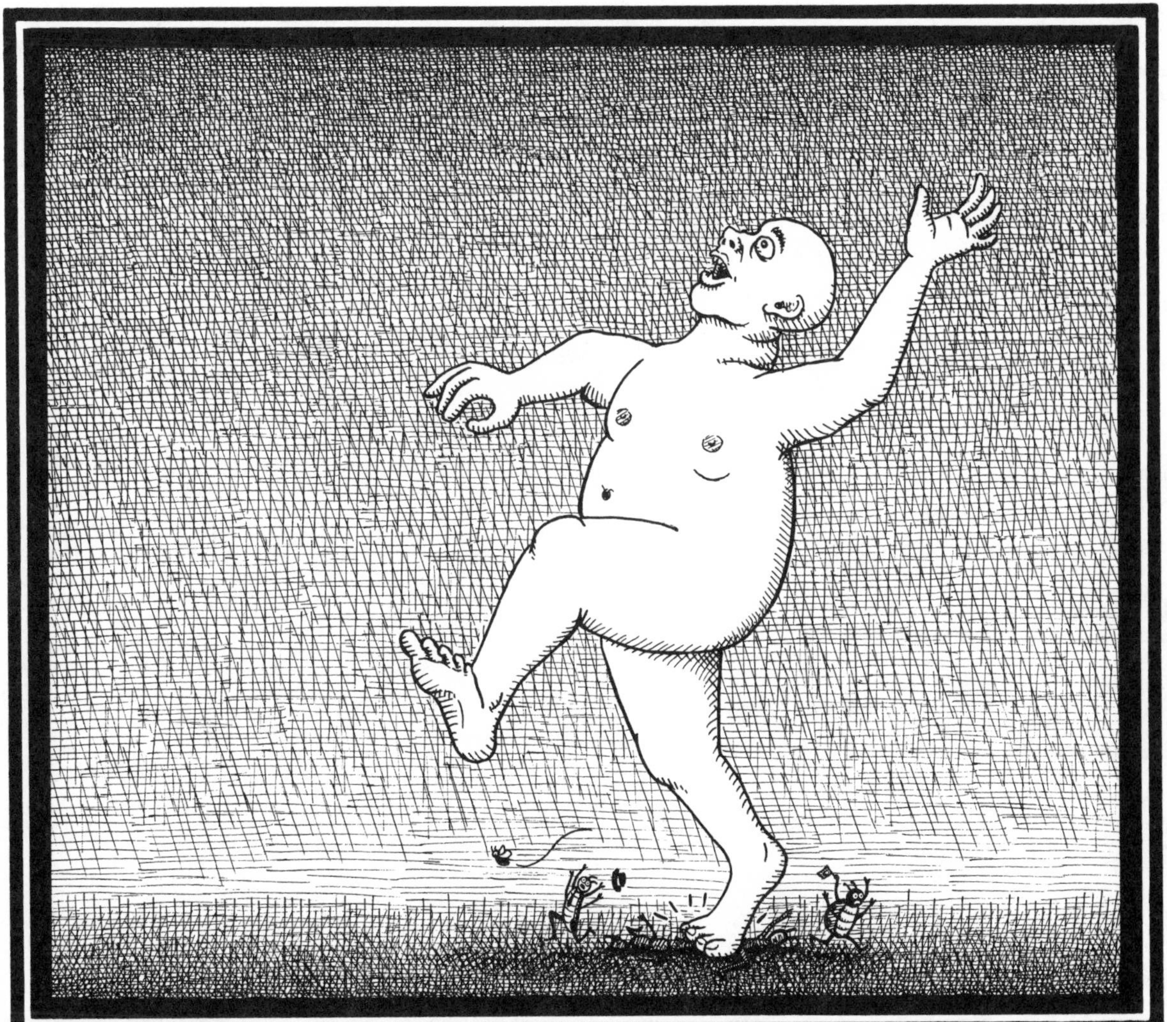

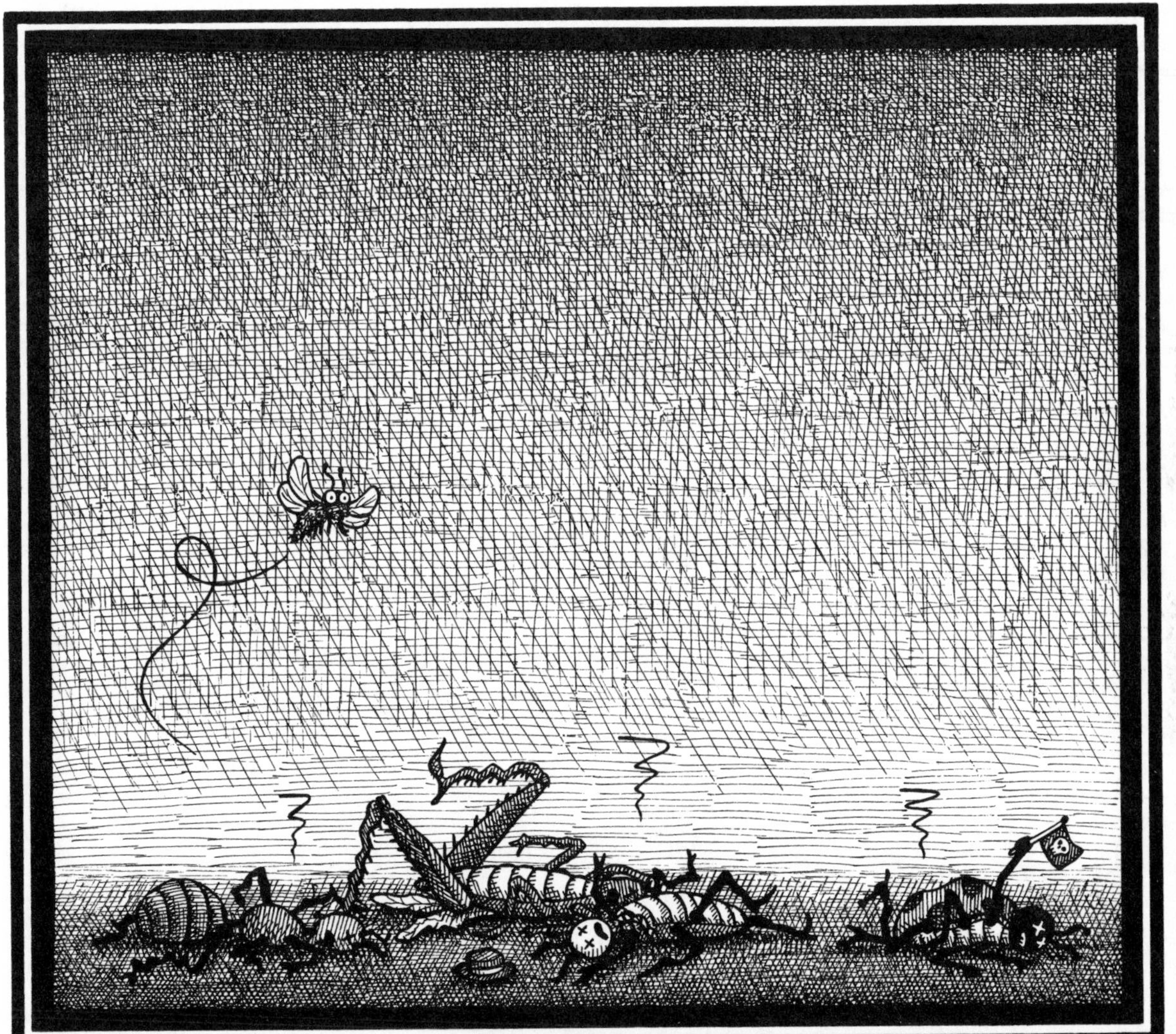

© Andi Linden

Landis Blair illustrated the prize-winning graphic novel *The Hunting Accident* and the *New York Times* bestseller *From Here to Eternity*, and has published illustrations in the *New York Times*, *Chicago* magazine, and *Medium*. He lives in Chicago, Illinois.

ACKNOWLEDGMENTS

She found my nonsense in its grime,
And he then made it worth your time.
Judy Hansen and Tom Mayer

There is no help she overlooks,
With life and cupboards, death and books.
Caitlin Doughty

This codger meets me on the brink,
Makes damn well sure I work and drink.
Eddie Campbell

They draw like gods, they save my hide,
And tease at where my boots reside.
Daniel Warren Johnson and Tyrell Cannon

A friend and guide far greater than,
Just prompting where this book began.
Laura Gonzalez

With all their publishing finesse,
They shaped this book from my distress.
Nneoma Amadi-obi, Steve Attardo,
Lauren Abbate, Becky Homiski, Don Rifkin,
and Erin Sinesky Lovett

He's shown me life in all it's worth,
Through story, wisdom, art, and mirth.
Ken Probst

My fav'rite pair that when combined
Are bookends to my tott'ring mind.
Robert Wringham and Samara Leibner

She lends her ear, ignores my flaws;
I'm envious of how she draws.
Angela Azmitia

She keeps me sane and grins at fate;
A witch, a cat, a walking mate.
Andi Linden

And these as well lent their support,
And/or keep me alive, in short.
Matthew Scott, Paula Billups, David Carlson,
Rachel Johnson, Ben Hatke, Meredith Blair, Stephen Pihlaja,
Elanor Leskiw, David Orr, Phillip Habel, Jennifer Solheim, Jacob Shier,
Audrey Niffenegger, Cheryl Tanner, Charlie Rizzo, Scott Kroll,
and Kerry Cochrane

To him my last grateful remark,
For coaxing me into the dark
Edward Gorey

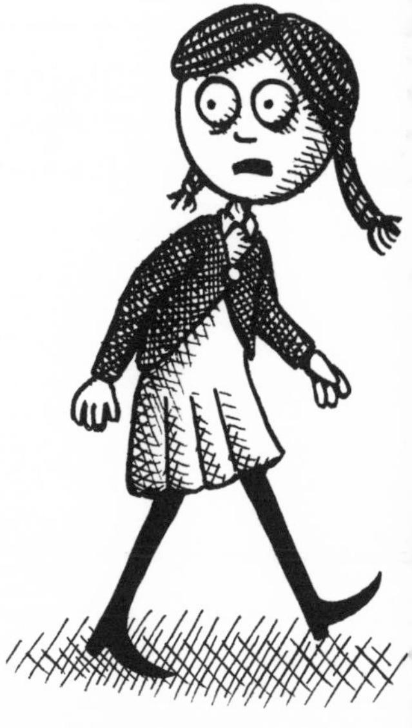

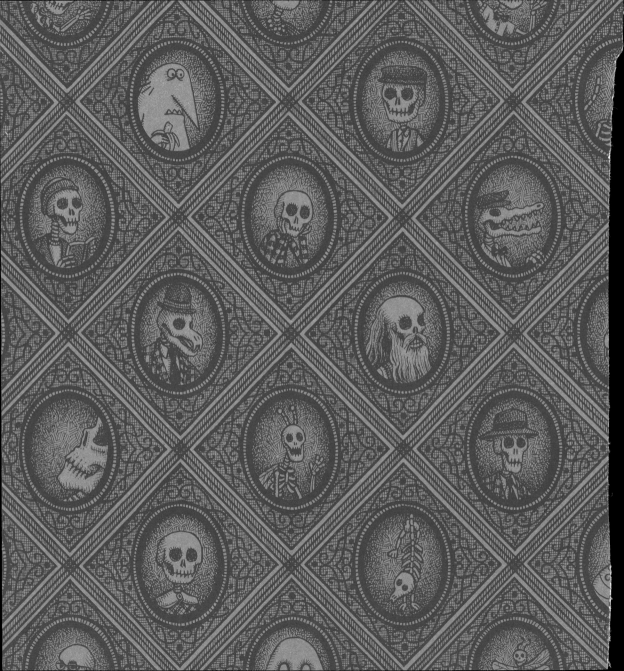